Preface

Almost every idea about speaking and writing was developed in some form or other over the period of a thousand years in Greek and Roman antiquity, from roughly the fifth century B.C. to the fifth century A.D. This complex of ideas has come down to us in the more than fifty rhetorical treatises, teaching manuals, handbooks, and student guides that are covered here. These works provided instruction not just for the creation of speeches in the law courts and political assemblies but for all forms of discourse, from conversational disputation to the writing of history, essays, letters, and fiction—and for poetry as well as prose. The classical works on epideictic rhetoric, the rhetoric of praise and blame, make no distinction at all between poetry and prose, and one finds at least as many exemplary citations from Homer and Virgil in ancient rhetorical instruction on style as from Demosthenes and Cicero. It was ancient rhetoric that taught methods of narration, vivid description, creation of dialogue, the stylistic shaping of language, and all kinds of figurative embellishment.

The works reviewed here represent ancient ideas about all kinds of composition. But these ideas did not die with the end of the Western Roman Empire. They continued to influence medieval instruction in preaching and letter writing and flourished again in the late Middle Ages and the Renaissance, when most of the ancient Greek texts represented here were recovered. This second period of influence lasted from the Renaissance through the eighteenth century in Western Europe. Consequently, classical rhetoric informs the literary developments of all the vernacular languages during the period that produced the greatest writers in French, Italian, Spanish, and English. Lyly's contribution to English prose in the celebrated novella *Euphues* cannot be assessed without a knowledge of the enormous influence of Ciceronian rhetoric in the fifteenth and sixteenth centuries. The topical content and structure of Spenser's *Four Hymns* and *Epithalamium* come ultimately from prescriptions outlined by Menander Rhetor in the third century A.D., and, as Sister Miriam Joseph demonstrated in *Shakespeare's Use of the Arts of Language* (1947)—excerpted in her popular *Rhetoric in Shakespeare's*

Time (1962)—the achievements of the greatest English writer are essentially framed by instruction in classical rhetoric.

The influence of classical rhetoric also extends to poetics, one of the defining developments of the late Renaissance, extending from the 1540s into the seventeenth century. Although a renewed interest in Aristotle's *Poetics* initiated this development, interest was also rekindled in Aristotle's *Rhetoric*, and Renaissance poetics remained intrinsically associated with classical rhetoric. Minturno's influential *De Poeta* (1559), written in Latin and Italian, is thoroughly and explicitly rhetorical in its orientation, and many of the details J. C. Scaliger accumulates in his scholarly *Poetices* (1561) come from such ancient rhetorical authorities as Hermogenes and Menander Rhetor. Scaliger had an enormous impact on critical theory for two hundred years; he is, for example, the theorist most quoted by Sidney in the late sixteenth century and by Dr. Johnson in the eighteenth.

But it is not just recognition of the importance of classical rhetoric for the understanding of Western literature that has been revived since the Second World War in the works of Sister Miriam Joseph, Wayne C. Booth, Brian Vickers, and many others. There has also been a renewed interest in ancient legal rhetoric. Cicero, who was one of the most influential rhetorical theorists, was also one of the greatest practicing attorneys of all time. American law schools now teach rhetoric, and the influence and echoes of classical rhetorical theory are to be found everywhere. A case in point is *How to Argue and Win Every Time* (1995), the best-seller by another immensely successful attorney, Gerry Spence. Part I of Spence's book is generally about the importance of what the ancients called ethical arguments. In particular, his lessons about not making judges and juries hate you while you are demolishing your opponents' positions (pp. 44–45) are discussed not only in the *Rhetorica ad Alexandrum* (sect. 37)—one of the earliest ancient treatises on rhetoric, written about twenty–five hundred years ago—but also in many later works of classical rhetoric.

The plan of this book is to provide comprehensive information about ancient rhetorical theory in the form of highly detailed, descriptive summaries of all the important authorities and works from Greek and Latin antiquity, including works as yet untranslated into English. These comprehensive summaries are not intended to

A
Guide
to
CLASSICAL
RHETORIC

Philip Rollinson
and
Richard Geckle

SUMMERTOWN

Signal Mountain, Tennessee

Published by Summertown Texts
P. O. Box 453
Signal Mountain, TN 37377–0453
1 (800) 742–5710
E–mail: rivrol@fmtc.net

Library of Congress Cataloging--in--Publication Data

Rollinson, Philip B.
   A guide to classical rhetoric / Philip Rollinson and Richard Geckle
      p.   cm.
   Includes bibliographical references (p.) and index.
   ISBN 1–893009–01–7. — ISBN 1–893009–00–9 (pbk.)
   1. Rhetoric, Ancient—Handbooks, manuals, etc. 2. Classical literature—History and criticism—Theory, etc.—Handbooks, manuals, etc. 3. Speeches, addresses, etc., Greek—History and criticism—Theory, etc.—Handbooks, manuals, etc. 4. Speeches, addresses, etc., Latin—History and criticism—Theory, etc.—Dictionaries. 5. Oratory, Ancient—Handbooks, manuals, etc. I. Geckle, Richard, 1966– . II. Title.
PA3038.R65 1998
808'.00938—dc21   98–31617
                                                CIP

Cover artwork by Janet Katz
Printed in the United States of America

Contents

replace the originals but rather to make them more accessible and useful. Each entry contains systematic parenthetical references to the passages and sections in the original work that contain the information described. Using these citations, the reader can quickly go to the passage and see what it has to say in full. These parenthetical citations are to the traditional parts and sections dividing the texts, so that any edition or translation may be referred to. In those cases where a particular edition has been used, page numbers are indicated.

The summaries are neither commentaries nor analyses. Rather, they combine paraphrase and description, and occasionally evaluation, so as to provide all the basic information in the works covered in a readable and interesting way. Equal space and attention are not given to every part of every work. Had that been done, several of the entries would have become bogged down with minutiae and the information rendered less accessible. Consequently, some parts of the works are treated in more detail than others. We have, however, tried to take some account of everything in each work. Key Greek and Latin terms are parenthetically indicated throughout all the entries.

The comprehensive index provides another important use of this guide. All concepts and topics are cross-referenced, so that one can quickly discover what was said in ancient rhetorical theory about any particular subject and by whom.

The terminus for works that are included is roughly the end of the fifth century A.D. Some of the works in Halm's edition of *Rhetores Latini Minores,* a collection of late classical and early medieval derivative compilations from ancient authorites, are before that cutoff and some after. We include an entry for Halm, briefly reviewing each of the works there, and have separate entries for two of them, those by Martianus Capella and Priscian. Martianus's treatment of the liberal arts contains probably the most widely known exposition of rhetoric in the Middle Ages; it also reflects material in now lost Greek and Latin sources. Priscian's *Praeexercitamina* is not just a translation but a reworking of the Greek *Progymnasmata* of Hermogenes and was the only Latin text on early rhetorical exercises available in Western Europe from the end of the Western Roman Empire until the reappearance and translation of the Greek text of Aphthonius in the Renaissance.

Finally, there are no entries for either St. Basil or St. Augustine. Both of these churchmen started their careers as teachers of rhetoric; but Basil's defense of the utility of reading pagan literature in the essay "To Young Men on Reading Greek Literature," which is sometimes included in treatments of classical rhetoric, actually lies in the realm of grammar. Similarly, the first three books of Augustine's *On Christian Doctrine* are about reading and interpretation and hence are grammatical rather than rhetorical in orientation. The fourth and final book is a preaching manual for the Christian minister and is the archetype for the numerous arts of preaching (*artes praedicandi*) of the Middle Ages, none of which are treated in this book.

This work does not compete with or duplicate any existing treatment of classical rhetoric. Rather, it fills an important gap as a tool for students and teachers of rhetoric, composition, literature, and the law, for the classroom and reference desk, for scholars and lay persons—for anyone, in fact, who wants to find out quickly and accurately who says what and where.

A number of scholars have reviewed various drafts of this work, and early versions have been used for several years by graduate students in the literature and the composition and rhetoric programs at the University of South Carolina. From these sources we have received valuable assistance that has enabled us to make the guide a much better and more accurate tool than it otherwise would have been. In this regard, we especially want to thank George Kennedy and Patricia Matsen.

Authors and Works

ALCIDAMAS
On Those Who Write Speeches
ALEXANDER   100 AD
On Figures of Thought and Speech
On Rhetorical Subjects
ANONYMOUS SEGUERIANUS   200 AD
Art of Political Speech
APHTHONIUS   350 AD
Progymnasmata
→ APSINES   190 AD   no msu
Art of Rhetoric
ARISTIDES RHETORIC   117 AD
On Political Discourse
On Simple Speech
ARISTOTLE
Prior Analytics
Posterior Analytics
Topica
Rhetoric
→ CICERO   106 BC
On Invention
The Best Kind of Orator
Topics
On the Orator
*On the Division of Rhetoric   *De Partitione Oratoria*   no msy
*Brutus   msu   PA 6156 C5 v. 5
*Orator   no msu
CORAX and TISIAS
DEMETRIUS
On Style
→ DIONYSIUS OF HALICARNASSUS   30 BC
On Literary Composition
Two Letters to Ammaeus
Letter to Gnaeus Pompeius
Dinarchus
Thucydides
✴ *On Ancient Orators*   msu   PA 3612 D 53   vols. 1-7   ?
"   "   " 54   vols. 1-2   ?

Introduction: Words and the Ancient Greco-Roman World

The Homeric epics reflect a political culture of kings and tribal leaders, who were usually superior warriors atop a basically military aristocracy. But the geography of the lands that the Greeks colonized after the ninth century B.C. seems to have initiated a shift from tribal unities into a myriad of individual communities. The Greeks expanded to the east throughout the islands in the Aegean Sea and onto the coasts of western Asia Minor and the Black Sea, as well as west into Sicily and southern Italy. And Greece itself, except for the plains of Thessaly and the Peloponnesus, is mountainous and difficult to get around. Consequently, most of the cities were much more isolated from each other than, say, the cities in the ancient Near East. Commerce and communication by sea became a necessity. Furthermore, the dozens of islands in the Aegean could only communicate with the rest of the world by sea.

The political identity of these communities tended to come from the individuals and families gathered in them, and the earlier tribal kind of government, the monarchial-military aristocracy, gave way in the new "city-state" (*polis*) to a variety of more democratic institutions, from conservative merchant or money-based oligarchies to representative administrations and fully participatory legislation. The size of the city-states played a part here as well. Many of the populations were so small (by our terms, at least) that all the adult male citizens were frequently involved in governance and, of course, in the courts as well. Even the largest, Athens, at the height of her power in the fifth century B.C. had only about 30,000 citizens (excluding slaves, women, and children). Here courts regularly had juries of over two hundred men, and in the smaller cities, important legal cases, as with legislation, might be heard by the entire citizenry.

Legislative, judicial, administrative, and even military functions were controlled by voting. In many city-states even generals were elected, and the electorate directly controlled recruitment for the navies and armies. Here, then, arose the acute need for oratorical powers. This need had existed in the earlier heroic world of tribe and clan as depicted in the Homeric epics, but with a tremendous difference. In the heroic world the military aristocrats argued with each other and gave advice to their kings and leaders, but the kings and leaders made the ultimate decisions; the power rested in their hands. In the typical city-state power rested with the electorate, all the adult male citizens voting as individuals for a collective will. The same was true judicially. In the older heroic world the king or ruler and his magistrates (the aristocrats under and supporting him) were the judicial authorities. In the city-states the male citizens, as a whole or divided into smaller groups, exercised legal authority; they were themselves the courts. There was, then, a democratic equality of all citizens.

In the environment of the *polis* the power of words took on an importance unprecedented in the history of the world. For the individual citizen to influence legislation in public assemblies and verdicts in the courts, he had to have rhetorical powers of persuasion. Clearly, the most effective speakers got their legislation adopted and won their cases in court, where litigants usually represented themselves (women, of course, could not; and later, in Roman culture, litigants were regularly represented by advocates). Over much of the Greek world, then (with some exceptions, such as Sparta), came the demand for education for all free men in gaining and perfecting argumentative and persuasive skills with words. And, as usually happens, this demand was met by a supply of teachers.

One can learn to argue and persuade by the manipulation of language without knowing much about words or the basic structure of language, but it is obviously much easier if one does know about these things. And so the earliest educational development seems to have been a proliferation of local and itinerant teachers of grammar. It is also true that one can learn the basics of language and the uses of it without being literate, i.e., orally, but it is much easier and more effective to use writing as an instructional tool. Consequently, the spread of grammatical education and teachers in ancient Greece went hand in hand with the spread of literacy.

Grammar is the study of letters, and by the time of its fullest development, around the first centuries B.C. and A.D., it was remarkably comprehensive and sophisticated. Parts of speech and usage were the core of grammatical education. But it also involved training in reading (*lectio*) and interpretation (*enarratio*), including editing and emending texts (*emendatio*), and literary criticism (*iudi-*

catio). Poetry was comprehensively covered; students were taught metrics and figurative language. The result of grammatical education was a thorough grounding in all the basic skills of reading and writing.

With those basic skills mastered, the student could begin to learn how to argue and persuade effectively with words in preparation for a career in public life and the courts, into which virtually every free male was forced (except the few philosophers who characteristically withdrew from the affairs of public life). In ancient Greece this rhetorical instruction seems to have begun from the argumentative side, i.e., with eristics or disputation, and is associated with another kind of teacher called sophists or learned persons (at that time an honorable appellation). The sophists traveled wherever there were students and interest in their skills.

Protagoras of Abdera (fifth century B.C.), who is featured prominently in two of Plato's *Dialogues*, was supposedly the first teacher to identify himself as a sophist and the first to charge for his services. Abdera was a prosperous commercial city (one of the many cities colonized in the seventh century B.C.) on the northeast coast of Greece near the island of Thasos. Protagoras was a skeptical pragmatist (he insisted that he could never know whether the gods exist or not) and the originator, according to Plato, of the famous relativist dictum "Man is the measure of all things" (*Theaetetus* 152a). Many anecdotes were told about him in antiquity, including one (also told about Corax and Tisias) concerning a former pupil suing to recover his instructional fees on the grounds that Protagoras had failed to teach him anything. Protagoras argued successfully in court that the pupil had no case, since if the pupil won the suit he would have demonstrated that he had profited from his instruction, whereas, were the pupil to lose the suit, he would have done just that, lose.

It is not Protagoras or Abdera, however, but the names Corax and Tisias and the fifth-century Greek colonies in Sicily with which the origins of the teaching of rhetoric are associated. Gorgias (483–376 B.C.) was probably the most famous sophist-rhetor. Taught by Tisias, he came to Athens in 427 B.C. as an ambassador from Leontini in Sicily. He made a sensational impact with his embellished speeches, characterized by figurative language and artfully constructed clauses and sentences. He thereby went beyond argumentative content and established the significant power of style.

The sophists seem to have developed two different instructional techniques. One, associated with Tisias and referred to by Aristotle (*On Sophistical Refutations* 183b), consisted of learning rules, i.e. theoretical instruction. Other sophists taught primarily by practice and example, forcing their students to memorize and imitate specimen speeches as well as commonplace arguments. They also differed sharply over the value of writing down speeches ahead of time versus speaking purely extemporaneously. Alcidamas (fourth century B.C.), a sophist from the city of Elaea in Asia Minor who studied under Gorgias, argues strongly that writing down and memorizing speeches is not just useless but actually counterproductive.

With these sophistic beginnings, rhetoric established itself even more firmly in fourth-century Greek culture. First, rhetoric itself became the basis of what we would call higher education, especially in the famous school of the Athenian rhetor Isocrates (436–338 B.C.), who is the father of what is today still known as a liberal education (i.e., in ancient times, the education of "free" men). Out of his school came a steady stream of statesmen, historians, and poets. Second, the philosophic schools themselves largely endorsed rhetoric and accepted it as a legitimate field of study (although exactly what kind of study was involved remained a subject of debate throughout antiquity). Although the *Dialogues* contain Socratic attacks on rhetoric, they also include enthusiastic support of it, and Plato himself (c. 429–347 B.C.), as the ancients noted, was a master stylist who kept revising his works down to his dying days. The greatest pupil of Plato, Aristotle (384–322 B.C.), enthusiastically endorsed the value of eristics, and out of his Peripatetic instruction in philosophy came the defining treatise on rhetoric. The Stoics also adopted rhetoric, with only their opponents, the Epicureans, dissenting, as can be seen in the fragmented works of Philodemus (c. 110 B.C.–40 B.C.).

Gradually Greek culture spread over the entire Mediterranean and Near Eastern worlds. First, two serious threats were turned back. To the east a powerful empire evolved in Persia that overwhelmed the Greek city-states in Asia Minor and ruled the Near Eastern world from Asia Minor and Egypt to India. The Persians invaded Europe and Greece proper in the early fifth century B.C. but were repulsed. At the same time in the west, the Semitic colony of Tyre at Carthage, on the central coast of North Africa, attempted to subdue the Greek city-states in Sicily. The Carthaginians were also beaten back. Subsequently the thoroughly Hellenized Macedonians to the north of Greece under King Philip conquered Greece in the fourth century B.C. Philip's son, Alexander, tutored by Aristotle, followed by conquering the Persian Empire. The resulting kingdoms set up by Alexander's generals and their heirs led to the Hellenization of most of the ancient world to the east of Greece. Although a new Parthian empire developed in Persia, Greek-speaking governments and culture remained dominant from Egypt throughout Palestine and Syria and Asia Minor.

In the West, meanwhile, by the late third century B. C. the Romans had conquered all of Italy and Sicily, as well as the Carthaginians in North Africa and the former Carthaginian colonies on the east coast of Spain. The Romans also expanded to the east and by the first century B.C. had subdued all of Greece and the Near East.

The continuation of Greek culture was fostered by the method of Roman rule. The Romans preferred to leave local and regional governments in place under the watchful eye of their own governors, supported by contingents of Roman soldiers, who were quartered all over the empire. The Romans exercised complete control of the military and foreign relationships; but as long the subjects lived peaceably and paid the requisite taxes to the Romans (for ordering their lives and protecting them militarily), their internal affairs were left alone. Roman rule worked because of its limited intervention in and control of local affairs and also because rebellion or any kind of challenge to the Roman imperium was severely dealt with (e.g., the destruction of Jerusalem).

The Romans also, as did most other ancient people, took slaves. Educated Greeks were the most prized, because they could manage estates and households—i.e., do business for their masters. In Rome "free" (liber) men were free from the necessity of having to work for a living; for them a "liberal" education was appropriate. And although in the ancient Greek, Hellenistic, and Roman worlds many ordinary men, farmers, shopkeepers, tradesmen, etc., participated to varying degrees in civic life, much and in many cases most of the economic work was done by women and slaves. Politics, the law, the military, and religion were the customary spheres of free male activity—the bases of subsequent European upper-class life.

Greek culture, then, thoroughly infiltrated Roman family and business life, as well as the life of learning and education. As early as the end of the third century B.C., Greek education and educators were present in Rome herself. The great Roman orator and statesman Cato (234–149 B.C.) was already objecting to the excessive Hellenization of Rome in the early second century B.C., and by the time of Cicero's education early in the first century B.C. elementary and intermediate instruction in rhetoric at Rome was followed by what we would call gradaute education at the great Greek centers of learning: Athens, Pergamum in Asia Minor, the island of Rhodes off the southwestern coast of Asia Minor, and Alexandria in Egypt. By that time most educated Romans knew Greek as well as Latin, and Greek was just about everyone's first or second language in the eastern Mediterranean. In the provinces north and west of Rome, e.g., Gaul, Spain, and Britain, Latin was, of course, the official language of the empire, and only the educated knew Greek as well as Latin, along with their own native languages.

When the barbarian invasions ended the Roman Empire in the west in the fifth century A.D., Latin remained as the basic language because of the superiority of imperial Latin culture, while in the east the Roman Empire survived as the Byzantine Empire for another thousand years with a Greek-based culture.

The theoretical works on rhetoric represented in this guide are all in Greek or Latin, and they cover a period of some one thousand years, from the golden age of Athens to the fall of the Western Roman Empire. This body of theory reflects the most important aspects of ancient civic life: the use of words and ideas a) politically to influence public affairs in assemblies of every kind (deliberative or political rhetoric), b) to defend or accuse in the courts (judicial or forensic rhetoric), and c) to inform and entertain, from conversational exchanges, letters, history, fiction, and poetry to all sorts of ceremonial speeches and funeral orations (epideictic rhetoric). Consequently, rhetorical theory is central to ancient life and to the accomplishments of ancient culture.

As it developed, rhetoric came to have five separate areas of instruction: invention (Greek *heuresis* or Latin *inventio*); arrangement (*taxis* or *dispositio*); style (*lexis* or *elocutio*); memory (*mnêmê* or *memoria*); and delivery (*hypokrisis* or *actio*). From the earliest extant treatises invention, or finding what to say, is of central importance, and it represents a fundamentally different way of thinking about composition from our own. This method of composition may have been originated by Aristotle. Since it appears not only in his work but also in the contemporaneous *Rhetorica ad Alexandrum,* however, it was probably a method already in use that was given defining status in his *Rhetoric.*

Aristotle saw rhetoric as education in finding the appropriate means of persuasion. One "finds" persuasive arguments in pre-learned "places" (*topoi* in Greek, *loci* in Latin) or seats (Latin *sedes*), and the fundamental instruction in rhetoric involved teaching the student what these places are. The student then practiced finding appropriate arguments from the appropriate places in composing speeches, either in writing or extemporaneously—this system was designed for and worked equally well for both. The successful result of this process was the presentation of proofs that created conviction in audiences and thereby persuaded them. Interestingly enough, the term used for "conviction"—*pistis* in Greek, *fides* in Latin—was used interchangeably for "proof" (both words also mean faith, as used in the New Testament), although there were other terms for proof as well, *probatio, confirmatio,* etc.

Aristotle identified and codified for all subsequent rhetorical theory three separate sources of proofs or areas of conviction. The first source is the character of the speaker (*êthos*), the second the content of what he has to say (*logos*), and the third the emotional reaction of the audience (*pathos*). These three areas are all part of the art of rhetoric (i.e., can be taught) and are created by the speech itself. This creation includes the speaker's own ethos. While Isocrates and later Quintilian emphasize how important the actual character of the speaker is, they and all other theorists accepted the fact that the character or the "voice" in any speech is also created by and in the speech itself.

Ethical proofs are most important at the beginning of a speech; logical proofs are mainly for the exposition of one's arguments, and pathetic proofs are generally reserved for the conclusion. In the introduction to a speech, then, we propose our topic (directly or indirectly) while persuading the audience with ethical proofs that we are worth listening to. Then we make our case as logically convincing as possible (Aristotle's *Rhetoric* has a primary focus on logical proofs). Finally, we conclude by appealing to our audience's emotions, so that they will not only be convinced rationally and logically but emotionally as well, i.e., they will not only think the same way we do about the subject but feel the same way, too.

These topical rules of finding proofs became prescriptive. The early first-century B.C. *Rhetorica ad Herennium* is typical. In it we learn that every legal case will involve one of the following four: the honorable, the disgraceful, the doubtful, or the inconsequential (1.3.5). The speaker must decide which and proceed to use the appropriate topoi of the introduction, of which there are two kinds, the direct and indirect (1.4.6). The speaker will choose the kind appropriate to the case, e.g., the direct introduction for a doubtful case (1.4.6). The idea here is to make the audience receptive, well disposed, and attentive. A brief overview of our position will make the audience receptive (1.4.7). Their attention will be aroused if we promise to disclose new or unexpected material. We make them well disposed to us by favorable remarks about ourselves, unfavorable remarks about our opponents, flattering remarks about the audience, and references to the facts of the case showing that we know what we are talking about (1.4–5.8).

According to the *ad Herennium* the conclusion should do three things: give a summation of our argument, amplify, and appeal to the audience's pity (2.30.47). Ten further topoi are given as means of amplification (from a prosecutorial point of view): the significance of the case; who has been affected; the danger to the body politic of overlooking such a crime; the bad example and precedent of leniency; the once-for-all nature of judgment, which means that the correct judgment must be made; premeditation; the heinousness of the crime generally; any unique aspects of heinousness; comparison to other heinous crimes, showing that the present one is worse than something else generally acknowledged to be evil; and a vivid description of the horrible details of the crime (2.30.48–49). The appeal for pity (from a defense point of view) will take up such topoi as the horrible effect on our lives if we lose, our grief, misery, etc., and will include, as appropriate, direct groveling for mercy (2.31.50).

The topoi here of amplification are initially identified as commonplaces (*loci communes, RAH* 2.30; *konoi topoi* in Greek). In both the *ad Herennium* and Cicero's contemporaneous *De inventione* places that may be used on either side of an argument are defined (*RAH* 2.5.9 and *De inv.* 2.48) and frequently, but not exclusively, referred to as commonplaces. The association of commonplaces with amplification designed to arouse the emotions of the audience in the conclusion of a speech, however, seems to tilt their use toward the prosecutorial side of attack (*RAH* 2.30, 48–49; *De inv.* 2.48–50), and by the time of Quintilian in the late first century A.D. commonplaces refer to attacks on vices generally or typically as distinguished from attacks on particular vices in particular people (2.4.22, as an early exercise, and 5.13.57). This sense continues to be reflected in the early rhetorical exercises outlined by Theon (who, however, uses *topos* alone more frequently than *koinos topos*), Hermogenes, Aphthonius, etc.

As can be seen from the *Rhetorica ad Herennium*, rhetorical theory came to be dominated by forensic rhetoric, although Aristotle's *Rhetoric* gives a great deal of attention to deliberative or political material, and this is the main focus of the early *Rhetorica ad Alexandrum*. The chief development in inventional (topical) composition that occurred after Aristotle, however, was made by Hermagoras of Temnos (second century B.C.) as an improvement to instruction in judicial rhetoric. Hermagoras's works are lost but, his *staseis* (*status* or *constitutiones* in Latin) were universally adopted as an additional tool to assist the speaker in the organization of arguments in any legal case.

The *staseis*, or issues, are comprehensively reviewed in Cicero's early *De inventione*, in the *Rhetorica ad Herennium*, later by Quintilian (late first century A.D.) and Hermogenes (*On Staseis*, covering political as well as legal issues, late second century A.D), and last of all by Menander Rhetor (third century A.D.), who applies the issues to epideictic rhetoric. There are four of them, providing the speaker with a sequential pattern for grasping the basis of any dispute: the conjectural, definitional, qualitative, and translative (*De inventione* 1.8–11). First, the area of dispute may be over the facts of a case themselves (conjectural). If there is agreement about the facts, then the question may be about how the facts (i.e., what has happened that is at issue) are to be construed or defined (definitional). If there is also agreement here, the point of controversy may be over the nature or quality of what happened (qualitative). If there is no dispute here either, then the point may be what we would call legal applicability, i.e., whether the correct accusation has been made, whether it has been made before the correct court, whether the correct defendant has been accused, etc. (translative). There are then species and subspecies of these basic issues, providing even more precise qualification of the point of dispute, which students were required to learn and practice using, as well.

While the ancient method of inventional composition was quite different from our modern pedagogical theories (at least until recently, when interest has been revived in them), the bases of argumentation and proof reflected an essentially different attitude toward life from ours. Ancient sophistic and rhetoric dealt with probabilities, accepting the fact that almost nothing is certain in life. This position seemed true to the ancients in both the legal and the political areas, which, as Aristotle was the first to point out, treat, respectively, questions of the past and the future.

As to the future, no political or legislative assembly can determine how laws will actually work out. In practice laws may not have the effect we imagine or hope, and decisions to make war, peace, commercial treaties, etc., may not achieve the goals we desire. In every case the deliberations can only aim at what will probably be the best course. There can be no certainty about the future.

But the same is true of the past. Even today it is apparent, as it was to the ancients, that proving that someone did something "beyond a reasonable doubt" is hard to do. The big difference between ancient and modern practice of the law is in the reliance on what we call evidence. The ancients had a lower view than we do of evidence per se. While we tend to think of evidence as self-evident and obvious, the ancients knew well that evidence never speaks for itself. Aristotle points out in his *Posterior Analytics* and *Rhetoric* that evidence or "signs" must always be construed in some context of probable conclusions that can be drawn from them. There are only a few "necessary signs" that may be assumed to be conclusive in their own right, but even these must be argued and put into a context of more or less probable proofs, and thus are within the domain, not of the factual or self-evident, but of the artistic control of the orator.

Aristotle, again, was the first to note that persuasive proofs or sources of conviction are either artificial or inartificial. By artificial he meant those that are subject to the inventional powers of the speaker, i.e., that are made by the art of rhetoric—including evidence, or what the ancients called the facts of a case, which only take on meaning in the artistic representation of them by the orator. Inartificial proofs are not directly subject to, and are essentially outside of, the realm of the art of rhetoric. These proofs are: the content of laws and contracts; testimony of witnesses; the results of torture (in ancient Greek and Roman law, slaves, low-class persons, and noncitizens were regularly subjected to torture as an inducement to get them to tell the truth); and oaths. Even though we still know today that the testimony of witnesses may be unreliable and that evidence is subject to interpretation, our much higher view of inferential or inductive reasoning, the so-called scientific method, has led our culture to view these kinds of proofs as providing far more certitude on their own than the ancients allowed.

Aristotle pointed out that the results of inductive, inferential reasoning never achieve absolute, only relatively more or less, certain conclusions. Hence he developed a system of what he called scientific reasoning whereby, given absolutely true premises, one could arrive at absolutely certain conclusions, i.e., apodictic truths. The success of this now well-known process of syllogistic reasoning actually depends, as Aristotle recognized, on inductive observation to provide the premises for the syllogism. Although we can be almost completely confident in the certainty of many premises (Socrates is a man, the sun rises every day), nonetheless, inductively based observation yields only more or less probable truths; and many inferences are not conclusively certain at all, since all observation depends on how things appear.

Consequently, Aristotle divided deductive or syllogistic reasoning itself into two basic kinds. One, based on true premises (i.e., as true and certain as can be realized), was the primary tool of philosophy. The other, based on probabilties (i.e., inferences that are not at all certain), was, along with inductive reasoning itself, the tool of rhetoric and the law. Aristotle's views prevailed in Western culture down to the scientific revolution of modern times, and his system of deductive reasoning, adopted by the Stoics and practically everyone else in antiquity, realized its greatest achievements in the Scholastic theology of the late Middle Ages. The reason was that the Scholastics had a source of absolutely true propositions and premises in the Bible, which was believed to have been divinely inspired. From these premises absolutely true conclusions could be deductively drawn.

Aristotelian predominance was challenged immediately after the heyday of Scholasticism and was gradually eroded as the successes of scientific technology and the industrial revolution transformed the Western world. Finally, Aristotele's realism and his methods of deduction were scrapped in favor of inferential reasoning based on scientific observation. We all recognize, to take just one example, the stunning and continuing effect of Charles Darwin's *On the Origin of Species,* which is used to this day to deny deistic creation as described in the Bible on the basis of inductively reached conclusions from observation of natural phenomena.

With the continuing triumph of scientific technology, our culture has come to believe that inferential observation using inductive reasoning results in the closest thing one can find to absolute truth, i.e., that evidence from observation is true. Even though the "laws" (conclusions) of science are continually being altered by new methods of observation and better means of testing scientific hypotheses, we still put our primary trust in inductive inferences based on observation. These hypotheses, which for Aristotle and the ancients were no more than educated guesses based on probabilites, have become for us, thanks to the technological capabilities of experimental confirmation, the source of reliable truth. As far as the law is concerned, public confidence in the uses of evidence has been powerfully reinforced by advances in forensic science and pathology (e.g., DNA testing). Consequently, in our court system, we have a much higher view of, and rely far more on, legal evidence.

In antiquity, where everything was a matter of probabilities, and evidence was not privileged above other kinds of forensic proofs, the preferred kind of proof was what we would call group prejudice. In his treatment of ethical and pathetic proofs in Book 2 of the

Rhetoric Aristotle gives an extensive account (the first in antiquity) of human psychology and behavior (2.1–17). This study is continued in a work by Aristotle's most famous pupil and successor, Theophrastus, whose book *Characters* gives detailed vignettes of thirty, mainly negative, types of human behavior. Again, ancient culture followed this Aristotelian lead in viewing human beings and human behavior as typical in certain defined ways. Thus, a drunk, any drunk, will have certain typical traits that define him and all others like him (note the use of inductive analogy here).

Today we view such stereotyping as inherently wrong, but the ancients relied on it. The results of actual and hypothetical legal cases, recorded in numerous anecdotes, especially by Cicero and Quintilian, can be astonishing to us. But the method is apparent from the earliest beginnings of rhetoric.

A nice example is the *Defense on Behalf of Palamedes*, written by Gorgias as a model forensic speech. Palamedes had been accused of treason against the Greeks by Odysseus, who planted two pieces of damning physical evidence: a forged letter from the Trojan king Priam arranging for the betrayal, and a sack of gold—the payoff—in his tent. Palamedes' defense, as constructed by Gorgias, rebuts the force of this evidence with an ethical defense but without attacking the evidence itself. Although he does point to such contradictory evidence as the language barrier, he spends most of his effort on the ethical proof of the recognized quality of his own simple virtue and reputation for integrity, arguing that notwithstanding any evidence to the contrary, he is incapable of comitting such a deed. Clever rhetorical twists are added to this basic defense. His "spin" on the accusation, for example, is that he is being accused of two contradictory things: one, that he is crazy enough to attempt a betrayal of his own cause, and two, that he is clever enough to accomplish it. Such contradictions in his view, nullify the effect of any and all actual evidence. And, astonishingly for us, Palamedes accuses Odysseus of basing his accusation on opinion, not truth, because the truth is that Palamedes is obviously not the kind of person who could do such a thing.

How persuasive this hypothetical defense would have been is impossible to ascertain (in the story that has come down to us, the Greek leader Agamemnon discovered the damning evidence and had

Palamedes summarily executed by stoning). Nonetheless, it is true that in defense or prosecution ancient Greeks and Romans depended more than we on ethical proofs and less on the self-evident impact of the "facts" (with all the "scientific" implications of that term) of the case at hand. This is not to say that in the ancient world, if a crime were committed, and you were the type of person who did such things and had the opportunity to commit the crime, you were probably guilty. But you would have appeared more likely to be guilty than in our day and would have had a more difficult time defending yourself with or without factual evidence. Certainly, the accomplishments of Roman justice were great, and in most Greek and Roman courts the truth probably did prevail most of the time; but it is also true that the rhetorical skills of invention were more important in the ancient world, where the typical probabilities of behavior largely determined how one's particular actions were evaluated.

And these probabilities were closely related to a third cornerstone of ancient rhetoric, decorum or propriety. Aristotle had used the concept of decorum in his discussion of style (*Rhetoric* 3), but it was Cicero who identified and codified it as a primary element underlying the very essence of rhetoric and, indeed, as he says, life itself. Cicero was led to this strong conclusion about the significance of decorum in the context of a major argument about styles of speaking late in his public career at the end of the Roman Republic. Some younger orators, and particularly one Calvus, were arguing that consistent use of a plain, unembellished style was the true reflection of classic Attic (Athenian) style, as opposed to the florid, often highly embellished style of Cicero and other Latin speakers of his generation and earlier. The style of Calvus was more like that of the Athenian Lysias, whereas Cicero preferred Demosthenes, accepted almost universally as the greatest Greek orator (and to whom Cicero's own style could be more favorably compared), as representative of true or authentic Atticism.

Now it was true that most speakers in antiquity, as Quintilian and others affirm, spoke in basically one style—i.e., they had their own style of speaking, their own voice, as it were, on whatever occasion, about whatever topic, and in whatever venue. Cicero's rejoinder is that true Attic style was, indeed, practiced by Demosthenes and a few other Athenians but that it was not characterized by uniformity and sameness but rather by variation. Cicero points out that Demosthenes significantly varies his style according to the occasion, the topic, and the audience and that he himself does the same thing. Yes, sometimes—to some audiences and on some subjects—a plain, unembellished style is appropriate. But on other occasions or even in different parts of the same speech, a grandiloquent, elaborate style is best and most effective. This ability to vary one's style is for Cicero the main accomplishment of the successful speaker and is defined by decorum, which, according to him, rules not only rhetoric but all other aspects of life as well. We dress appropriately for whatever function we are attending; there are the appropriate times to laugh, make war, be angry, etc.—a position that echoes the famous statement on decorum in the Old Testament book of Ecclesiastes (3.1–8).

Stylistic versatility is the key to decorum, but there was something equally important about style throughout ancient rhetorical theory, from the the *Rhetorica ad Herennium* (Book 4) and works of Cicero (*De Oratore* 3, *Brutus,* and *Orator*), Dionysius of Halicarnassus (especially *On Literary Composition*), Alexander, Aristides, Demetrius, and Longinus, to the later works of Hermogenes (*On Types of Style, On the Method of Force*). Style was not viewed by the ancients as something separable and added to content. Rather they thought, much like the New Critics of the twentieth century, that form and content are inseparable. The best articulation of this point is in the treatise identified with the name Longinus, which remains one of the most sophisticated discussions of style ever written. Centuries before Marshall McLuhan opined that "the medium is the message," Longinus sets out in detail why and how the style of written or spoken expression not only carries the content but enables it to have meaning and effectively informs whatever impact it has, and so is a determinant of meaning.

Stylistic matters included diction and syntax (correct usage; coined words; figurative language; the structure of phrases, clauses, and sentences) and even the rhythmic sounds of language; style was, consequently, the third element of rhetorical instruction, following invention and arrangement. Arrangement, or organization of one's thoughts, does not receive much direct attention in ancient rhetorical theory because the order and sequence of thoughts was already implied in topical invention. The customary five parts of a forensic speech (introduction, statement of the facts of the case, proof, refutation, and conclusion) not only had their prescribed topoi but a sequential order, as well. Thus, we should marshall our arguments in the proof in a certain order, and similarly in the refutation of our opponent's position.

Order and sequence in the application of topoi were also prescribed in the rhetorical exercises (*progymnasmata*) for beginning students of rhetoric. Several texts of these exercises survive, from the oldest extant one by Theon (first century A.D.) to those by Hermogenes (second century), Aphthonius (fourth), Nicolaus (fifth), and Priscian (c. A.D. 500), whose *Praeexercitamina* is a Latin reworking of Hermogenes.

The twelve or fourteen exercises show how important writing had become by the end of the Roman Republic and how rhetorical instruction served not just orators but historians, essayists, poets, and dramatists, as well. In Aphthonius the exercises are in writing: fables; any narrative account; anecdotal stories; aphorisms; argumentative refutations; proofs; amplification of evil behavior (commonplace); praise of anything; invective; characterization; vivid description; comparison; thesis and hypothesis; and proposing a law.

Theatrical skills were also important in the final two areas of rhetorical instruction, memory and delivery. Like the actor, the speaker who writes down a set speech before he delivers it must learn it. Here again the method of topical invention aided in two additional ways beyond the creation of the written composition itself. Some speakers only made topical notes beforehand, remembered these, and then spoke extemporaneously from them. And, of course, as the opponents of writing down speeches ahead of time observe, forensic and deliberative interchange always demands that the orator be able to think on his feet and speak extemporaneously anyway.

Whether the speech was completely memorized or completely extemporaneous, delivery was inherently a theatrical performance, one to which the ancients gave much attention. They were the first to discuss body language and the implications of pose and gesture, facial expression, etc. The Romans of the Republic had a special problem here in that one hand, the left, had always to hold on to the toga to keep it from falling apart in the front and exposing the speaker (actors on the stage wore the much more convenient Greek tunic).

The active uses of rhetoric in the Roman Republic paralleled the life of rhetoric in the Greek city-states. But with the advent of the empire, deliberative and even forensic rhetoric declined, as Tacitus complains in the late first century, and it became a frequent butt of satire (e.g., in Lucian and Sextus Empiricus). Although some emperors occasionally solicited senatorial advice, they were, in fact, absolute rulers, and no policies were made by the Senate. On the legal front, although there was probably no less litigation, the effect of a top-down hierarchy of power seems to have stifled the full and open uses of forensic rhetoric and encouraged the importance of bribes and political associations. Practice or display speeches on political and legal topics, which had been around, of course, at least since Gorgias, now became more important than the real things in real assemblies and real courts. Early in the imperial period Seneca the Elder (c. 50 B.C.–A.D. 40) assembled a collection of such speeches from memory—revealing just how hollow and meaningless they could be.

The decline of political and legal rhetoric was paralleled in imperial times by the increasing importance of the third kind of rhetoric: epideictic, the rhetoric of praise and blame. Display speeches celebrating gods, emperors, governors, regions, cities, etc., became a principal medium for oratorical skills. Gifted speakers commanded large crowds to listen to these kinds of speeches, which were essentially forms of artistic entertainment (and possibly edification), and, as such, were more like prose poems. Indeed, the most important ancient authority on epideictic rhetoric, Menander, who has left us two treatises on the subject from the third century A.D., makes no distinction between poetry and prose.

But rhetoric survived in all its forms, especially in encyclopedic compendia of the seven liberal arts, of which the most important for the Middle Ages was that by Martianus Capella from late antiquity. Even instruction in the two prominent new areas of composition in the Middle Ages, preaching and letter writing, was thoroughly topical and followed the patterns of prescriptive, formulaic invention of ancient rhetoric. Furthermore, all the revivals of learning in France and England before the Renaissance (e. g. the Carolingian and twelfth-century "renaissances" and the "new" poetics of the fourteenth century) were essentially informed in some way or other by the methods of ancient rhetoric.

The foundations of Renaissance Humanism also lie in classical rhetoric. Ancient texts were recovered and printed, and educated men and women attempted to write and speak good classical Latin, rather than the stylistically inferior church Latin of the Middle Ages. And this Latin superculture, which, in the sixteenth century, ruled all over Europe from England and Portugal to Poland, profoundly influenced the vernacular literatures of Central and Western Europe, poetry and prose, from the Renaissance through the eighteenth century. One cannot assess the achievements of Ariosto, Tasso, Ronsard, Racine, Spenser, Milton, Dryden, or Pope without reference to ancient rhetoric.

In this sense classical rhetoric is far more significant for our understanding of literary art in the West than are the relatively few extant poetics from antiquity. Of the two best known and most influential, Horace's "Letter to Piso," the so-called *Ars poetica,* is itself largely informed by the rhetorical concept of decorum, and its famous dictum that poetry should please and instruct comes straight from rhetorical theory about the function of any speech. Aristotle's *Poetics* is also informed by the rhetorical concept of decorum in the definition of tragedy and its parts, and his important idea about the organic wholeness of a poetic work comes from Plato's standard for the composition of a speech (*Phaedrus* 264c). Consequently, the more than fifty works reviewed here reflect all of the essential points about the use and manipulation of words not only in ancient Greco-Roman culture but throughout Western culture down to the nineteenth century.

ALCIDAMAS was a fourth-century B.C. sophist from Elaea in Asia Minor. He studied under Gorgias and was a rival of Isocrates, whose advocacy of polished written oratory he opposed. His genuine writings are lost (an extant speech titled *Odysseus against the Treason of Palamedes* is falsely attributed to him) except for the short treatise *CONCERNING THOSE WHO WRITE WRITTEN SPEECHES OR CONCERNING SOPHISTS (PERI TÔN TOUS GRAPTOUS LOGOUS GRAPHONTÔN Ê PERI SOPHISTÔN)*.

A. begins by saying that he writes in response to those of the sophists who write out speeches before delivering them. These men are pretentious and not very knowledgeable in rhetoric and speaking. The practice of writing speeches should be secondary to speaking; indeed, it is inferior to rhetoric and philosophy, and those who do it would be better called writers than sophists. Writing speeches is easier than speaking extemporaneously, amassing arguments, etc., and those who speak well could certainly write speeches well, but not vice versa. Speaking is always useful, while writing seldom is; speaking is a quick and nimble activity, writing a slow and ponderous one; and speeches appearing to have been written beforehand seem insincere and inspire disgust (1–13).

To have memorized written speeches on a variety of topics makes the speaker appear inconsistent, for sometimes his speech will be polished, at other times rough, depending on which parts were taken from memory and which were improvised. Those who habitually write out speeches become less and less able to respond extemporaneously. Remembering written speeches is difficult, and it is embarassing and obvious when one forgets something. When such people are forced to alter something in the middle of a lawsuit, they find it difficult. Extemporaneous speech can better adapt to the audience's desire for brevity, length, etc. Again, written speeches do not allow for quick alteration, since the speech would become choppy and disjointed. Written speeches should not be called speeches at all, but images (*eidôla*), forms (*schêmata*), or copies (*mimêmata*) of speeches, and should be thought of the way we think of statues, paintings, etc., which are enjoyable for a moment but have no practical use (14–28).

A. admits that it may be absurd to *write* an argument against written speeches, to criticize the act of writing when he wants to be esteemed as a writer, and to have respect for knowledge while denigrating preparation. But while writing is inferior to extemporaneous speech, he wants those who do not know him to learn about him from his writings, and it is easier to judge someone's intellectual development from writing than from extemporaneous speech, for speech is soon forgotten. Finally, A. stresses that he favors extemporaneous speech but not speaking randomly without coherent organization. Orators should exercise forethought. All-around excellence in oratory requires practice in extemporaneous speech (29–34).

Text: *Artium Scriptores (Reste der voraristotelischen Rhetorik)*, ed. Ludwig Radermacher (Vienna: Rudolf M. Rohrer, 1951), 132–47. Translation: *Readings from Classical Rhetoric*, ed. Patricia P. Matsen, Philip Rollinson, and Marion Sousa (Carbondale: Southern Illinois Univrsity Press, 1990), 38–42.

ALEXANDER, son of Numenius, was an official under Hadrian who lived in the second century A.D. He wrote a treatise on figures, of which an epitome survives called *ON THE FIGURES OF THOUGHT AND SPEECH (PERI TÔN TÊS DIANOIAS KAI TÊS LEXEÔS SCHÊMATÔN)*, as well as a general handbook of rhetoric, *ON RHETORICAL SUBJECTS (PERI RHETORIKÔN APHOR-MÔN)*, of which a portion survives.

In the epitome on figures A. begins by remarking that figures (*schêmata*) are a difficult subject because of the sheer number of them. He will arrange them according to thought (*dianoia*) and diction (*lexis*). As for the difference between a figure and a trope (*tropos*), a figure involves more than one word, a trope only a single word. Further, a trope involves a word not used in its proper sense, whereas the figure preserves the proper sense. The figures of diction differ from those of thought in that if the arrangement of words in figures of diction is altered by moving, removing, or adding, the figures are lost, but if the words are altered in figures of thought, the figures remain intact. A. defines figure as an alteration for the better in diction or thought, and one that is not a trope. Figures serve to embellish speech (Spengel, vol. 3, pp. 9–14).

A. discusses figures of thought first, giving one or more examples from poetry or prose (usually from Demosthenes) for each. His definitions are often vague, obscure, and idiosyncratic compared to those of other writers. He reviews, in order (pp. 14–27), *prodiorthôsis* (preparatory apology); *epidiorthôsis* (correction of a previous expression); *amphidiorthôsis* (guarding both before and after); *prokatalêpsis* (anticipation); *hypexairesis* (removal); *aetiologia* (giving the cause); *synathroismos* (collection); *epimonê* (delay); *leptologia* (subtle discourse); *prosôpopoiia* (personification); *epanalêpsis* (repetition of words or phrases); *epanaphora* (repetition of words beginning clauses); *êthopoiia* (characterization); *aposiôpêsis* (passing over something in silence); *epitrochasmos* (hurried accumulation); *eirôneia* (irony); *paraleipsis* (omission); *apostrophê* (turning back or shifting the attack); *diaporêsis* (perplexity of multiple or feigned thoughts); *erôtêma* (a "yes" or "no" question); *pysma* (a more than "yes" or "no" question); *diatypôsis* (vivid description); *anteisagôgê* (contrastive substitution); *diasyrmos* (ridicule); and *metastasis* (removal by shifting the blame).

Then to figures of diction. Diction is secondary to thought; it makes the thought clear. The most important figures of diction are the period (*periodos,* full sentence), colon (*kôlon,* clause), and comma (*komma,* phrase); these are the elements that make up diction. A period is an expression that by combination of cola produces a thought complete in itself. A colon is part of a period, which either stands by itself or completes an antithetical period. A comma is smaller than a period or colon. It is used by itself or in reference to something else. Some periods have two, three, and even four cola. Periods that have more than four lack good proportion and have the arrangement not of periods but of detailed speeches. Periods can be complete in themselves or joined together (pp. 27–29).

Other figures of diction are *anadiplôsis, palillogia,* or *epanalêpsis* (repetition of words); *epanaphora* (beginning clauses with the same words); *antistrophê* (ending clauses with the same words); *symplochê* or *synthesis* (combining *anaphora* and *antistrophê*); *synônymia* (synonym); *epanodos* (fuller statement); *climax* (ladder, ending a clause and beginning the next one with the same phrasing); *prosdiasaphêsis* (added explanation); *periphrasis* (circumlocution); *pleonasm* (redundancy); *asyndeton* or *dialysis* (leaving out connective words); *elleipsis* (omission of one or more words); *alloiôsis* or *allagê* (change of number, case, tense, or voice); *polyptôton* (variation of case); *metabolê* (change of sentences, clauses, and phrases); *zeugma* (joining); *homoioteleuton* (like endings of clauses); *homoioptôton* (use of the same case); *paronomasia* (pun, slightly altering the sense); *antithesis* (opposition, use of antithetical expressions); *antimetathesis, synkrisis,* or *plokê* (interchange, use of same words to indicates different things); *antimetabolê* (transposition of the same words); *antenantiôsis* (counter-contradiction, positive statement made in negative form) (pp. 36–38); *hyperbaton* (transposition breaking up parts of words); *parembolê* (interpolation); *parison* (even balance of syllables in two or more cola); *prosynapantêsis* (meeting beforehand, putting modifiers of a later noun with an earlier one); and *epitimêsis* (censure) and *hypallagê* (interchange), which both censure (pp. 29–40).

ON RHETORICAL SUBJECTS begins with the point that the two chief rhetorical problems are thesis and hypothesis. Thesis is a general inquiry without a defined person, while hypothesis involves a defined person. Hypotheses inquire into events past, present, or future. Political oratory (*politikos logos*) has three hypotheses: encomium, deliberation, and justice. These differ among themselves in the time, circumstance, end, and audience toward which they are directed (pp. 1–2).

On the difference between *epainos* (praise) and encomium (*engkômion*): some think that *epainos* refers to some specific virtue, but encomium to the whole of a man's life; further, that *epainos* is concise and simple, encomium far-reaching and great. But it is truer to say that *epainos* differs from encomium as the true differs from the persuasive; *epainos* involves that about which there is no disagreement, but persuasion is a necessary component of encomium. Some say that *epainoi* emphasize greatness of virtue, encomia noble achievements. We deliver *epainoi* to the gods for their virtue but encomia to the men who fought at Marathon or Salamis. It is said that eulogy is a type of *epainos*, and that a hymn is an *epainos* for a god (pp. 2–4).

On how it is necessary to praise (*epainein*) a god: you may start with the birth of the gods and, following Plato, say that they were born from the first god, who is unbegotten and immortal. Then discuss the begotten gods. Review births, habits, names, ages. Discuss versions given by various peoples; for example, Egyptians and Greeks say different things about Herakles. Say whether the god is worshipped by all or some nations. If by all, point that out; if by some, praise these nations by saying that they are the strongest, oldest, most well governed, etc. Discuss the god's powers and skills, and whether he is heavenly, marine, or terrestrial, as well as his relationship with the other gods (pp. 4–6).

Text: *Rhetores Graeci*, ed. Leonardi Spengel (1853–56; rpt. Frankfurt: Minerva, 1966), 3:1–40.

ANONYMOUS SEGUERIANUS refers to the unknown author of an *ART OF POLITICAL SPEECH (TECHNÊ TOU POLITIKOU LOGOU)*, from approximately the early third century A.D. In 1838 Séguier, Marquis de St. Brison, found a manuscript of the work in Paris's royal library. The work draws heavily from Alexander, son of Numenius (*q.v.*). Other sources mentioned include Apollodorus of Pergamum (first century B.C.), Theodorus (first century B.C.), and Harpocration, Neocles, and Zeno, all of whom probably lived in the second century A.D. Throughout the work, points are illustrated by references to Greek literature.

In the first chapter A.S. divides a political speech into four parts: introductions (*prooimia*), narration (*diêgêsis*), proofs (*pisteis*), and conclusions (*epilogoi*, 1). But he also accepts the opinion of ancient writers that an introduction is a speech that manipulates the emotions of the hearer. Sources are the speaker, the opponent, the judges, and the subjects (*pragmata*, 5–7). Speakers use three techniques in order to make the audience receptive: *proekthesis*, a statement of what one is going to say; *ananeôsis*, a review of points previously made, and *merismos*, an outline of the parts of the oration (10–13). The speaker should also be trustworthy (*axiopistos*), knowledgeable (*eidôs*), and experienced (*empeiros*); should use censure (*to epitiman*), claim to say what is legal (*nomima*), seem honorable (*endoxos*) or use the advice of honorable men, say that he will speak about important, noble, or advantageous things, and promise that he will speak briefly and wisely about what is new and relevant (14–15). He can create good will (*eunoia*) by his nature, way of life, or heredity, by saying what is advantageous or that he has similar desires, by being admired (*chrêstos*), modest, fair, and reasonable (*epieikês*, 16–18).

The introduction differs from the conclusion in that figures (*schêmata*) and style (*hermêneia*) in the former should be moderate (*metrion*) and tame (*tithasson*); but figures in the latter should be excited (*sungkekinêmena*), and the style should be metaphorical (*tropikê*), with a specialized vocabulary. Moreover, much of what is said in introductions should not be said in conclusions (19–20). A.S. thinks that the introduction is not always necessary, and mentions circumstances in which it should be omitted, citing the arguments of Alexander in support of this view. But he also presents the view of others, such as the followers of Apollodorus, that it is essential

(21–36). A.S. concludes this chapter with a brief discussion of the use of multiple introductions (37–39).

In the second chapter he presents definitions of narration from Neocles, Zeno, Theodorus, and Apollodorus, but he seems to favor Alexander's definition, which he gives last in this series: the narration is the speaker's account of the subject of the oration (46–51). There are four types: true, fictitious (*peplasmenê*), spoken to judges, and composed for their own sake. Narrations composed for their own sake may pertain to life (*biôtikai*), historical (*historikai*) or mythical (*mythikai*) materials, or the vicissitudes of fortune (*peripetikai*). Narrations addressed to judges may be straightforward, but some are incidental to the facts of the case (*paradiêgêseis*) or designed to counter the opponent (*antidiêgêseis*). Incidental narrations can be divided into preliminary ones (*prodiêgêseis*), those of other facts alongside the main facts (*paradiêgêseis*), and those after the proofs or in the epilogue (*epidiêgêseis*, 53–60).

Narrations should have brevity (*syntomia*), clarity (*saphêneia*), and persuasiveness (*pithanotês*). The speaker can be brief in the facts (*pragmata*) by avoiding redundancy, lengthy digressions, etc., and brief in style (*lexis*) by avoiding synonyms, long words, epithets, repetition, and periphrasis and by using ellipsis, a single word to govern several words or phrases (*epizeugma*), asyndeton, and emphatic omission (*emphasis paraleipseôs*, 63–78). The speaker can preserve clarity in content by avoiding obscure topics, confused chronology, repetition, etc., and clarity in style by avoiding foreign words, strange words, onomatopoeia, and so on (79–88). Persuasiveness is created by, among other things, attempting to make everything that is said resemble the truth, and using maxims (*gnomai*) and lofty language (*hypsêlê phrasis*, 89–100).

A.S. identifies seven tropes (*tropoi*) of narration: amplification (*auxêsis*), diminution (*meiôsis*), euphemism, omission (*paraleipsis*), reminder (*epanamnêsis*), exaggeration and understatement (*epi to kreitton ê cheiron phrasis*), and vividness (*enargeia*, 105–11). He reviews the arguments of the followers of Apollodorus that narration is always necessary and of Alexander and Neocles that it is not (113–23). As for placement, the followers of Apollodorus say that the narration should come only after the introduction, while Alexander and Neocles allow for various positions (124–31). A.S. also gives various arguments on the issue of whether the narration should be a single entity or divided, and on whether there should be one narration or many for a single question (*zêtêma*, 132–35). The chapter concludes with assorted remarks on the style (*hermêneia* or *lexis*) of narratives. In general, it should be bolder (*thrasytera*) than that of the introduction, as well as simple (*haplê*) and clear (136–42).

The third chapter begins by defining a proof as language that supports the proposed question. Some proofs are nonartistic, such as witnesses, decrees, and contracts, and others are artistic, requiring the art of rhetoric. Presenting the various (and sometimes quite different) views of his sources, A.S. discusses various types of artistic proof, including example (*paradeigma*), enthymeme, pathos, and evidence, which divides into proof from probability (*eikos*), sign (*tekmêrion*), and, again, example. An enthymeme, according to Harpocration, is language used for the demonstration (*apodeixis*) of the subject of the speech. The proposition (*prothesis*) of the demonstration is designed to make the audience receptive and to make clear the transition from the narration to the proofs; it may also be used for amplification and diminution (143–65).

A.S. next discusses the topics (*topoi*) of the proof, many of which have their own subdivisions. The most common topics are definition (*horos*), division (*diairesis*), comparison (*parathesis*), correspondence (*systoichia*), inclusion (*periochê*), likness (*homoion*), adjunct (*parepomenon*), inconsistency (*machê*), potentiality (*dynamis*), and judgement (*krisis*, 169–82). Then to affirmation (*kataskeuê*) and refutation (*anaskeuê* or *lysis*) of proofs, with a heavy emphasis on the latter. A. discusses the refutation of proofs based on examples and then refutation of nonartistic proofs, including laws, the testimony of witnesses, evidence taken under torture, and oaths (183–91). The chapter concludes with brief remarks on organization and style. The speaker, for example, should generally place weak points after strong points. The style of proofs should be concise (*synestrammenê*), pointed (*kônoeidês*), and argumentative (*agônistikê*). Delivery (*hypokrisis*) should fit the character of the speech (192–97).

The fourth and final chapter on conclusions begins with a discussion of various definitions. Alexander, A. says, defines the conclusion as a speech strengthening what has been said. There are two aspects: the practical (*praktikon*), which involves recapitulation (*anakephalaiôsis*), and the pathetical (*pathêtikon*), which involves preparing the emotions and strengthening the speech. Both may be omitted when appropriate (198–206). After brief comments on the function of the conclusion, A.S. focuses on the practical aspect and discusses recapitulation, which he defines as a brief summary of what has been said. The diction (*lexis*) in recapitulation should be exact (*akribês*) and the figures varied (207–21).

As for the pathetical aspect, A. identifies four primary emotions: distress (*lypê*), which divides into pity and envy; fear (*phobos*), which divides into shame and anguish (fear of failure); desire (*epithymia*), which divides into anger (desire for revenge) and wrath (impulse to evil); and pleasure (*hêdonê*), which divides into delight at the misfortune of a neighbor (*epichairekakia*) and enjoyment (222–28). Amplification and diminution are important in pathetical conclusions, as are vividness (*diatypôsis*) and conversation involving deceased persons. A. explains that the diction (*phrasis*) of the introduction should be plain; that of the narration more spirited (*thrasytera*) and more daring (*mallon kekindyneumenê*); that of the proofs combative (*enagônios*) and pointed (*pikra*), with periods and *kôla*; and that of epilogues emotional (*pathêtikê*) and more daring (*tolmêrotera*) and passionate (*peripathestera*, 229–43). A. concludes with a recapitulation of his earlier comments on diction, based here on Harpocration and Dionysius of Halicarnassus (243–53).

Text and translation: *Two Greek Rhetorical Treatises from the Roman Empire: Introduction, Text, and Translation of the Arts of Rhetoric Attributed to Anonymus Seguerianus and to Apsines of Gadara*, by Mervin A. Dilts and George A. Kennedy (Leiden: Brill, 1997).

APHTHONIUS (c. A.D. 350–400) has left us the longest of the *PROGYMNASMATA* and the most important, because it not only outlines the exercises but also gives exemplary models for each. There is no introduction or conclusion. Fourteen exercises are treated: story or fable (*mythos*); narrative (*diêgêma*); chreia (*chreia*); aphorism (*gnômê*); refutation (*anaskeuê*); confirmation (*kataskeuê*); commonplace (*koinos topos*); encomium; invective (*psogos*); comparison (*synkrisis*); characterization (*êthopoiia*); vivid description (*ekphrasis*); thesis; and proposing a law (*nomou eisphora*).

Fable or story is defined as "a false statement giving the appearance of truth." Well-known creators of fables have given their names to them: Sybaritic, Cilician, Cyprian, and especially Aesopian. There are three kinds: rational (about humans), ethical (about animals), and mixed. The point or advice of the story (*parainesis*) may be put either before or after the story. The model is the story of the ants and crickets showing that young people ought to work hard (Spengel, 2: 21).

Narrative (*diêgêma*) tells of actions that have happened or as if they had happened. It differs from narration (*diêgêsis*) in the same way that poem (*poiêma*)—e.g., the making of the arms of Achilles—differs from a poesy (*poiêsis*), such as the whole *Iliad*. Narratives are dramatic, historical, or political. A's exemplary narrative is the myth of how the rose became red (22).

Chreia is defined as an anecdote about a person with some exemplary significance. There are three kinds: verbal (a saying); active (referring to actions); and mixed, combining words and action. A further division, with examples provided, involves "encomiastic, paraphrastic, statement of the cause, from the contrary, by comparison, by example, with testimony of ancients, [and] with a brief epilogue" (23–25).

Aphorism is a general statement urging us either to do something or not to do something. The first division, with examples, is into protreptic, apotreptic, declarative, simple, compound, persuasive, true, and hyperbolic. Then A. adds that you can also divide it like the chreia (25–27).

Refutation should focus on what is neither obviously in error nor irrefutable. A definite procedure is involved. First comes what is wrong with the position you want to refute. Next is a statement of the way you see it. Five topoi are involved: from what is unclear, from what is impossible, from what is inappropriate, from what is illogical, and from what is inexpedient. Examples are given in reference to the poetic myth of Daphne (27–30).

Confirmation also should focus on what is neither obviously true nor apparently unprovable. The procedure and topoi are the obverse of those in refutation. Emphasize the correctness of your position, treating what is probable, clear, possible, logical, appropriate, and expedient—examples from the same story of Daphne (30–32).

Commonplace amplifies what is obviously evil or wrong. It gets its name *common* because the amplification applies generally to all those who participate in the evil in question. Again, sequence is involved, with examples against a tyrant: two introductions, the headings from contraries, exposition, comparison, intention, digression, rejecting pity (for the tyrant), legality, justice, expedience, and practicality (32–35).

Encomium is praise of the good in persons, things, times, places, animals, and plants. Again, sequence is involved in the numerous topoi taken up (an extensive list). Two lengthy exemplary encomia praise Thucydides and Wisdom (35–40).

Invective, like commonplace, attacks what is obviously evil, but it aims only at blaming, while commonplace attempts to achieve legal punishment. The model is an invective against Philip of Macedon (40–42).

Comparison puts things, either equal or unequal, side by side for effect. Thus it is either a double encomium or an invective combined with an encomium (i.e., contrast). The example compares Achilles to Hector as equals (42–44).

Characterization imitates the character of a person. There are three variations: *êthopoiia*—of a known person; *eidôlopoiia*—of a dead person; and *prosôpopoiia*—of an invented, fictitious person. It is also divided into the pathetical (i.e., emotional), ethical (showing character only), and the mixed. The model is a pathetical *êthopoiia* of what Niobe might have said over her dead children (44–46).

Description is vivid, i.e., it verbally brings whatever is described to view. It is simple or compound and should use a relaxed style and many figures. The example describes the acropolis at Alexandria (46–49).

Thesis is a general examination of political or theoretical questions. Thesis is general (e.g., should a city be fortified), and hypothesis specific (e.g., should the Spartans fortify their city in anticipation of the Persian invasion). The headings are legality, justice, expedience, and practicality. Extensive examples consider the question of marriage (49–53).

Proposal of law combines features of thesis and hypothesis. Lengthy examples are given about various laws on adultery (53–56).

Texts: *Rhetores Graeci,* ed. Leonardi Spengel (1853–56; rpt. Frankfurt: Minerva, 1966), 2:19–56; *Aphthonii Progymnasmata,* ed. Hugo Rabe (Leipzig: Teubner, 1913). Translation in *Readings from Classical Rhetoric,* ed. Patricia P. Matsen, Philip Rollinson, and Marion Sousa (Carbondale: Southern Illinois Univ. Press, 1990), 267–88.

APSINES was born around A.D.190 in Gadara in Syria. He taught rhetoric in Athens and wrote declamations, a treatise on figures of speech, and an *ART OF RHETORIC (TECHNÊ RHÊTORIKÊ)* survives, although the text has many interpolations. Throughout this work A. illustrates his points with references to classical Greek literature, especially the orations of Demosthenes.

In the first chapter A. says that introductions (*prooimia*) are constructed from topical theorems (*theôrêmata*), and he proceeds to discuss varieties. In the theorem from praise (*epainos*), the speaker, when introducing a second point, may praise the audience for having been persuaded on the first, or, when recommending a second course of action, may praise the audience for performing the first action. In the theorem from what follows (*ex akolouthou*) the speaker will persuade the audience to agree with a point that logically follows a prior point. In from defeat (*barytês;* literally, "heaviness"), the speaker, defeated on an earlier proposal, introduces another (often contrary), thereby playing on the sympathies of the audience (1–19). This theorem may also be used by someone repeatedly brought to trial (24–30). In from prejudicial attack (*diabolê*) the speaker jabs at an opponent who has previously prevailed on some issue (20–23). Other theorems focus on the accuser and include from what is excessive (*perittotês*), where, if the accuser has repeatedly been brought to trial and acquitted, the speaker may criticize the judges for allowing such a bad man to manipulate them (31). Another theorem involves things that trouble the speaker, such as the number or cleverness of his opponents (32–34).

Then to adverse factors in a case. First, a person (*prosôpon*) may be forced to speak against someone respected, or a relative or friend, or to an unsympathetic audience. Second, something (*pragma*) that is troublesome, paradoxical, or unpleasant may have to be said. Third is a fault (*aitia*), when we appear to speak out of hostility, favor, or self-interest (35–42). Another theorem concerns the speaker's seemingly undue delay in bringing a charge against someone (43–45). Next is the theorem from result (*apobasis*); it takes various forms, designed for both the accuser and the defendant. Other theorems described earlier may also be useful for prosecutions based on result (46–68). Then to theorems from advantage to the city, when the speaker wants to deflect attention from his own self-interest; from an inappropriate proposition (*atopos protasis*), when the speaker suggests an alternate way to rectify a problem; from prayer (*euchê*), when he says that he would have "prayed" that something had not in fact occurred; and from an honorable judgment (*endoxos krisis*), when he cites the good advice of others (69–76).

A. concludes the chapter with strategies for speeches involving coloring (*chrôma*); counteraccusation (*antengklêma*); advocacy of someone (*synêgoriai*), depending on whether they are honorable or dishonorable; disputes about the facts (*amphisbêtêseis*) and identities of those involved (*amphisbêtêmata*); figured problems (*eschêmatismena*); the theorem from personal judgment (*oikeia krisis*), when the speaker interjects his own opinion; the theorem from self-denunciation (*prosangelia*), when the speaker rebukes himself (78–87); procedural exception (*paragraphê*, 88, 92); attempts to make restitution (90–91); and preliminary concession (*kata syndromên*, 94–100).

The second chapter is on the preparation for the proof (*prokatastasis*), which can take various forms. There is examination of intention (*exetasis dianoias*), which divides into three types: examination of the intent of ourselves, of the audience, and of the opponent (1–10). Removal of an objection (*antipiptontos anairesis*) is designed to counteract the audience's negative attitude toward the speech. A preliminary statement of the issue (*prosystasis*) is used to note a main point in advance, while a preliminary prejudicial attack (*prodiabolê*) is designed to attack the deeds or character of the opponent (11–13). Preliminary division (*prodiorismos*) organizes the charges of the accuser. Contrast (*antexetasis*) is used to compare the present to the past. The first heading (*kephalaion*) can be used as the statement of the case (*katastasis*). Tropes (*tropoi*), such as irony, are especially useful for some figured problems, and a promise (*epangelia*) is designed to assure the audience that the speaker will do some particular thing (14–20).

Chapter 3 begins with general remarks on narration (*diêgêsis*). First is the exposition (*ekthesis*) of things that have happened, where persuasiveness (*pithanotês*) and clarity (*saphêneia*) are required. Some narrations set out plain facts, others are more critical; some are historical, others are argumentative. The facts should not be set out in too much detail. Narration differs from *aphêgêsis* (also usually translated as "narration") in that narration pertains strictly to the question at hand, while *aphêgêsis* refers to other narrative in the speech (1–3).

Next are strategies for particular types of narration. When seeking some honor for himself or another, the orator should seem to speak unwillingly and quickly. Asyndeton and calling attention to something while explicitly passing over it (*paraleipsis*) are effective. Contrast (*antexetasis*) should be used in questions of result, in order to compare the past with the present (4–8). When composing a speech based on what follows (*ex akolouthou*), the speaker should briefly narrate what has been done and then introduce some next course of action. The prosecution of a scurrilous person requires a narration with accusation (*katêgoria*), but that of an honorable person requires at least some praise. The speaker seeking to prevent something that has repeatedly been done should explain why he has not taken action previously. When prosecuting someone who appears to be doing something good, the speaker should scrutinize the person's intent (9–18). A discouraged tone (*barytês*) is helpful to the prosecutor who has been defeated previously, as is graphic description (*hypographê*) to one who attacks someone's great injustice, although small injustices require more caution. Graphic description is also fitting for a case involving some suffering or disaster; it appeals to the emotions of the audience (19–23).

The chapter concludes with remarks on categories of narration. Some narrations are highly ponderous (*panu en barytêti*), others intermediate (*mesai*), involving public or private affairs. Encomiastic (*engkômiastikai*) narrations are rather magnificent (*pompikôterai*) and panegyrical (*panêgyrikôterai*) but also somewhat annoying (25–26). Those that are pathetical (*pathêtikai*) should be relatively unembellished; they profit from feigned perplexity (*diaporêsis*), hesitation (*mellêsmos*), contrast (*antexetasis*), silence (*aposiôpêsis*), complaint (*schetliasmos*), repetition (*epanalêpsis*), and graphic description. Vehement narrations are directed against persons of ill repute; they often involve personal attack (*katêgoria*) done with moderation, examination of intent, employment of detached phrases (*apostatika schêmata*), and graphic description (27–28). Ethical (*êthikai*) narrations are either figured (*eschêmatismenai*) or have an underlying ethos, that is, they relate in some way to character.

The fourth chapter concerns objections (*antitheseis*) and ways to refute them. A. says that some objections are artistic (*entechnoi*), which the speaker himself has invented, and some nonartistic (*atechnoi*), i.e., historical examples, laws, decrees, etc. Because the speaker invents them and they must be judged, artistic objections are the stronger of the two (1–4). Objections may be stated, or we may use the propositions (*protaseis*) of the objections as objections themselves. Objections may also be raised by joining supporting reasons (*kataskeuai*) to the propositions. Finally, we may effectively pursue what logically follows from the objection. A. discusses each of these three approaches, as well as ways to refute them (5–9). He adds that sometimes the speaker, without stating the objection explicitly, can refute it without seeming to do so. The speaker may also introduce the same objection many times, or he may introduce two objections joined as one and refute each separately. Finally, sometimes contradictory objections may be introduced (10–17).

The fifth chapter begins by identifying two types of refutation (*lysis*): by reversal (*kata anatropên*) and by method (*kata methodon*). Refutation by reversal, which involves denial of the charge, is supported from the underlying facts, when they appear to contradict the charge; from probabilities (*ex eikotôn*), when the charge is not likely to be true; or from nonartistic proof (*ex atechnou pisteôs*), e.g., the evidence of a witness. Refutation by method may involve hyperbole, contradictory statements (*synkrousis*), diminution of the charge (*meiôsis*), amplification (*auxesis*), or counterobjection (*antiparastasis*, 1–6). Counterobjection, which usually involves some appeal to results, may be derived from the "final headings" (*telika kephalaia*) of justice, advantage, honor, means (*tropos*), or judgment of what is honorable (*kat' endoxou krisin*).

Other possible elements of refutation by method are: scrutiny of intent (*dianoias exetasis*), e.g., of a law; the opposite of the hypothesis (*tou enantiou kath' hypothesin*), when the speaker shows that the opposite of the charge is not desirable or possible; making a distinction (*diaphora*); similarity; reduction to the absurd; omission (*to ellipês*); procedural exception (*paragraphê*); time; place; person; objection (*metalêpsis*); pardon (*syngnômê*); and external factors (7–20). A. remarks that all these refutations will not be suitable for any one case and provides the example of a couple brought to court because they swore not to marry. The couple argues that marriage involves hazards, and here refutation by reversal does not work; method must be used, and A. gives examples of how to do so. The chapter concludes with assorted comments on the placement of weaker and stronger refutations, refutations introduced with objections, and the distinction between particular and universal refutations (21–26). It is possible that there is a lacuna in the text here or that a whole chapter has been lost (see Dilts and Kennedy, p. 167).

In chapter six A. takes up example (*paradeigma*). Comparison (*parabolê*) deals with inanimate or irrational living things, or inanimate objects, while example deals with persons from the past. An example is domestic (the more useful type) or foreign; it should be well known, clear, and concise (1–6). They are rarely used in the introduction and are taken from like (*homoion*), contrary (*enantion*), greater (*meizon*), and lesser (*ellaton*). They may be specific or not, they demand a rapid style (*gorga schêmata*), and sometimes it is most effective to leave them incomplete (7–15).

The seventh chapter concerns the refutation of examples in more detail. This always involves reversal (*anatropê*) and sometimes method. Refutation by method may involve: difference, based on intent, occasion, person, etc.; result; and counterobjection (*antiparastasis*).

Enthymemes are the subject of chapter eight (A. uses *enthymeme* in Aristotle's sense to mean a rhetorical syllogism). Some are derived from the lesser, a topic that naturally lends itself to amplification; the speaker may appeal to a lesser thing, person, impiety, fact, occasion, place, or manner. Enthymemes from the parallel (*apo parakeimenou*) involve things that are equivalent, such as various public offices (1–8). A speaker may also use enthymemes from the greater, syllogistically (*syllogistikôs*); from a dilemma (*dilêmma*); from the contrary; from what follows syllogistically; from result by suggesting the possible (*kath' hypothesin tou endechomenou*); from what is left out (*ek tou ekleiphthentos*) by additional assumption (*proslêpsis*); from what is essential (*ek tês ousias*); and from past time (i. e., how something that did not happen might have turned out if it had happened, 9–18). A. observess that an enthymeme gives an impression of sharpness (*drimytês*) and is contestive (*agônistikon*) and refutative (*elengtikon*). He concludes the chapter with other types of enthymeme: from inconsistency (*machê*), from an honorable judgment (*ek kriseôs endoxou*), from difference, and by comparison (*parabolikôs*, 19--24).

In the ninth chapter the focus is primarily on the final headings (*telika kephalaia*): the legal (*nomimon*), custom (*ethos*), just (*dikaion*), advantageous (*sympheron*), possible (*dynaton*), and honorable (*endoxon*). A. mentions, but does not discuss, the clear (*saphes*).

The legal can be derived from time, the quality (*poiotês*) of the lawgiver, the intent of the lawgiver, common judgment, and the thing itself that the law declares to be right. A law may also be attacked by reversing these arguments (1--10). Custom, which may be used in place of the legal, involves what has happened. It comes either from the particular person at issue or from common qualities (*koinotês*); here the speaker may also use arguments from what is left out (*to elleipon*), from an honorable judgment, from a difference, or from the lesser (11--15). The just is derived from either a person or a thing (16). Advantage is derived from results (*apo tôn ekbaseôn*) and should entail what the advantage will be for those persuaded and the disadvantage for those not persuaded. The speaker may also appeal to arguments from time, from an example (*paradeigma*), and from the opposite (17--18). The possible is constructed from external things such as friends, money, allies, place, opportunity, and the goodwill of the gods, but also from examples (19). The honorable is derived from what corresponds to the opinions of many. A. concludes the chapter with brief remarks on nonartistic proofs and arguments based on them (20--21).

The lengthy tenth, and final, chapter is on the conclusion or epilogue (see Dilts and Kennedy for the argument, based on style, that this chapter may have been written by one of A.'s students, pp. xvi--xvii). A. divides epilogue into three parts: reminder (*anamnêsis*) or recapitulation (*anakephalaiôsis*), pity (*eleos*), and indignation (*deinôsis*). He discusses reminder and pity in the first two sections of the chapter; the third section concerns emotion (*pathos*) in general, although indignation is included.

A judicial speech has pragmatic aspects (the narration and proof, or *apodeixis*) and pathetical aspects (the introduction and conclusion). Reminder belongs to the pragmatic aspect of the speech, even though it is found in a pathetical part (1--2). The focus shifts to techniques for making a reminder by headings. Impersonation (*prosôpopoeia*) introduces a person not in the courtroom and so recalls things that have been said, while vivid description (*hypotypôsis*) is useful when something is about to happen (3–6). Another kind of characterization (*êthopoeia*) attributes speech to persons imagined to be present. Other techniques are comparison (*synkrisis*) of what seems just to both sides; introduction of a decree (*psêphismatos eisphora*, 7–9); [imagined and ironic] statement of the jurors (*gnôsigraphia*); introduction of laws (*nomôn eisphora*); [imagined] inscription, likeness, statue, tomb, etc.; and rhetorical question (*peusis*, 10–13).

As for pity, A. says that the speaker's first job is to prepare the judges by using commonplaces (*koinoi topoi*) about the need for pity and humaneness and about Athenians' humane judgment and past actions, and by reminding the judges of what the defendants have done for them and others (15–18). After these preparatory commonplaces the speaker may use the topic of contrary to what is deserved (*para tên axian*), when he suffers something that he does not deserve, or the topic of contrary to hope (*para tên elpida*) when his hopes for reward, thanks, etc. are foiled. Another means of exciting pity is to amplify someone's previous good fortune, thus heightening the contrast with present misfortune (19–22). To arouse pity for certain persons, the speaker may use topics from mind (*psychê*), which involves grief, love, and so forth; from body (*sôma*), which involves wounds, floggings, and so on; and external things (*ta ektos*), such as food or money. In using these three topics the speaker should also describe clearly what has resulted from these misfortunes (23–27).

Mentioning someone's unseemly (*aprepê*) or shameful (*aischra*) experiences also creates pity, particularly when disgrace is involved. Vivid description (*enargeia*) of the unfortunate and attributing words to someone (*êthopoeia*) also arouse pity, as does producing sympathy (*homoiopatheia*) by asking the judges to imagine themselves in a similar situation—although the speaker should use anticipatory correction (*prodiorthôsis*) in order not to appear to wish misfortune upon the judges (28–34). Self-accusation also creates pity, as does addressing a speech to a place, or mentioning that events have not turned out as they should. The speaker may also address the possessions of a dead person, or address the fatherland about the dead person, or the children, parents, or wives of the dead (35–41). Other techniques for arousing pity include the recollection (*anamnêsis*) of someone's good deeds; revealing enemies' delight at someone's misfortune; showing the emotions of the relatives; disclosing the words, actions, and condition of the unfortunate; lamenting one's own loneliness; and finally, the command (*entolê*) before dying, by which the speaker makes clear someone's final wishes (42–47).

The brief third section is on emotion, which arises when the speaker mentions evils happening to a city or a person beyond what is deserved. The diction (*lexis*) should be unaffected (*aplastos*) and unembellished (*akallôpistos*), the syntax (*synthesis*) relaxed (*anetos*), and the figures (*schêmata*) rather rapid (*gorgotera*) and vigorous (*akmaiotera*). The speaker can create emotion through contrasts (*antexetasis*), comparison (*parathesis*), unlimited hyperbole (*hyperbolê en tôi aoristôi*), examination of the qualities of persons, expression of perplexity (*diaporêsis*), indignation (*deinôsis*), passionate complaints (*schetliasmoi*), exclamations (*anaklêtika*), doublings (*diplasiasmoi*), detached phrasing (*apostasis*), short phrases (*kommata*), asyndeton, expressing fear, and imaginary speech (*plasis*). A. concludes that, since hearers are suspicious of appeals to emotion, the speaker should make it clear that he has faith in his reasoning but is compelled to speak emotionally also (48–58).

Text and translation: *Two Greek Rhetorical Treatises from the Roman Empire: Introduction, Text, and Translation of the Arts of Rhetoric Attributed to Anonymus Seguerianus and to Apsines of Gadara,* by Mervin A. Dilts and George A. Kennedy (Leiden: Brill, 1997).

ARISTIDES RHETORIC is a collection of two works preserved with the genuine works of the famous sophist Aelius Aristides (c. A.D. 117-189), but not written by him. *ON POLITICAL DIS-COURSE (PERI POLITIKOU LOGOU)* is mainly an examination of twelve aspects of style not unlike Hermogenes' *On Types of Style*, while *ON SIMPLE SPEECH (PERI APHELOUS LOGOU)* examines the differences between "simple" and political speech. The illustrations in *ON POLITICAL DISCOURSE* are primarily taken from Demosthenes. Scholars have suggested that Basilicus of Nicomedia, a rhetorician of the second century A.D., was the actual author of the work. In The model for *ON SIMPLE SPEECH* is Xenophon, and it has been suggested that Zenon, also a rhetorician of the second century, was the author of that work.

ON POLITICAL DISCOURSE opens with a review of the types (*ideai*) and virtues (*aretai*) of political speech: solemnity (*semnotês*), gravity (*barytês*), amplification (*peribolê*), sincerity (*axiopistia*), vehemence (*sphodrotês*), directness (*emphasis*), force (*deinotês*), diligence (*epimeleia*), sweetness (*glykytês*), clarity (*saphêneia*) and purity (*katharotês*), brevity (*brachytês*) and concision (*syntomia*), and prudence (*kolasis*). Each is discussed in terms of thought (*gnômê*), figures (*schêmata*), and expression (*apangelia*).

Discourse will be solemn in thought when it involves honorable (*endoxa*) things, things concerning the gods or men (offspring, ancestors, freedom, justice, etc.), or things involving life and death. One should avoid, however, excessive pedantry in discussing these concepts. Safer topics include honorable deeds and thoughts and rare and incredible acts, as well as old things. Declarative (*apophantika*) figures are among those that add solemnity, as do the employment of detached phrases (*apostasis*), use of oblique cases (*plagiasmos*), speaking in maxims (*to gnômologein*), substitution of more respected things for those less respected, aphorisms (*aphorismoi*), deflecting attention from oneself, and asyndeton. Nouns should be favored over verbs. Also desirable are the use of metaphor (*tropê*), redundancy, suppression of person in favor of action, and speaking in specific terms, e.g., referring to gold and silver instead of money (Spengel, vol. 2, pp. 459-69).

Gravity in thought occurs when someone accuses himself, his relatives, or his friends. Characteristics are hyperbolic expression, the introduction of the strange and extraordinary, and mention of the deaths of honorable persons. Figures that produce gravity include critical thought (*dianoia*), expressions of anger (*schetliastika*), declarations of pain, expressions of doubt, and dubious expressions of anger, but gravity does not occur according to expression (pp. 469–72).

Abundance or amplification occurs according to thought: when undefined elements are added to defined elements; when something is set forth in general terms (*genos*), then discussed in specific terms (*eidos*); when other thoughts are added in the middle of a thought or thoughts; and so forth. In general, facts should be built up and added to. Among the figures creating abundance are the expansion of an idea (*hypostasis*), enumeration (*aparithmêsis*), omission (*paraleipsis*), division (*merismos*), and juxtaposition (*parathesis*). Abundance especially occurs according to expression when synonyms are used (pp. 472–86).

Sincerity occurs according to thought when the speaker makes claims for his fairness; uses oaths and prayers; refers to the judgments of the audience; confirms or denies resolutely; vehemently distances himself from certain things; anticipates the opponents' arguments; says things as if they were just remembered; agrees with certain comments of the opponent, and so forth. Figures that produce sincerity include those that suggest the agreement of the speaker and audience, promises (*epangeliai*), concession of the opponent's point (*syndromê*), and omission. Sincerity does not occur according to expression (pp. 486–92).

Vehemence occurs according to thought when someone censures esteemed persons or deeds; represents someone or something as bizarre and monstrous; displays great anger; speaks about obvious crimes, etc. The figures producing vehemence include impetuous (*epiphorika*) figures and direct address (*apostrophê*). Vehemence in expression arises from hyperbole, emphatic vocabulary, and metaphor (492–95).

Directness in thought can be created by enumerating things one after another and by using modifiers. Among the figures for directness are demonstrative (*deiktika*) and hortatory (*symbouleutika*) figures, question (*erôtêsis*), and constant refutation (*anairesis*).

Directness in expression is created in the same way as harshness (which is not discussed) and vehemence in expression (pp. 495–97).

Force occurs only according to thought, by the adoption of external arguments that are beneficial to the speaker and by anticipating and refuting the arguments of the opponent (pp. 497–98).

Diligence occurs according to thought when thoughts are combined with each other, when mixed and diverse thoughts are employed, when material related to the matter at hand is presented, and when metaphor is used. Among the figures creating diligence is division (*merismos*). Diligence in expression is produced by density and repetition and by the use of verbs instead of nouns (p. 499).

Sweetness is created in thought by external thoughts, such as history, proverb, and myth; in figure when novel means of expression are used (*apangeliai kainoprepeis*); in expression by metaphors that are subdued (*hypheimenai*), not harsh (p. 499).

Clarity and purity occur in thought when events are related in order; when external material is not introduced, only the facts themselves; when things known and things disputed are presented as such, and so forth; in figure when the speaker, moving from one point to another, completes one and promises to complete the other; in expression when common and clear nouns are used, as well as narratival (*aphêgêmatika*) figures; also, when synonyms are avoided and gentle, not harsh, words are used (pp. 499–500).

Brevity and concision are created in thought when the necessary matters are presented at once, and antecedents are discussed judiciously; in style (*lexis*), when direct, nonparaphrastic speech is used, synonyms are avoided, and the subject, not the style, is the first concern (p. 500).

Prudence is produced in thought when external thoughts are avoided, or at least identified as such, and when detached thoughts are avoided; in figure when the expansion of ideas is interrupted, and earnest prayer (*paraitêsis*) and the correction of previous expressions (*epidiorthôsis*) are used; and in expression when metaphor and hyperbole are avoided (pp. 500–01).

Brief mention follows of other types of style in speech and poetry, and the characteristics of the ideal orator. Then to a brief discussion of the three kinds of speech: panegyric (*engkômiastikon*), deliberative (*symbouleutikon*), and forensic (*dikanikon*). Judicial speeches may involve property and quality (*poiotês*) and may be very short, very long, or somewhere in between. Deliberative speeches are naturally shorter than judicial; their subjects include the just, beneficial, possible, easy, necessary, safe, beautiful, pious, holy, pleasant, and their opposites. Subdivisions of each of these subjects are given (pp. 501–04). The subjects of panegyric involve person and deed. Types of panegyric include praise (*epainos*), encomium (*engkômion*), hymn (*hymnos*), and invective (*psogos*). Praises are taken up according to amplification (*auxêsis*), omission (*paraleipsis*), comparison (*parabolê*), and euphemism (*euphêmia*). Then to advice on how to praise in a nonvulgar manner, and brief comments on invective, of which there are three types, according to amplification, omission, comparison, and bad language (*dysphêmia*). Composition (*synthesis*) and diction (*phrasis*) are discussed next. The colon (*kôlon*) is a combination of two or more words, while the period (*periodos*) is composed of one or more cola. Diction may be unclear, redundant, or trifling (*mataia*). The remainder of the section is unclear because of a lacuna (pp. 504–08).

At the end of the treatise certain sections are summarized, other material on style is added, Aristides' twenty-ninth speech is summarized, and portions of the *Iliad* and *Odyssey* are paraphrased (pp. 508–12).

ON SIMPLE SPEECH divides speech into thoughts (*epinoêmata*) and expression (*apangelia*) and subdivides the latter into style (*lexis*), figures (*schêmata*), and rhythm (*rhythmos*). These components differ in political speech and simple speech. Political thoughts are rougher (*trachytera*), more glorious (*endoxotera*), and sharper (*drimytera*), while simple thoughts are not only simple (*hapla*) but also common (*epikoina*) and inglorious (*adoxa*). Political speeches must be clearer than simple speeches. The figures in political speech are rough, vehement (*sphodra*), refutative (*elengktika*), and forceful (*biaia*), while in simple speeches they are relaxed (*aneimena*), simple, and show no refutation or examination. As for style, the political speech must be delivered with confidence and intensity, while simple speech is more relaxed. The rhythm of political speech is smoother than that of simple speech (pp. 512–14).

Characteristic of simple speech is reference to manner (*tropos*) and character (*êthos*). Simple speech employs all kinds of thought but, unlike political speech, admits thoughts lacking strength, ones that are trivial and even risible. Then to a restatement of many of the points above (pp. 515–19). Simple speeches involve changing vocabulary and lack force (*bia*), anger (*thumos*), and vehemence; unlike political speeches, they employ external thoughts. The simple speech should be multifaceted; it should have solemnity, abundance, dignity (*axiôma*), characterization, and charm (*charis*) and be laugh-provoking (*gelôs*, pp. 519–22).

Then to character, with reference to Xenophon. Thoughts that have characterization differ; they may convey charm, goodness, sweetness, kindness (*chrêstotês*), or solemnity (pp. 522–27). Characterizations create solemnity when the opinion (*gnômê*) of the speaker is emphasized. Then to brief discussions of characterization involving kindness, the invisible and hidden, sweetness, irony, etc. Simple speech also employs unemphatic (*anemphatos*) style, figures, and rhythm (pp. 527–30). Characterization produces solemnity by emphasizing piety to the gods or solemnity toward friends. Other means of creating solemnity are changing the emphasis from persons to deeds, the interweaving of styles (*symplokê*), the representation of future or present events as past, mentioning revered (*semna*) names, and speaking in general rather than particular terms (pp. 530–32).

Amplification is next. It can be created by the combination of defined and undefined elements, as well as the combination of oblique and nominative constructions, and sweetness, which is created by poetical diction, metaphor, describing trivial things grandly and grands things trivially, etc. Generally, sweetness is more common in simple speech than in political speech (pp. 532–35). Then comes beauty (*kallos*), created in simple speech by geographical description and the juxtaposition of similar elements. Brief comments on sincerity, arrangement (*oikonomia*), interpretation (*hermêneia*), and epicheiremes follow (pp. 535–39). The introduction (*archê*) should be brief, should avoid extraneous information, and should set forth facts in a basic manner.

A somewhat redundant discussion follows of various matters, such as rhythm, metaphor, passages that combine elements of simple and political speech, avoidance of displays of emotion, use of the nominative case, avoidance of harshness, use of slow instead of fast rhythm (pp. 539–45), avoidance of hyperbole, comparison, asyndeton, interweaving of styles, creating fictions (*to tas plaseis poiein*), novel means of expression (*kainoprepeiai*), arrangement of lesser events before greater, and change of tense (pp. 545–54).

Text: *Rhetores Graeci,* ed. Leonardi Spengel (1853–56; rpt. Frankfurt: Minerva, 1966), 2:469–560.

ARISTOTLE (384–322 B.C.) studied under Plato but, as is well known, developed his own system of philosophy, which in many important ways diverged from his teacher's. Two dramatic differences between A. and Plato are their responses to poetry and to rhetoric. Plato's response ranges from suspicion to hostility, while A. includes both within the friendly focus of his comprehensive analyses of everything in the universe. And in both cases A.'s views have prevailed. His discussion of poetic imitation and tragedy remains one of the most important works ever written on critical theory, and his *RHETORIC* established most of the basic concepts of subsequent rhetorical theory and instruction.

A.'s understanding of rhetoric is based on its position in the scheme of kinds of knowledge, which are (1) theoretical (e.g., metaphysics), (2) practical (e.g., ethics), or (3) productive—i.e. guides to the creation of objects of use or artistic contemplation (e.g., poetics and rhetoric). Rhetoric is also related to analytics (later called logic by the Stoics), which is a special knowledge of the *logos,* a tool or instrument of inquiry into the various sciences. A.'s *Organon* comprises the *CATEGORIES, ON INTERPRETATION, PRIOR ANALYTICS, POSTERIOR ANALYTICS,* and *TOPICA.* The last three of these relate directly to rhetoric.

The *PRIOR ANALYTICS* develops the theory of syllogistic reasoning, and the *POSTERIOR ANALYTICS* shows how knowledge is logically or scientifically acquired, verified, and systematized: either syllogistically (i.e., deductively) or inductively. Rhetoric is analogically related to this kind of reasoning through its use of enthymemes and examples. The enthymeme is a kind of syllogism in that it uses the method of the syllogism but is developed from probabilities and signs. Probabilities are generally accepted truths, e.g., that envious people are evilly disposed. The sign is the foundation of a demonstrative premise that is based on something that has happened (factual evidence) and is generally accepted as true, e.g., the presence of smoke indicates that something is burning. Example, on the other hand, is a kind of induction (*PRIOR. AN.* 2.23–27).

Rhetoric is also related to Aristotle's dialectic, which is discussed in the *TOPICA.* For A. dialectic is not Plato's process of philosophic inquiry into truth but rather a conversational and argumentative logic, which lacks the definitive precision of analytics and is based only on probabilities; and so it is A.'s appropriated version of the argumentation of sophistry and disputation or eristic. Analytical reasoning begins with true premises and syllogistically realizes absolute demonstration (*apodeixis*). Dialectic operates in the same intellectual way but deals with premises that are only thought to be true or are probably true. So, the same kind of reasoning is demonstrative, i.e., apodictic, when it proceeds from premises that are true, but dialectical when it is based on generally accepted opinions.

A. is not afraid of or opposed to dialectical reasoning just because it does not lead to absolute, demonstratively true conclusions; rather, he encourages its practice. Dialectic, he observes, helps train the mind. It is also a necessary tool of conversation. It even has a direct application to analytical reasoning, since he who is proficient in dialectical argument will be better able to recognize fallacious arguments, and since the first principles of true knowledge, the basic premises, cannot be demonstrated anyway (*TOPICA* 1.2). The tools of dialectic that the *TOPICA* discusses are places (topoi) of argument, general principles of probabilities, and commonplace rules of procedure in arguing about dialectical problems. The final book (8) has an illuminating treatment of fallacies and a brilliant overview of techniques of argument.

Although suggestions have been made over the years that the **RHETORIC** is not a treatise but a series of lecture notes assembled by students, or that it is incomplete, an overview shows just how systematic it is and how definitive it was for all subsequent rhetorical theory: rhetoric defined (1.1–2); three kinds of speakers (1.3); deliberative or political rhetoric and its topoi (1.4–8); epideictic rhetoric and its topoi (1.9); forensic and its topoi (1.10–15); inartificial proofs (1.15); ethos and pathos, introducing a study of human psychology and behavior (2.1.1–7); pathetic proofs (2.1.8–2.11); ethical proofs (2.12–17); logical proofs and arguments common to all three kinds of rhetoric (2.18–19); examples, rhetorical inductions (2.20); maxims or wise sayings (2.21); enthymemes, rhetorical deductions, and twenty-eight topoi (2.24); apparent enthymemes, fallacies, and nine topoi (2.24); refutations (2.25); style and arrangement (3.1); figurative language and epithet (3.2); frigidity of style (3.3); simile and metaphor (3.4); purity of style (3.5); loftiness of style (3.6); stylistic propriety or decorum (3.7); sentence structure and prose rhythm

(3.8–9); smart and popular sayings, especially involving metaphor and simile, and vividness of expression (3.10–11); different styles (3.12); parts of a speech (3.13); introduction (3.14); removing prejudice (3.15); narrative in epideictic rhetoric (3.16); the proofs in a speech (3.17); interrogation (3.18); the conclusion of a speech (3.19).

The opening defines rhetoric as the "counterpart of dialectic," which seeks not to persuade but to find the appropriate means of persuasion in any given situation (1.1.1–4 and 1.2.1). These means are to be found in various kinds of proof or conviction (*pistis*). The proofs do involve art, while everything else involved in rhetoric is ancillary (1.1.3). Proofs are of two kinds: inartificial (not involving rhetorical art—e.g., in forensic rhetoric: laws, witnesses, contracts, torture, and oaths) and artificial (involving the art of rhetoric). These rhetorical proofs are, of course, distinct from the apodictic proofs of syllogistic reasoning (1.1).

The three basic kinds of artifical proof or areas of conviction depend on three different sources (1.2.3–6). One source of conviction is the character of the speaker, his *êthos*. Another is the content of the speech, the *logos*. The third is the response, mainly emotional (*pathos*), of the audience. These three basic kinds of proof, ethical, logical, and pathetic, relate to the three kinds of rhetoric: deliberative (*symbouleutikos*), forensic (*dikanikos*), and epideictic (*epideiktikos*). The ethos of the speaker is most important for deliberative speeches. The response of the audience is most significant for forensic (2.1.4). The demonstration of the speech itself is important to all three but implicitly is the main point of epideictic rhetoric.

While these three parts, speaker, subject/content, and hearer, define the three kinds of rhetoric (speaker–deliberative, subject–epideictic, and hearer–forensic, 1.3.1), there are other fundamental distinctions, as well. The deliberative either exhorts or dissuades, the forensic either accuses or defends, the epideictic either praises or blames (1.3.3). Each kind has its own special focus of time: the deliberative looks at the future, forensic the past, epideictic the present (1.3.4). Each also has its own purpose (*telos*): deliberative what is expedient and best or what is harmful, forensic the just or unjust, and epideictic what is honorable or shameful (1.3.5–6).

The orator must have a ready supply of propositions (*protaseis*) relating to each of these three areas of purpose: expediency, justice, and honorable actions. The kinds of propositions pertinent to each area are also developed (1.3.7–9). Thus the main subjects of deliberative rhetoric are "ways and means, war and peace, defence of the country, imports and exports, and legislation" (1.4.7).

This sort of categorization characterizes A.'s *RHETORIC,* but his emphasis is on the development of rhetorical proofs as the means of persuasion. Here enthymeme and example (*paradeigma*) are again identified as rhetorical versions of the syllogism and induction, the former based on probabilities, signs, and necessary signs and the latter on examples (1.1.11 and 1.2.8–9), and again the dialectical or rhetorical syllogism is connected with topoi (1.2.21). Aristotle distinguishes two kinds of topoi, those which are general or universal and those which are particular (1.2.21–22). General topoi can apply to more than one discipline, particular ones cannot. Rhetorical reasoning with the enthymeme mainly uses particular topoi.

The precise relationship of propositions, rhetorical proofs, enthymemes, and topoi in the *RHETORIC* is, however, a bit confused at times. The topoi refer to at least four related categories of things: subject areas, occasions for arguments, contexts for arguments (facts, relationships, and factual domains of questions), and strategies and tactics for arguing, including, as in the *TOPICA,* recognition of opponents' fallacies. At one time enthymemes and examples are the two primary rhetorical proofs (1.2.8), but later they are two of three (the third being amplification, *auxêsis*) kinds of reasoning common to all forms of speaking (1.9.40–41), and still later they are joined by a different third, the maxim (*gnômê*), as the three proofs common to all three kinds of rhetoric (2.20–22). But it is propositions about the possible or impossible, future or past, and size or greatness that are said to be common to all speaking (2.18.3–4) and all three kinds of speakers (1.3.8–9). Finally, enthymemes are said to be constructed out of specific topoi (1.2.22) and have elements of topoi (2.22.1–13), and yet the topoi may have several enthymemes (2.26.1).

Regardless of some overlap and confusion of these terms, the *RHETORIC* is overwhelmingly topical in its approach to rhetorical argument and persuasion. After an important discussion of the enthymeme in general, which includes a rationale for topical thinking (2.22), A. elaborates on twenty-eight topical arguments (2.23) from opposites (*enantia*), similar inflections (*homoioi ptôseis*), relative terms (*allêla*), more and less (*mallon kai hêtton*), considerations of time (*to ton chronon skopein*), shifting the attack (*ta eirêmena kath' hautous pros ton eiponta*), definition (*horismos*), different meanings (*posachôs*), division (*diairesis*), induction (*epagôgê*), precedent (*krisis*), enumeration of parts (*meroi*), consequences (*akolouthounta*), reversing a dilemma (*blaisôsis*), paradoxical contradiction (*paradoxa*), analogy (*analogon*), cause and effect (*ex hôn symbainei tauta*), change of mind (*ek tou mê tauto . . . aei haireisthai . . . all' anapalin*), possible cause (*to hou henek' . . . an genoito*), human motives (*hôn heneka kai prattousi kai pheugousin*), improbabilities (*apista*), contradictions (*anomologoumena*), reasons for false opinions (*aitiai paradoxôn*), cause (*aitia*), possible better actions (*pôs ên praxai beltion*), contraries (*enantia*), errors committed (*hamartêthenta*), and meaning of a name (*onoma*).

The *RHETORIC* is not limited, however, to the treatment of topical proofs or invention (*heuresis*). Memory is not covered, but Book 3 treats style and arrangement after a passing comment on delivery (3.1). A. singles out clarity (*to saphes*) as the chief ornament of style (3.2) and spends most of the subsequent discussion on figurative language, especially the metaphor. He closes with a review of stylistic variations based on whether the speech is written, is used in debate, is a public address, or is involved with legal pleadings (3.12); the underlying principle here is decorum or appropriateness in governing variation. As for arrangement (3.13–19), A. recognizes only two main parts of a speech, the statement of the case (*prothesis*) and the proof (*pistis*). To these may be added two more, the introduction (*prooimion*) and conclusion (*epilogos*).

Texts and translations: Aristotle, *Categories, On Interpretation,* trans. H. P. Cooke, *Prior Analytics,* trans. Hugh Tredennick (Cambridge, Mass.: Harvard Univ. Press, 1938); *Posterior Analytics,* trans. Hugh Tredennick, *Topica,* trans. F. S. Forster (Cambridge, Mass.: Harvard Univ. Press, 1960); *The "Art" of Rhetoric,* trans. John Henry Freese (Cambridge, Mass.: Harvard Univ. Press, 1926). Translation: *Aristotle on Rhetoric: A Theory of Civic Discourse,* by George A. Kennedy (Oxford: Oxford Univ. Press, 1991).

CICERO (106–43 B.C.) was the greatest practicing orator in the history of Rome. He also made important contributions to rhetorical theory in addition to treating and assessing the contributions of others to rhetoric. Consequently, the several works he wrote on rhetoric (*DE INVENTIONE, TOPICA, DE OPTIMO GENERE ORATORUM, DE ORATORE, BRUTUS, ORATOR,* and *DE PARTITIONE ORATORIA*) are of the utmost significance.

ON INVENTION (DE INVENTIONE) is probably the incomplete juvenile work referred to in C.'s mature *DE ORATORE* 1.5. Its two books, which focus on judicial or forensic invention, are closely related to the first two books of the contemporaneous *Rhetorica ad Herennium,* but exactly how is not clear. Both refer to the same Hellenistic (especially Stoic) tradition of rhetorical instruction and possibly to an identical (now lost) textbook and/or instructor.

Book 1 of the *DE INVENTIONE* opens with a calm, evenhanded introduction to rhetoric, which praises Aristotle's conceptualizations and Hermagoras's organization (1.1–9). The three kinds of subject matter of speeches, epideictic (*demonstrativa*), deliberative (*deliberativa*), and judicial (*iudicalis*), are accepted, as are the five traditional areas of instruction, invention (*inventio*), arrangement (*dispositio*), style (*elocutio*), memory (*memoria*), and delivery (*pronuntiatio*). The treatment of judicial invention begins with the four issues (*constitutiones*) of Hermagoras, the bases of any dispute, which are conjectural (*coniecturalis*), definitional (*definitiva*), qualitative (*generalis*), and translative (*translativa*, 10–16). These four are conceptually sequential. Thus, we may first of all have a dispute over the facts of a case (conjectural). If there is agreement about the facts, the dispute may then be over how what has happened is to be construed or defined (definitional). If there is agreement here, too, the point of controversy may then be over the nature or character of what happened (qualitative). Finally, the issue may be the applicability or propriety of the legal processes, whether the correct accusation has been made, whether it has been made before the right court, or whether the correct defendant is accused, etc. (translative).

Since he has rejected Hermagoras's conceptualization of the parts of rhetoric (8), C. rejects (12–14) the first two of the four Hermagorean species of the qualitative issue—deliberative, epideictic, equitable (*iuridicialis*), and legal (*negotialis*), leaving questions of equity and of strict legality (15–16). The former, equitable species itself has two subspecies, the absolute (concerning right and wrong) and the assumptive (concerning defense against inapplicable circumstances). The assumptive is subdivided into confession (*concessio*), shifting the charge (*remotio criminis*), reply to the accusation (*relatio criminis*), and comparison (*comparatio*). Confession has two further parts: *purgatio*, when guilt is admitted but intentionality is denied, and *deprecatio*, when intentionality is admitted and forgiveness is asked for.

After a brief review of other introductory aspects of a case, e.g., whether written documents are involved or whether the case is simple or complex (17–19), the remainder of the first book reviews the topoi for the six parts of a speech: the introduction (*exordium*, 20–26); narration of the supposed facts of the case (*narratio*, 27–30); division (*partitio*, 31–33), which isolates the areas of agreement and difference and presents the main points to be made in the speech; proof (*confirmatio*, 34–77), including treatment of rhetorical induction (51–56) and deduction (57–77); refutation (*reprehensio*, 78–96), which considers four different approaches, including recognition of the fallacious arguments of one's opponent; and conclusion (*conclusio*, 98–109), which has three parts, the summation, arousal of indignation (*indignatio*) and arousal of pity (*conquestio*). In passing from the refutation to the conclusion C. rejects a seventh part of a speech, the digression (*digressio*), which he claims Hermagoras inserts before the conclusion (97).

Book 2 begins with a graceful defense of the author's use of different rhetorical authorities for different points (1–11) and proceeds to elaborate on the treatments of proof and refutation with extensive discussion of hypothetical examples for all of the categories and sub-categories of the issues in judicial cases (12–115). In this process various topical approaches are fleshed out and explained, including the topoi common (*loci communes*) to each issue or aspect of an issue, i.e., from both prosecutorial and defense points of view (2.51, 55, 85–86, 91, 94, 101–02, 108–09, 143, and 152–53; sometimes these are simply referred to as "places," e.g. 2.16, 19, and 24). For example, under the translative issue, when the defense demands a change in the legal process, the common topos for the prosecution will be to claim that the defendant is making this plea because he has no confidence in his case. The common topos for the defendant's response will be that the whole judicial system will be jeopardized if cases are not tried under the proper jurisdiction, etc. (61). Commonplaces are defined as "those arguments which can be transferred to many cases" and refer to the amplification of certain kinds of statements (2.48–50). They also amplify doubtful statements or undisputed facts (2.68).

C. uses the same approach on the controversies over written documents (116–21) and over the letter and intent of laws (122–54) before turning to invention in deliberative and epideictic speeches (155–78). This much briefer discussion on the virtuous, honorable, and expedient includes an important passage on what were to become the four cardinal or natural virtues in Christian ethics: prudence, justice, courage, and temperance (159–65). The main focus is on deliberative speeches, but at the end C. refers to praise and blame (178).

The *TOPICS (TOPICA)* purports to be an attempt by C. to elucidate Aristotle's *Topica* for his friend Trebatius, who had found that work confusing to master on his own and had also discovered that a rhetorician recommended by C. was not familiar with it (1–3). C. says he wrote this elucidation from memory on a sea voyage (5). There is not, however, a very close connection of the work to Aristotle. Rather, C. treats the topoi the same way as he does in his own *DE ORATORE.*

C. begins by pointing out that all argumentation, Greek dialectic, is concerned either with finding arguments or judging their worth (6–7). Alluding to Aristotle, he defines topics or places (*loci*) as the seats or areas (*sedes*) from which arguments are drawn (7–8). Arguments are either extrinsic (*extrinsecus* or inartificial, i.e., not having to do with the art of rhetoric, 24) or intrinsic (*inclusa*). The topoi of the intrinsic are listed and briefly defined (9–23). There are arguments from definition (*definitio*); enumeration/division (*enumeratio*); etymology (*notatio*); and related circumstances, which include conjugates, genus, species, similitude, difference, contraries, adjuncts, antecedents, consequents, contradictions, causes, effects, and comparisons. After a pause to comment on the extrinsic, C. comes back to examine these topoi more fully (26–71).

He proceeds to comment briefly on extrinsic, inartifical places of proof, i.e., testimony, etc. (72–78). That is followed by brief discussions of practical and theoretical questions (79–86); the topoi appropriate to these questions (87–90); the three kinds of speeches (91); the issues (now identified as *status* in Latin from the Greek *stasis*, 93), only three of which are mentioned here—conjectural (*coniecturalis*), definitional (*definitiva*), and juridical (*iuridicialis*), combining the qualitative and translative (92–96); and the four parts of a speech: introduction (*principium*), narration (*narratio*), proof (*fides*), and conclusion (*peroratio*, 97–100).

ON THE BEST KIND OF ORATOR (*DE OPTIMO GENERE ORATORUM*) purports to be an introduction to C.'s (probably never completed) translations of the celebrated speeches by the two greatest Athenian orators, Aeschines (*Against Ctesiphon*) and Demosthenes (*On the Crown*), opposing each other at the trial of Ctesiphon in 330 B.C. Although brief and apparently in some draft form, the work is of interest.

It opens with a distinction between poets and orators (1–4). While there are different kinds of poets, depending on the different genres of poems, there is only one kind of orator. We look for the best epic poet, the best writer of tragedies, the best comic poet, etc., but we look for only one kind of best orator, who will best instruct, delight, and move his audiences to action (3).

Eloquence (*eloquentia*) consists of diction (*verba*) and expressions (*sententiae*). The rules of diction are basically the same: good Latinity, elegant words, the proper balance of figurative and literal language, etc., are generally required (4). The kinds of expressions vary, however, with the different kinds of speeches (5). There are also the considerations of prose rhythm (*numerus*), the best arrangement (*ordo*) for developing one's proof, memory, and delivery (5). The best orator will be the best in all these aspects (6).

There is also only one kind of oratory, Athenian or Attic (7–15). Versatility is the key to Attic oratory—the capability of using whatever style and logical development are appropriate or necessary in whatever situation. Asiatic style is consistently overdone and inappropriate (9), and those speakers who can master only one style are minor, not great, orators (9–10). C. himself speaks in the Attic manner, best characterized by Demosthenes: full (*amplus*), ornate (*ornatus*), and copious (*copiosus*). And in Greek the two speeches by Aeschines and Demosthenes, two giants of oratory, illustrate Attic oratory at its best (11–18). C. closes with a graceful introduction to the background of the dispute itself (19–23).

ON THE ORATOR (*DE ORATORE*) is a leisurely treatment of rhetoric addressed to C.'s brother, Quintus. It takes the form of a conversational dialogue (C. claims to have modeled it after the Aristotelian dialogue, *Ad. Fam.* 1.9.23), in which the principal speakers are two of the great Roman orators of the generation before C.'s, Lucius Licinius Crassus (140–91 B.C.), who is generally C.'s mouthpiece, and Marcus Antonius (143–87 B.C.), the grandfather of the famous Mark Antony. They are talking primarily to two younger men, Publius Sulpicius Rufus and Gaius Aurelius Cotta, but others join in for parts of the dialogue.

C.'s introduction to Book 1 (1–29) indicates that of all the disciplines and professions, poetry and oratory have produced the fewest really distinguished practitioners and rhetoric the fewest of all (8 and 11–12; later, Antonius agrees, 128) and that the competent orator must be knowledgeable in all branches of learning (20–22). Crassus then begins the first day's conversation with an encomium of rhetoric and especially of its power to move men to action (30). Scaevola, a legal expert and interlocutor only in Book 1, moderates Crassus's enthusiasm (39–44), and from the rejoinder by Crassus (45–73) the dialogue gradually proceeds. Crassus remarks on the irony of Plato's consummate rhetorical skills in making fun of rhetoric in the *Gorgias* (47) and observes that all other forms of knowledge need the skills of rhetoric to present their findings (62). Scaevola briefly objects again (74–79), but Antonius accepts Crassus's point and proceeds to review a disputation he had overheard at Athens about the nature of rhetoric and the respective importance of study, art, and natural capability (80–98). Crassus's response here (99ff.), eliciting many interruptions and comments, is to deny that rhetoric is an art if one defines an art as involving systematic, objective knowledge. What can be taught and discussed about rhetoric systematically, however, is the empirical record of what the best speakers have actually done and this is something like an art (107–09). And so, a bit later, the precepts of rhetorical instruction do not make great speakers; rather, the precepts are merely the reflection of what the best orators have done (146). For Crassus, then, natural talent (*ingenium*) is paramount (113–17). When asked what else is necessary (131–33), he responds with a thumbnail sketch of rhetorical instruction (134–59) in which he emphasizes the importance of extensive practice in writing speeches (150–53).

The remainder of the first day's dialogue is spent on the question of how important is an expert knowledge of the law. Crassus praises Scaevola and emphasizes the importance of profound legal knowledge, while the younger Antonius emphasizes the relatively greater significance of rhetorical skills (168–265).

Book 2 continues in the same leisurely fashion. A second introduction to C.'s brother, Quintus, praises the learning of Crassus and Antonius (1–11). The dialogue begins with two new interlocutors, Quintus Lutatius Catulus and his half brother, Gaius Julius Caesar Strabo Vopiscus (12–27). Antonius discourses at length about the whole of *eloquentia*. His high opinion of oratory generally (30–38) is similar to Crassus's. He downplays the importance of epideictic as opposed to the deliberative and especially to the most difficult, forensic branches of rhetoric (72), because it is easier (44–48)—although Catulus is praised for the funeral oration he delivered for his mother, Popilia, the first eulogy ever of a woman (44)—and, like history (which is also discussed, 51–64), does not really need or have separate rules.

With a disparaging glance at academic (i.e., impractical) Greek instruction (75), Antonius begins a review of the elements of rhetorical instruction from his pragmatic point of view (77ff). He rejects the theoretical division between controversial causes (*controversiae*) and questions for dispute (*quaestiones*), i.e. between forensic and deliberative rhetoric, and notes the arbitrary nature of the four or five or six or seven parts of a speech (78–79). His instruction begins very differently by suggesting that the student should most importantly be assigned a good model to imitate and then practice imitating him extensively (90–98).

In actual practice before the bar, the first thing is to know your case thoroughly (99–103). That will naturally lead you to a correct focus on the particular issues involved (questions of fact, of the nature of acts, and of their definition, 104–13). Then find your proofs, ethical, logical, and pathetic (114–306). This rambling section on invention pauses briefly on inartificial arguments (116–20) before Antonius objects again to the normal distinction in rhetorical instruction between deliberative proofs involving generalizations and universals and forensic proofs involving particulars of time and persons (133–34). In fact, the determinations of particulars in forensic cases will also be decided by general and universal truths (134–47)—reflecting an Aristotelian view of the typicality of human nature and human behavior.

There are three sources of success in the invention of proofs: natural genius (*acumen*), theoretical instruction (*ratio*), and hard work (*diligentia*). The first and especially the third of these are most significant (147–51). The remainder of this book is taken up with the presentation of a multitude of specific examples and anecdotes illustrating different points of invention, including an extensive section on wit and humor delivered by Vopiscus (217–90).

The treatment of arrangement is, as is typical of ancient rhetorical theory, much briefer (307–32). Antonius recommends that the strongest arguments be put first (313–14), that introductions be pointedly pertinent to the case (316–25), and that lucidity and entertainment are the true goals of the narration, not brevity (326–30).

Neither the deliberative, here a speech of recommendation or exhortation (*suasio*), nor the epideictic need separate rules (333), but each is briefly reviewed (333–40 and 341–49, respectively). Topical memory, using the orderly arrangement of mental images, is also briefly discussed (351–60) before the book ends with the anticipation of Crassus's discussion of style.

This discussion opens Book 3 in the same leisurely way as the earlier books. C.'s third introduction to his brother Quintus notes the untimely death of Crassus shortly after the dialogue, and indeed, the unfortunate ends of most of the interlocutors (3.1–16). When Crassus begins, he rambles on about different styles of speaking, different speakers, and different modes of instruction tailored to particular students (18–36) before asserting that the orator should speak correctly (*Latine*), lucidly (*plane*), ornately (*ornate*), and appropriately (*apte*, 37).

Since most correctness in language is learned from others [e.g., grammarians] and has been mastered by every literate person, Crassus's treatment of Latinity (39–47) is devoted mainly to pronunciation, to which he will return later in the discussion of delivery, where the most important element is the voice (224–27). Since the need for lucidity or clarity in speaking is so obvious, that, too, is quickly dispatched (48–51). After a brief introduction to ornateness (52–55), Crassus digresses on the intrinsic relationship of the form and content of speaking (56–89), regretting that Socrates severed the expression of sentiments from the sentiments themselves and so necessitated separate teachers for thinking and speaking (60–61). The Stoics are praised for being the only philosophic school to grant that eloquence is a virtue and part of wisdom (65). The point is that the orator must be both learned and a capable speaker (80).

Crassus then returns to ornateness and appropriateness, the last two requisites of good style (91). The introduction to ornamentation or embellishment discusses the impact of the beauty and charm of speech on an audience (96–103). Amplification is hailed as the chief means of embellishment, but the discussion of the methods of amplification (104ff) includes the deliberate expansion of specific points into their broadest, most general context (120–21)—i.e., with the Aristotelian sense that particulars take on significance in the context of their typicality—and that leads back to still another discussion of philosophy, sophistry, learning, and education (122–47).

Finally, Crassus turns to diction and syntax (149). Diction is embellished by the use of rare words, coined words, and metaphors (152–70). The discussion of metaphor includes allegory and metonymy. The implied comparison in a metaphor should be obvious and not strained; vehicle and tenor should be closely related. Most of the discussion of syntax that follows (171–98) is devoted to prose rhythm and is probably the most influential and best known part of *DE ORATORE.* The orator's prose should have definite rhythms, but never so regular as to become poetry. Specific feet (quantitative measures, not accentual) are even recommended for particular parts of clauses and sentences, and the importance of practice in both speaking and writing is stressed. This section closes with a discussion of the subconscious impact of prose rhythm on even an unlearned audience (195–98).

After mentioning the three general styles—full (*plena*), thin or meagre (*tenuis*), and the in–between or middle (*mediocris*, 199–200)—Crassus develops a brief but remarkable treatment of what he calls the almost innumerable ways of shaping words (*verba*) or speech (*oratio*) and thoughts or expressions (*sententiae*). About fifty ways of shaping or forming thoughts are catalogued (202–05)—the exact number is difficult to pinpoint, since Crassus's review is refreshingly free from the terms and categories of the grammarians. The shaping of thoughts includes interrogation, irony, impersonation, vivid description, rapid review, interruption, invective, raising the voice, and even falling into silence. The treatment of the ways to shape words (206–08) is equally freed from the traditional tags of elementary instruction. Approximately forty are mentioned, among which are repetition, climax, antithesis, abbreviation, running on, answering one's own question, metonymy, and periphrasis. The difference between the two categories is that the special shaping of words disappears if we change the actual words, whereas the shaping of thoughts can remain even if different words (with the same or similar meanings, of course) are substituted (200).

Crassus finally gets to appropriateness or decorum (210–12). He has already pointed out that one's style in a speech should be appropriate to the audience (97) and to the content of the speech (177). These points are reiterated, and it is emphasized that no one style is appropriate to every subject, every audience, every speaker, or every occasion.

Book 3 ends with delivery (213–27), which Crassus asserts is of the utmost importance and has, unfortunately, been largely abandoned by orators and left to actors (214).

ON THE DIVISION OF RHETORIC (*DE PARTITIONE ORATORIAE*) is a compact survey of rhetoric, reflecting, according to C., the teachings of the Middle Academy (139). Written very late in C.'s life, it takes the form of a dialogue between Cicero and his son; Cicero senior is the teacher and authority, while Cicero junior asks all the appropriately leading questions to elicit the details of instruction (a dialogue form to be widely imitated in the multitude of master-pupil manuals of the Latin Middle Ages). The subject is all the divisions or parts of rhetoric and rhetorical instruction. It contains a relatively (by the standards of ancient rhetorical theory) extensive and sophisticated treatment of arrangement, including organization, sequence, and order.

There are four parts of a speech: the introduction (*exordium*), narration (*narratio*), proof (*confirmatio*, which includes the refutation), and conclusion (*peroratio*, 4). Every question is either unlimited (*infinita*) or limited (*definita*). Arguments (nicely defined as "probable inventions designed to create conviction," 5) are divided in the customary way between the external (i.e., inartificial) and the internal (i.e., artificial) and are topically developed. The summary of artificial topoi (7) is superb, as is the longer discussion of the organization of the topoi (once found and decided on). Cicero senior treats organization, first in general, then in particular, for the four different parts of a speech and for the prosecution and defense in judicial cases (9–15). His focus is on the speaker. Diction (16–17) and syntax (18–24), including a nice discussion of the association of sound and sense and the rationale of schemes and tropes, follow.

After brief comments on delivery (*actio*) and memory (*memoria*, 25-26), Cicero senior focuses on the speech itself and reviews its four parts (27–60). The importance of amplification (*amplificatio*), which emphasizes what you want to get across, is especially stressed (27 and 52–60)—later, in a memorable definiton of eloquence, copiousness is the key rhetorical ingredient (*nihil enim est aliud eloquentia nisi copiose loquens sapientia*, "eloquence is nothing else than wisdom speaking copiously," 79). As for the proof (and refutation), every controversy is said to involve one of three issues (33): whether something happened (the conjectural issue), what happened (definition), and the particular quality of whatever happened (qualitative). Again C. includes an interesting discussion of the significance of sequence and the marshalling of arguments in creating conviction (46–47 and 59), which is followed by a refreshingly pragmatic review of the art (insisting that art is involved here, too) of handling inartifical arguments (48–51).

Cicero senior then turns to the two kinds of questions, the limited (*finitum*) and the unlimited (*infinitum*, 61–68). The former involves particular occasions, the latter general discussion of a thesis. Again, attention is paid to the organization of arguments (68).

Next come the three kinds of causes: epideictic (69–82), including further treatment of the particular organizational aspects of arrangement in speeches praising or blaming (74–75 and 82), and a discussion of the virtues and vices (76–81); deliberative (83–98), which is based on topoi of the expedient and the possible; and judicial (98–131), where the three stages of cases follow the three issues— again, the handling of witnesses and inartificial proofs is included. Finally, Cicero senior reviews the treatment of legal documents when they are the ground of dispute (132–38).

The *BRUTUS* is a fascinating dialogue reviewing the history of Greek and, especially, Roman oratory down to C.'s own day. The speakers are Cicero himself and his best and oldest friend, Titus Pomponius Atticus, whose recently published *Annals* (*Liber Annalis*) provided the historical basis of C.'s review by establishing an accurate sequential framework of people and dates. The other speaker, for whom the dialogue is named, is Marcus Junius Brutus, who, like C., was an ardent defender of the senatorial cause, and is represented here joining Cicero in a lament for the loss of deliberative rhetorical opportunities with the demise of the Republic (6–10, 22–23, and 328–32).

The discussion begins on the occasion of the death of Quintus Hortensius Hortalus, Cicero's senior by eight years and the greatest contemporary speaker after (implicitly) Cicero himself. It ends with a detailed critique of Hortensius as an orator and a fascinating autobiographical review of C.'s own rhetorical training. As usual with C., thinking and speaking are closely allied. One cannot, he has Brutus assert in the opening, speak well without being able to think wisely (*dicere enim bene nemo potest nisi qui prudenter intellegit,* 23).

The review of Greek speakers (26–52) disparages brevity (50). The much longer survey of Roman orators (52ff.) praises eloquence as the lamp by which genius is illuminated (59) and Servius Galba as the first Roman whose speeches are marked by six characteristic functions of the orator: digression for the purpose of ornamentation, delighting his audiences, moving them, amplifying his subject, using pathos, and employing commonplaces (82). These six functions are elaborated, and Galba is also praised for his great memory and abilities as an extemporaneous speaker (91–93).

It is noted in passing that most speeches are written down after they have been delivered and not before; therefore, the memorization of a speech is topical (91). Later, however, Hortensius is praised for his ability to memorize his speeches word for word, whether from his thoughts or written down (301). Brutus particularly praises one of his speeches in defense of Messalla, and Cicero says that according to his understanding the written copy exactly reproduces the speech that was delivered (328). Furthermore, in his own training Cicero recommends writing out speeches (i.e., ahead of time) as an exercise (321). Presumably such written products would become the basis for word-for-word memorization and delivery.

Oratory is basically about success (200), and success comes when the orator is able to effect three results on his audience: to instruct or inform them (i.e., to communicate what he has to say to them); to please them (i.e., both positively, to create a pleasing sound, rhythm, form of expression, etc., and negatively, not to annoy the audience with stilted language, confusing passages, cacaphony, awkward expressions, etc. that draw attention to the inadequacies of the speaker's style); and to move them (i.e., to get them to act on the information he has managed to convey in a pleasant way—usually effected by appeals to the listeners' emotions, 185). The foundation of this success is pure diction, i.e. good Latinity (258), which is primarily acquired by listening to others who speak properly, e.g., one's parents (210), and by reading good authors (322).

Antonius and Crassus are naturally praised, along with Sulpicius and Cotta, Scaevola, Julius Caesar (whose purity of diction is unmatched, as is his admirable clarity and brevity as a historian, 252 and 262), and many others. Along with the praises go pointed criticisms. Calvus, a younger contemporary of C. and the apparent founder of the Atticist movement in Rome, is scrutinized mercilessly and criticized for his misrepresentation of Atticism as a style consistently plain and meager rather than full, varied, and adopting as appropriate all the powers available to language—as best reflected in the greatest Attic speaker and the true model, Demosthenes (283–91).

Not only are speakers reviewed but also the philosophic schools that adopted and contributed to rhetorical instruction (Stoics, Peripatetics, and Academics, 114–21). And nonnative Roman speakers are also treated (169–72), all of whom lacked something in *Latinitas* and *urbanitas,* i.e., good Latinity and urbane, sophisticated expression.

In his last rhetorical treatise, the *ORATOR,* C. continues the conversation with Brutus, proposing to define the ideal orator, and particularly defends his own style of speaking against the attacks of the self-appointed Atticists. In the process he refers to many specific passages in his own speeches and discusses prose rhythm in greater detail than any authority before him. This long, sometimes rambling discussion remains the most extensive treatment of the subject in antiquity.

First of all, philosophy is an essential ingredient in the education of the orator (14–15). The three kinds of speaking are the grandiloquent (*grandiloqua*), the concise (*acuta* or *tenuis*), and the tempered or moderate in–between (*temperata, media,* 20–21). No one has excelled Demosthenes in any of the three, and his successes are the true measure of the Attic style (23–27). In C.'s day the self-proclaimed Atticists only speak in a rough, unpolished sytle (28), but there are really a variety of Attic styles—as in the speeches of Lysias, Aeschines, and Demosthenes (29–30).

After briefly mentioning the three kinds of speeches (37–42), C. hurriedly takes up invention, arrangement, and style (43ff.). A streamlined version of the issues (did anything actually happen, what was it, and how is it to be defined?) is reviewed under invention (45), before arrangement (50) and style (51ff.) are considered. After an introduction to style, delivery is covered (55–60), and then rhetorical style is distinguished from philosophic, sophistic, historical, and poetic styles (65–68). Through the proper eloquence, then, the orator will prove, delight, and sway (69).

The whole key to success is decorum or propriety. In a famous passage (71) C. observes:

> For the same style and the same thoughts must not be used in portraying every condition in life, or every rank, position or age, and in fact a similar distinction must be made in respect of place, time and audience. The universal rule, in oratory as in life, is to consider propriety. (Loeb, pp. 357–59)

To illustrate decorum C. gives detailed reviews of the precise characteristics of the three main styles of speaking: the plain or low style (*subtilis,* 75–90); the middle or more robust (*robustius*), but not the most ample and full (91–96); and the greatest of all, which is full, copious, serious, and ornate (*amplus, copiosus, gravis, ornatus,* 97–

101). The truly eloquent speaker, then, will "discuss trivial matters in a plain style, matters of moderate significance in the tempered style, and weighty affairs in the grand manner" (Loeb, p. 379). Illustrative references follow to various speeches, including many by C. himself (102–11). The ideal speaker should be well trained in logic, history, and the law (113–23). C. closes with another classic statement on decorum:

> This, indeed, is the form of wisdom that the orator must especially employ—to adapt himself to occasions and persons. In my opinion one must not speak in the same style at all times, nor before all people, nor against all opponents, nor in defence of all clients, nor in partnership with all advocates. He, therefore, will be eloquent who can adapt his speech to fit all conceivable circumstances. (Loeb, pp. 397–99)

After brief remarks on ethical and pathetic topoi (128–33), C. turns to the characteristics of style in single words and in the combination of words (134–35). For the former only metaphors are mentioned. But seventeen ornaments of combination are cited, such as repetition of the exact words, repetition of words with similar case endings, stringing together clauses without conjunctions, etc.

He then takes up ornaments of thought or expression (*sententiarum ornamenta*) and presents a remarkable list of almost forty of them (137–38), giving not their technical names (*descriptio, exemplum, distributio,* etc.), but a concise description of what actually happens with each—e.g., the orator "will urge his point by asking questions and will reply to himself as if to questions; he will say something, but desire to have it understood in the opposite sense; he will express doubt whether or how to mention some point" (Loeb, p. 411).

Rhetorical education is cursorily mentioned, along with the importance of literature, before C. takes up sentence structure (149ff). Three aspects are considered: how the sounds of the final syllables in a period (sentence or independent clause) correspond to the sounds of the initial syllables in the following period (149–64); each period should have a definite shape (164–67); and each period should have a definite cadence or rhythm (168–236).

After an introduction to the nature and origins of prose rhythm (168–82), C. establishes poetic feet as the means of discussing and judging prose rhythm (183–90). He then proceeds to the most technical part of this treatment, the determination of which meters to use and when (191–97) and in what combinations (197–203). This last question leads to three further questions for consideration (204–36). Should the whole period be rhythmical? What is the difference between a rhythmical quality to a period and the rhythm itself? And should each period be divided into equally rhythmical clauses (*kôla*)? The answers to these questions and a defense of the usefulness of prose rhythm (227–36) take up the rest of the treatise.

Texts and translations: Cicero, *De Inventione, De Optimo Genere Oratorum, Topica,* trans. H. M. Hubbell (Cambridge, Mass.: Harvard Univ. Press, 1949); *De Oratore, Books I–II,* trans. E. W. Sutton and H. Rackham (Cambridge, Mass.: Harvard Univ. Press, 1942); *De Oratore, Book III, De Fato, Paradoxa Stoicorum, De Partitione Oratoria,* trans. H. Rackham (Cambridge, Mass.: Harvard Univ. Press, 1942); *Brutus,* trans. G. L. Hendrickson, *Orator,* trans. H. M. Hubbell (Cambridge, Mass.: Harvard Univ. Press, 1939).

CORAX and TISIAS have for many centuries been identified as teacher and pupil, respectively, who "invented" rhetoric in Sicily in the second quarter of the fifth century B.C. Cicero (*Brutus* 46) reports Aristotle as saying (probably in the now lost *Synagôgê Technôn*, a collection of material from rhetorical handbooks) that after the expulsion of the Sicilian tyrants, when there was a rush to recover property through legal means, C. and T. wrote an "art" and "precepts" of rhetoric, which no one had done before. This work focused on judicial oratory, especially on arguments from probability (see Plato, *Phaedr*us 273c–274a and Aristotle, *Rhet*oric 2.24.11). Their doctrine was taken to Athens, perhaps with the help of fellow Sicilian Gorgias of Leontini (Pausanius 6.17.8). An apparently well-known story about C. and T. is found in prolegomena written in late antiquity (especially nos. 4 and 17 in Rabe, *Prolegomenôn Syllogê* [Leipzig, 1931], and see also Sextus Empiricus, *Against the Rhetoricians* 96–99). T., it seems, refused to pay C. for instruction, and they went to court. T. testified that if he lost, he need not pay because that would show that the rhetorical instruction that he received from C. was worthless. C. replied by reversing the argument. If *he* lost, it would show that he had in fact taught T. well. The court called the pair "a bad egg from a bad crow," *korax* being the Greek word for crow. Most modern scholars reject the crow story, accepting only that C. discussed persuasive techniques in judicial oratory, that the discussion of proof was dominated by argument from probability, and that T. expanded and improved C.'s work, perhaps writing it down for the first time.

But recent scholarship has cast doubt on the traditional identities of C. and T. It now seems likely that C. was nothing more than a nickname of T. This would explain several odd features in the sources. For instance, Plato (cited above) refers an argument from probability to T., but does not mention C. Aristotle (cited above), on the other hand, refers an argument from probability to C. while not mentioning T. Also, the sources themselves seem uncertain about the identities of T. and C., or refer to Corax with contempt. Plato (cited above), for example, says "Tisias, or whoever it really was and whatever he is pleased to be called" (cf. Cicero, *De Oratore* 1.91, 3.81; Lucian, *Pseudologistês* 30). Moreover, Corax does not appear to have been a Greek name in actual use in antiquity—understandable, given its meaning. A passage from a poem by Pindar dedicated to a Sicilian tyrant (*Olympian odes* 2.86–88) reads, "The true poet is he who knoweth much by gift of nature, but they that have only learnt the lore of song, and are turbulent and intemperate of tongue, like a pair of crows (*korakes*), chatter in vain against the godlike bird of Zeus" (Loeb), suggests that in fifth-century Sicily loud and annoying discourse was associated with crows. T., as a teacher of rhetoric, may have been dubbed "The Crow."

For collected references to Corax and Tisias in ancient writers, see L. Radermacher, *Artium scriptores* (Vienna, 1951), 28–35. In general, see S. Wilcox, "Corax and the 'Prolegomena'" *AJP* 64 (1943): 1–23, and G. Kennedy, "The Earliest Rhetorical Handbooks" *AJP* 80 (1959): 169–78; for the argument denying the separate existence of Corax, see T. Cole, "Who was Corax?" *Illinois Classical Studies* 16 (1991): 65–84.

DEMETRIUS is the reputed author of *ON STYLE* (*PERI HER-MÊNEIAS*), a rhetorical treatise that concentrates exclusively on one of the five traditional parts of rhetoric, *lexis* (style), under the Greek name *hermêneia* (Latin = *elocutio*). The date of composition of this work is disputed. Estimates range from early Hellenistic times, even as early as the fourth century B.C., all the way down to the Roman Imperial period. More important than date, however, is the fact that this treatise differs from the usual treatments of style under three headings, high, middle, and low (but cf. *Rhet. ad Her.* 4.11–14), by developing its own fourfold classification of plain (*ischnos*), grand (*megaloprepês*), polished (*glaphyros*), and forceful (*deinos*) styles (*charactêres*). D. also tacks on an additional epistolary style (*epistolikos*) as an adjunct to the plain style.

Book 1 focuses on the foundation of all prose styles, periodicity, the parts of a period and their definitions (1–34). First, the *kôlon* is defined as a whole thought or complete part of a whole thought (2). Next, illustrations are offered to support the effective use of short or long *kôla* in various contexts. The sub-colon or phrase, the *komma*, is defined as smaller than the *kôlon*. A period (*periodos*), then, is developed out of a combination of *kôla* and *kommata* (10). D. sums up his discussion of the period and its elements by quoting Aristotle's definition of a period: "a period is a portion of speech that has a beginning and an end" (*Rhetoric* 3.9). Next, by way of illustrating the origin of periodic style, D. contrasts the "rounded" style (*katestrammenê*) of Isocrates with the "loose" or "disjointed" style (*diêirêmenê*) of Herodotus. The virtues of both manners are briefly discussed (12–18). Then to another classification of the period on a different level associated with function or genre; here periods are narrative (*historikê*), conversational (*dialogikê*), or oratorical (*rhêtorikê*, 19–21).

Next D. turns to various devices of style useful for the formation of periods: antithetical cola (*antikeimena kôla*); cola of equal length (*isokôla*); and cola ending in similar sound patterns (*homoioteleuta*), 22–27. D. warns that these devices can smack of artificiality and may not be suitable for forceful oratory (28–29). Finally, as a way of clarifying that the period is a form of words, D. contrasts the period with the enthymeme, which may be expressed in various verbal shapes, periodic or otherwise (30–35).

Book 2 introduces the four basic styles: plain or simple, grand or magnificent, polished or elegant, and forceful or powerful (36). The main subject is the grand style, which is treated under three headings: thought (*dianoia*), word choice (*lexis*), and the appropriate arrangement of words, later called *synthesis* (2.38).

First D. enters into a long, technical discussion of prose rhythms, colometry, and special stylistic features of word placement (*synthesis*) appropriate to the grand style (39–67). Sections 39–44 treat the paeon, hexameter, and iambic feet as bases of prose rhythm. Discussion follows of the length of cola (44–48), the arrangement of words (49–52), and the management of connectives and particles to effect dignity (53–58). Next comes a list of figures of style (*schêmata tês lexeôs*, 59–67), including *anthypallagê*, an unusual shift in grammatical case; *epanaphora*, repetition of the same word at the beginning of phrases; *dialysis*, omission of conjunctions, whose opposite is *synapheia* or the repeated use of conjunctions; and *anadiplôsis*, the double use of a word in the same phrase for emphasis. D. ends his treatment of synthesis by looking at euphony, with a special focus on the concatenation of vowel sounds, or *synkrousis* (68–74).

After briefly commenting on the subject matter appropriate to the grand style (75–76), D. turns to diction (77–114). He begins with extensive comments on metaphor (*metaphora*) and simile (*eikasia*, 78–90). Treatment follows of compound words (*syntheta onomata*, 91), words created to imitate sounds (*pepoiêmena onomata*, 94), and indirect expressions (*allêgoria*, 99–102). Finally comes a miscellany of stylistic devices that may effect elevation of style, e.g., concision (*syntomia*, 103), a capping line (*epiphônêma*, 109), maxim (*gnômê*, 110), and the use of poetic words in general (112–14). Book 2 concludes with comments on the frigid style (*psychron*), which is the vice corresponding to the grand style. Frigidity arises from awkward or inappropriate diction or synthesis unsuccessfully aiming at the grand (114–24).

Book 3 (128–92) discusses the elegant or polished style (*glaphyros logos*). After a general description of this style (128–39) in terms of subject matter (*pragmata*), diction (*lexis*), and arrangement (*taxis*), D. treats in more detail the figures that can be used to create the polished style. Some of these figures are the same ones which are used for the grand style: *anadiplôsis* (140); anaphora (141); metaphor (142); *syn-*

theton onoma (143), the ordinary word (*idiôtikon onoma*, 144); striking comparison (*parabolê*, 146); shift in thought (*metabolê*, 148); intertextual allusions (150); indirect expressions (*allêgoriai*, 151); unexpected, witty twists of phrase (152–53); and the bantering accusation (155). All these figures fall under the heading of *lexis*.

The next topic is subject matter (*pragmata*), where certain selections may contribute to the charming style (156). D. mentions the proverb (*paroimia*), the tale (*mythos*), the comparison (*eikasia*), and exaggeration (*hyperbolê*) as sources of charm (*charis*). He also distinguishes charm from bald humor (*geloion*), which is inappropriate to a charming or graceful context (163–72). Finally come other forms of graceful ornamentation, e.g., lovely-sounding words (*kala onomata*), and the principles of alphabetic euphony (173–78).

The book ends with hasty treatments of arrangement or composition of words (*synthesis*) and prose rhythms appropriate to the graceful style (179–85), with a parting look at the stylistic vice opposite to *logos glaphyros*, a style of (literally) "bad imitation" (*kakozêlon*), sometimes translated as the "mannered" style (186–87).

Book 4 (190–239) covers the plain style (*charactêr ischnos*). Quickly passing over subject matter, D. moves into a discussion of diction, suggesting the avoidance of compound words (*dipla onomata*) and coined words (*pepoiêmena onomata*) in the plain style. The plain style especially needs to be clear (*saphês*, 191). After an excursus on stage mannerisms (193–95), clarity (*saphêneia*) is discussed further (196–202) and then the proper use of prose rhythms, hiatus, and the avoidance of peculiar or strange figures (203–08).

After clarity, vividness (*enargeia*) is the quality of plain style to be pursued (209–21). Various techniques contribute to vividness: the precise and accurate rendering of events (*akribologia*, 209), repetition of words (*dilogia*, 211), clashing of vowel sounds (*kakophônia*, 219), and even words that sound like what they mean (*pepoiêmena onomata*, 220).

Before he gets to the vice corresponding to the plain style at the end of this book—the arid style (*xêros*), which arises from defects of word choice, inappropriate narrative of a serious event as trivial, or tasteless thought itself (236–39)—D. interpolates a brief discussion of letter writing (*charactêr epistolikos*, 223–35), the only consideration of it in ancient rhetorical manuals. The style of letters needs to be more carefully crafted than that of dialogue, but it is unlike the style of a declaimed courtroom speech. The epistolary style should, however, capture the *êthos* or natural character of its writer. Letters need to be more formal when addressed to royalty.

Book 5 (240–304) deals with forcefulness in style (*deinotês*). Passing over subject matter (*pragmata*), D. begins a long section on compostion (*synthesis*, 241–71). Various observations are made, e.g., the use of *kommata* in place of *kôla* for a stabbing effect (241), symbolic phrases (*symbola*), avoidance of archaic style (245), avoidance of excessive antithesis (250), the use of periods closely packed together (251), harsh–sounding words (*kakophônia*, 255), conjunctions displaced to the end of sentences (257–58), and wit with sarcasm (259–62). Next D. moves to figures of thought (*schêmata tês dianoias*, 263–66): passing over (*paraleipsis*), falling silent (*aposiôpêsis*), and impersonation (*prosôpopoiia*). Figures of speech or style are (*schêmata tês lexeôs*, 267–71): *anadiplôsis, anaphora, asyndeton, homoioteleuton, dialysis* (a type of asyndeton), and *klimax* (the ladder figure). Here figures of speech are treated under the heading of synthesis, whereas in Book 3 they were treated under diction (*lexis*), which is now taken up for the forceful style.

The forceful style (272–97) involves metaphor (272), simile (273), compound words (275), *epimonê*, a newly mentioned verbal device increasing the force or power of any given fact (280), and euphemism (281). D. then discusses *emphasis* along with hyperbole and allegory (282–86). *Emphasis* seems to mean a stress on words such that they imply more than they mean on the surface. Then dissimulation (*eschêmatismenon en logôi*) is treated at length (287–98).

D. now briefly returns to word arrangement (*synthesis*), advising the avoidance of smoothness of language (*leiotês*) in the forceful style and recommending spontaneity and vigor (299–301). He closes with the vice of graceless or unpleasant style (*acharis*), the negative correlative to the forceful style (302–04).

Text and translation: Aristotle, *Poetics,* trans. Stephen Halliwell; *Longinus,* trans. W. Hamilton Fyfe, rev. Donald A. Russell; Demetrius, *On Style,* trans. Doreen C. Inness, based on trans. by W. Rhys Roberts, 2nd ed. (Cambridge, Mass.: Harvard Univ. Press, 1995).

DIONYSIUS OF HALICARNASSUS was a historian and rhetorician who came to Rome in 30 B.C. and lived there for more than two decades. His works include *ON LITERARY COMPOSITION* (*PERI SYNTHESEÔS ONOMATÔN*), three literary letters (two addressed to *AMMAEUS* and one to *GNAEUS POMPEIUS*), essays on *DINARCHUS* and *THUCYDIDES,* and a work later entitled *ON ANCIENT ORATORS* (*PERI TÔN ARCHAIÔN RHÊTORÔN*) that comprises essays on Lysias, Isocrates, Isaeus, and Demosthenes. D. also wrote the extremely fragmentary *On Imitation* (*Pêri Mimêseôs*), as well as treatises on political philosophy and figures, neither of which has survived.

ON LITERARY COMPOSITION, addressed to a certain Rufus Metilius, begins with D.'s claim that the treatise will be useful for all aspects of life that are conducted through speech, particularly political oratory (*politikos logos*). Almost every kind of discourse (*logos*) requires study in ideas, which pertain to content (*to pragmatikon*), and words, which pertain to style (*to lektikon*). The present study on the arrangement (*synthesis*) of words, directed toward the young, has no comparable predecessor, and D. will later produce a treatise on the choice of words should he live long enough (1).

First, composition (*synthesis*) is defined as the arrangement of the parts of speech. Aristotle and Theophrastus considered them to be three (nouns, verbs, and conjunctions), though successors further divided these. The combination of these parts creates clauses (*kôla*), and the combination of clauses creates periods (*periodoi*), which comprise the complete discourse. Composition, while naturally subsequent to the choice of words, is nonetheless more important (2). D. then sets out to prove this assertion. He quotes a passage from the *Odyssey* and one from Herodotus and argues that each passage is made pleasing not by the words themselves, which are unremarkable, but by their combination (3). Then to how rearrangment of the words alters the rhythm, meter, and character of lines from the *Iliad.* D. demonstrates a similar effect in Herodotus. Almost all the ancient writers paid special attention to composition, but later it was completely neglected, and many writers are barely readable (4). Previous theories are simplistic, inaccurate, and basically worthless. Since ancient poets, historians, etc. gave much thought to composition and had a system of rules that they followed, D. will attempt to outline their system (5).

The science (*epistêmê*) of composition has three functions: 1) to observe which combinations are likely to create a beautiful and pleasant union; 2) to judge how each part should be arranged in order to make the harmonious composition better; and 3) to judge whether any alterations are necessary and to make them. This applies to poetry as well as prose; D. gives examples (6). Then to the proper combination of clauses (7), their form (whether statement, question, prayer, order, etc., 8), and additions and subtractions to them, illustrated by passages from ancient writers. The same precepts apply to the use of periods (9).

The second main topic of the treatise is what should be the aims of the writer wishing to compose well, and how to achieve them. The two greatest aims, pleasure (*hêdonê*) and beauty (*to kalon*) are distinct: Thucydides' writings, for example, are beautiful but not especially pleasant, while Xenophon's are extremely pleasant but not especially beautiful. Herodotus has both qualities (10). Four elements comprise an attractive and pleasant style: melody (*melos*), rhythm (*rhythmos*), variety (*metabolê*), and the appropriate use of those three. Under pleasure are included freshness (*hôra*), charm (*charis*), eloquence (*eustomia*), sweetness (*glykytês*), persuasiveness (*to pithanon*), and the like; under beauty are impressiveness (*megaloprepeia*), gravity (*baros*), seriousness (*semnologia*), dignity (*axiôma*), and the like. D. discusses the importance of each of these four elements and then proceeds to a rather technical discussion of melody, rhythm, interval, pitch, and quantity (11). Different parts of the sentence strike the ear in different ways, and good taste is a matter of judgment, not science, but the writer should link together words that are melodious and rhythmical or interweave those that are with those that are not, thereby diminishing the effects of the latter. Further, he should use variety and arrange the content appropriately and naturally (12). Beauty should be pursued by the same four elements, which are ultimately determined by the letters themselves and the phonetic effect of the syllables (13).

This leads D. to a more detailed examination of speech, which he divides into basic parts called elements (*stoicheia*) and letters (*grammata*). A technical discussion on linguistics, particularly phonetics, follows. D. examines vowels and semivowels, voiced and voiceless letters, and so forth (14). Then to the nature of syllables and the different effects created by their use, with illustrations from Homer (15–16). In sum, various letters create syllables, various syllables words, and various words a discourse. A style is beautiful when it has beautiful words, syllables, and letters. Examples of different effects created by Homer follow (16).

A detailed discussion of rhythm and meter is next. Every word that consists of more than one syllable is spoken in some sort of rhythm, or meter. D. analyzes the virtues, or faults, of various metrical feet, with examples from writers of both poetry and prose. The rhythmic incompetence of the historian and orator Hegesias of Magnesia is attacked, in contrast to the felicities of Homer (17–18). Variety is the third factor of beautiful arrangement. Poets are less at liberty to vary their meter, but prose writers have complete freedom. The finest style has periodic and nonperiodic sentences, clauses of varying number and length, different figures, etc. Herodotus, Plato, and Demosthenes were good at this, but not Isocrates and his followers (19). Next D. discusses appropriateness (*to prepon*), which is essential. Words must be combined in different ways according to character and situation. This point is illustrated with detailed analyses of passages from Homer (20).

There are three kinds of composition, which D. calls the austere (*austêra*), polished (*glaphyra*), and well-blended (*eukraton*). The austere style demands that the words hold firm position and that the parts of the sentence be separated by intervals; it allows harshness and dissonance and long words. Its clauses may be unparallel and free, while its rhythms should be dignified. It uses periods sparingly, a variety of cases and figures, and so forth. It is unadorned, antique, and not at all flowery. Among its models were Pindar in lyric, Aeschylus in tragedy, Thucydides in history, Antiphon in oratory. Passages from Pindar and Thucydides are analyzed in extreme linguistic detail (21–22). The polished type, which displays rapidity, has an exact fit between words with no interval, melodious and smooth words, and an avoidance of harshness and dissonance. The clauses should be woven into periods that can be spoken in one breath. The rhythms should be moderate in length, or somewhat short. The figures should be delicate and pleasant. In sum, it is generally the opposite of the austere type. Among its models are Hesiod in epic, Sappho in lyric, Euripides in tragedy, and Isocrates in oratory. Passages from Sappho and Isocrates are analyzed in detail (23). The third type of composition, the well-blended, is a mixture of the other two, and therefore may be the best. Homer is the greatest example of its use. Other models are Sophocles in tragedy, Herodotus in history, Demosthenes in oratory, and Democritus, Plato, and Aristotle in philosophy (24).

The next consideration is to how prose is made to resemble poetry, and poetry prose. As an example of poetic prose D. takes Demosthenes. In order to resemble, but not be, poetry, prose must have varied and unobtrusive rhythms and meters but not actually be in a regular meter or rhythm. Passages from Demosthenes are analyzed in detail. To those who scoff at the idea that Demosthenes and others would take such painstaking care over the rhythms and meters of their prose, D. issues a hearty rejoinder (25). As for poetry that resembles prose, the most important factor is the fit of the words, then the composition of the clauses, and finally the symmetry of the periods. There must be enjambment, and the clauses and periods should be unequal in length. Lyric poets can, and should, use many meters and rhythms in a single period in order to produce this effect. Just as not all prose resembling poetry is worthy of respect, so too is some poetry resembling prose good, some not. D. gives examples of his points from Homer and Simonides. D. concludes the treatise by advising Rufus to study and practice the lessons within (26).

The ostensible purpose of the *FIRST LETTER TO AMMAEUS* is to prove that Aristotle's *Rhetoric* was written after Demosthenes had delivered his greatest orations, not before, and so that Demosthenes had not, as some Peripatetics claimed, learned his rhetorical skills from Aristotle (1–3). Biographical and chronological information on Demosthenes and his speeches is reviewed, along with a brief sketch of Aristotle's life (4–5). Aristotle's works on rhetoric and logic are analyzed to prove that the *Rhetoric* was composed late in Aristotle's career (6–7). Historical events mentioned in the *Rhetoric* prove the anteriority of some of Demosthenes' greatest speeches (8–11). D. concludes the letter by arguing that Demosthenes also wrote his single greatest speech, *On the Crown*, before the publication of the *Rhetoric* and by declaring that Aristotle in fact wrote the *Rhetoric* with reference to the works of Demosthenes and other orators (12).

The *LETTER TO GNAEUS POMPEIUS* purports to defend D.'s previous criticism of Plato, to which Pompeius has objected. D. assures Pompeius that he has great admiration for Plato, but that his criticisms were a natural result of comparison with Demosthenes, whom he judges the finest rhetorician of all (1). D. then quotes his own remarks on Plato from the treatise on Demosthenes, noting that his criticisms pertain only to style, not content (2). He turns to history, using a lengthy quotation from his own treatise *On Imitation*. Five aspects of content are considered, with specific comparisons of Herodotus and Thucydides. The historian must choose a noble subject, decide where to begin and end, decide what to include, arrange properly what is included, and present it impartially (Herodotus is superior in all five). Both historians display a pure (*kathara*) style in their respective dialects. After a lacuna, D. gives a random list of comparative virtues of style. Thucydides is superior in conciseness (*syntomia*); they both exhibit vividness (*enargeia*); Thucydides is better at depicting emotion (*ta pathê*), etc. (3). A comparison of Xenophon and the historian Philistus follows. D. critiques Xenophon in the context of his model, Herodotus (4), and Philistus in the context of Thucydides, with whom he has more in common (5). Finally, the historian Theopompus is critiqued in the contexts of his teacher, Isocrates, and of Demosthenes (6).

The *SECOND LETTER TO AMMAEUS* responds to Ammaeus' dissatisfaction with D.'s method elsewhere of analyzing the style of Thucydides. D. quotes his own remarks on style from the essay on Thucydides (1–2), then comments on each of these remarks, adding illustrative passages as requested by Ammaeus. Topics discussed include Thucydides' use of obscure vocabulary, expression of phrases by nouns and vice versa, transformation of nouns into verbs and vice versa, substitution of singular for plural and vice versa, ostentatious figures of speech, and so forth (3–17).

The essay on *DINARCHUS* reviews that orator's career. Dinarchus had not been included in D.'s treatise *On Ancient Orators* because he neither created an individual style nor perfected one created by somebody else. Nonetheless, he is worthy of study.

Biographical information comes first, along with comments about the need to distinguish the genuine speeches of Dinarchus from the ones spuriously attributed to him (1–4). Dinarchus is the best of the imitators of Demosthenes, but he still falls somewhat short in every aspect of style and content (5–8). Then to questions of dating and ascription. D. gives a list of the approximately thirty public speeches that he considers genuine (9–10), then a list of spurious speeches with the reasons for rejecting their authenticity (11), then approximately thirty genuine private speeches (12), and, finally, spurious private speeches, again with the reasons for rejection (13).

The essay on *THUCYDIDES* proposes to elaborate on the brief discussion in the essay *On Imitation*. Topics include the scope and method of Thucydides (5–8); his arrangement (9–12); his elaboration of details (13–18); and his introduction, which D. improves by rewriting (19–20). Then to a detailed discussion of Thucydides' style (21–23). Thucydides forged a new style—metaphorical, obscure, archaic, and bizarre. It is very figurative and extremely concise. His style has four main aspects: artificiality of vocabulary (*to poiêtikon tôn onomatôn*), variety of figures (*to polyeides tôn schêmatôn*), harshness of word order (*to trachu tês harmonias*), and rapidity of signification (*to tachos tôn sêmasiôn*). Special features of his style include compactness and solidity (*to striphnon kai to pyknon*), pungency and severity (*to pikron kai to austêron*), vehemence (*to embrithes*), dreadfulness (*to deinon kai to phoberon*), and above all, emotional power (*to pathêtikon*, 24).

D. proceeds to quote and comment on specific passages. He begins with the introduction again and then focuses on two long passages of narration (25–33). Then to the speeches (*dêmêgoriai*) in the work, a discussion that D. divides into content (*to pragmatikon*) and style (*to lektikon*). Thucydides is very good at the invention (*heuresis*) of arguments and ideas but not so good at the use (*chrêsis*) of invention, because some of his speeches are inappropriate to the occasion (34–35). Various speeches and parts of speeches are examined; some are good, some bad, and some both (36–48). D. reiterates that Thucydides is best when he uses normal language. His style is obviously not suited to political debates or private conversations. Some say that he wrote only for the very educated. Indeed, it is sad that only a few can understand everything that he writes. The assertion that his language was familiar at the time is clearly not true. The writing in historical works should be only a step removed from ordinary usage (49–51). Although no historian has imitated Thucydides, Demosthenes has imitated him in many ways. Students of political oratory should take Demosthenes as their guide. As for Thucydides, we should admire his clear passages, not his obscure ones (52–55).

ON ANCIENT ORATORS begins by observing that D. and Ammaeus, to whom the work is addressed, should be happy about the current revival of political oratory (*politikos logos*). Vulgar, frigid oratory is not now admired except in a few Asian cities. Rome's conquest of the world has caused this situation, for her leaders are discriminating and sophisticated. D. says that his present task is to choose the most important ancient orators and historians, examining how they lived and wrote. He will select the most elegant (*chariestatoi*) of them and examine them chronologically, beginning with the orators and moving to the historians if time permits. First will be Lysias, Isocrates, and Isaeus, then Demosthenes, Hyperides, and Aeschines [he does not, in fact, write on Hyperides and Aeschines] (1–4).

The essay on Lysias opens with biographical information and proceeds to the virtues of Lysias's style. First, his vocabulary is pure (*katharos*), a perfect model of the Attic dialect. He is also praised for powerful use of ordinary language (1–3); clarity (*saphêneia*) and conciseness (4–6); vividness (*enargeia*); effective characterization (*êthopoiia*); spontaneity; propriety (*to prepon*); and charm (*charis*), his most important quality (7–10). The genuineness of Lysias's speech on the statue of Iphicrates is discussed (11–12). Then comes a recapitulation of his style and a defense against the accusation by Theophrastus that he uses artificial language (13–14). Next is Lysias's treatment of content. He is good at invention (*heuresis*)—discovering the arguments inherent in a situation—but his arrangement (*taxis*), while simple and generally uniform, is not as good (15). Of the three types of oratory, Lysias has especially made his mark in forensic. Then to commentary on Lysias's oratory according to the parts of speech in the Isocratean school. His introductions (*prooimia*) are most skillful, varied, and original (16–17). In the narration (*diêgêsis*) he is the best of all orators, for his are clear, concise, pleasant, and persuasive. As for proofs (*pisteis*), there are three types, involving fact (*pragma*), emotion (*pathos*), and character (*êthos*). Lysias is the best in factual proofs, skillful in proofs of character, but rather weak in proofs involving emotion, since he lacks strength in amplification and arousing pity. His conclusions (*epilogoi*) are moderate and pleasing, but not particularly powerful (18–19). D. illustrates his observations by quoting sections from forensic, epideictic, and deliberative speeches by Lysias (20–34).

Isocrates style is as pure as that of Lysias, but he has a tendency to be too ornate. His full periods make his work better for reading than for practical use and, consequently, more suited for ceremonial occasions than for the courts. Isocrates chooses his words well, but his arrangement is somewhat unharmonious, and he uses figures poorly. He lacks the charm (*charis*) of Lysias but is superior in being more impressive and dignified (1–3). As for content, his invention (*heuresis*) of arguments is equal to that of Lysias, and he is better at arranging and dividing topics. D. praises his superiority in virtuous content (4) and quotes several illustrative passages from speeches and letters (5–10). Then to a summary of the similarities and differences between the style and content of Lysias and Isocrates, and the observation that in political and judicial oratory the words naturally follow the thought, not vice versa (11–13). Next is Isocrates' excessive use of figures, with specific examples (14), and passages that display Isocrates' best points from both political and forensic speeches (15–20).

Isaeus, like Lysias, is a specialist in forensic oratory (1). Isaeus's language, like that of Lysias, is pure, clear, standard, persuasive, and appropriate to the subject. But Lysias employs a more simple, moral, and natural style, which is extremely charming. Isaeus displays more technical skill and a more elaborate, artistic style. His content is divided and arranged more precisely and artistically, and his arguments are highly developed (2–4). Comments on Isaeus's style are illustrated by extensive comparisons of passages from Isaeus to similar ones from Lysias (5–11) and Demosthenes (12–13). D. praises Isaeus's skillful arrangement of content, which is marked by variety. The narrative parts of Isaeus seem contrived and deceitful rather than natural. As for proofs, his epicheiremes and enthymemes go into more detail, amplify more, and make the emotions seem more noble than do Lysias's (14–17). In summary, Lysias aims more for truth, Isaeus for art. Lysias pursues charm, Isaeus force. D. then mentions or comments briefly on Gorgias of Leontini, Alcidamas, Theodorus of Byzantium, Anaximines, Antiphon, Thrasymachus, Polycrates, Critias, Zoilius, and others (18–20).

The introduction of the essay on Demosthenes has apparently been lost. At the beginning we find D. illustrating a discussion of the grand (later referred to as *hypsêlon*) style (*lexis*) with a passage from Gorgias of Leontini. Thucydides is the standard example of that style (1). The second style is the plain (*aphelês*, later referred to as *ischnon*), used most successfully by historians, philosophers, and orators and perfected by Lysias. The third style is the middle (*mesotês*), a mixture of the other two. Its models are Isocrates and Plato (2–3). Then come reviews of the stylistic characteristics of Isocrates and Plato (4–7). Finally to Demosthenes himself, who blended the three types into a perfect, composite style. Passages are discussed that illustrate Demosthenes' uses of the grand (8–10), simple (11–13), and middle style (14–32), the last perfected by him. Extensive comparisons are made to passages in Lysias, Isocrates, and Plato, including a detailed critique of Plato's *Menexenus* (23–29), with comparative quotations from the conclusion of the *Menexenus* and from Demosthenes—D. argues for the superiority of the latter (30–32). After recapitulating his points thus far, D. discusses Demosthenes' arrangement of words, which is the best among orators and never criticized even by his enemies (33–35).

Then to Demosthenes' harmonious composition (*harmonia*). There are three main types of literary composition (*synthesis spoudaia*). First is the austere and old-fashioned type (*austêra kai philarchaios*), which aims at dignity, not elegance, and has long words, hiatus, harshness, elevated rhythm, dignified figures, simple periods, and asyndeton. Thucydides is the best example of it among historians (36–39). The second type is polished (*glaphyra*) and spectacular (*theatrikê*), which aims at adornment rather than dignity. This type features smoothness, musical sounds, no hiatus or other harshness, poetical clauses, frequent use of periods, and figures that arouse emotion. Its models are Hesiod, Sappho, and Anacreon in poetry and Isocrates and his followers in prose (40). The third type is a mixture of the first two. The model is Homer, who combines pleasantness (*hêdonê*) and dignity (*to semnon*). Herodotus among historians and Plato among philosophers imitated him (41–42). D. then quotes from Demosthenes, who used a mixed type of composition because he knew that forensic and panegyric required different modes. In general, he realized that the introduction and narration (*diêgêsis*) needed to be pleasant, while the proofs and epilogues should be austere. Different styles were needed in different situations (43–46). Demosthenes mastered the principles of the mixed type. He knew that the austere type aimed for beauty (*to kalon*) and the polished type for pleasure (*to hêdu*), which are the two objectives of almost every speech. Beauty and pleasure have the same elements: tone (*melos*), rhythm (*rhythmos*), variation (*metabolê*), and propriety (*to prepon*). D. next discusses the relationships among these elements, which Demosthenes thoroughly understood and exploited differently at different times. One can recognize Demosthenes' style of composition by its great concentration (*syndromê*), amplification (*pleonasmos*), and melody (*emmeleia*, 47–50).

Then come general remarks on the importance of harmonious composition in speeches and the great effort needed to achieve it (51–52). A discussion of how Demosthenes embellished his speeches in delivery (*hypokrisis*) follows. There are two considerations: modulation of the voice (*ta pathê tês phônês*) and movements of the body (*ta schêmata tou sômatos*). Demosthenes mastered both. After arguing that different delivery, e.g., ironic, angry, question and answer, and urbane, is required in different situations (53–54), D. concludes by discussing criticisms of Demosthenes. He lacked charm, but the criticisms of Aeschines, e.g., that Demosthenes used harsh and vulgar language, are unfounded. Those who censure Demosthenes for pleonasm are misguided, for it is actually a virtue (55–58).

Text and translation: Dionysius of Halicarnassus, *The Critical Essays in Two Volumes,* trans. Stephen Usher (Cambridge, Mass.: Harvard Univ. Press, 1974–85).

GORGIAS, a native of Leontini in Sicily, was born before 480 B.C. He was said to have studied under the philosopher, physician, and orator Empedocles. One of the most famous of the sophists, Gorgias was especially known for his pioneering use of figurative, especially antithetical, language; his trip to Athens on an embassy in 427 B.C. was an important event in the history of rhetoric. He died an extremely old man after 380. A fragmentary philosophical treatise, *ON THE NONEXISTENT OR ON NATURE (PERI TOU MÊ ONTOS Ê PERI PHYSEÔS)* argues in a skeptical, paradoxical vein: nothing actually exists (71–76), and even if it does, it is unknowable (77–82); were it knowable, it could not be communicated to others by means of linguistic statement (*logos*), which is both revelatory and nonexistent (83–87). Gorgias also wrote several oratorical works, two of which survive intact: *ENCOMIUM OF HELEN (Helenês Engkômion)* and *DEFENSE ON BEHALF OF PALAMEDES (HYPER PALAMÊDOUS APOLOGIA)*. Both have implications for rhetorical theory.

G. begins the *ENCOMIUM OF HELEN* by saying that the praiseworthy should be praised and the blameworthy blamed. Those who criticize Helen for going to Troy are wrong in doing so, and G. wants to set them straight (1–2). He praises Helen for her lineage, beauty, etc. (3–4) and asserts that he will justify her actions (5). She acted either by the will of fate (*tychê*), for which she is not responsible (6), or on account of compulsion, for which she also is not responsible (7), or under the seduction of words. Speech (*logos*) is powerful. It operates at the level of opinion (*doxa*). The persuader did wrong, and Helen is wrongly charged (8–13). Speech is like a drug for the soul that causes distress or delight, fear or boldness (14). Another possible reason for Helen's behavior was love. Men fear, desire, etc. that which they see. Helen may have desired Paris, but that is the fault of human nature and not a sin but a misfortune (15–19). G. ends by reviewing the main points and objectives of his speech (20–21).

The *DEFENSE ON BEHALF OF PALAMEDES* involves the enmity between Odysseus and Palamedes. Odysseus forged a letter from Priam to Palamedes that arranged for Palamedes to betray the Greeks, hid gold in Palamedes tent, and then accused Palamedes of treachery. G. speaks as Palamedes and says that the question is whether he will die justly or with dishonor, for everyone dies. If Odysseus accuses him out of concern for Greece, he is the best of men. But if he acts out of envy, conspiracy, or villainy, he is the worst of men. He will show that Odysseus accuses him falsely for two reasons (1–5). First, he, Palamedes, is not capable of the act charged. There are many reasons why it would be impossible for him to have done it, e.g., the language barrier (6–12). Second, there was no motive for him to do it even if he were able. He puts forth many supporting arguments, e.g., that he does not need the money (13–21). Then Palamedes addresses his accuser, asking what kind of man he is and proclaiming that his accuser operates not from knowledge, but from opinion (*doxa*). Opinion is less trustworthy than the truth (*alêtheia*, 22–24). He is accused of two contradictory things: madness, for betraying Greece, and intelligence, for being clever enough to do it. But the same man cannot possess both. Palamedes then refuses to recount all the foolish remarks of his accuser (25–27), turning instead to the good deeds of his life and his blamelessness (28–32). He urges his audience to pay more attention to actions than to words, for words cannot make actions free of doubt (33–35). If they convict him, they will make the greatest error. Since they are the best judges, there is no need to say more (36–37).

Text: Gorgias, *Reden, Fragmente und Testimonien*, ed. and trans. Thomas Buckheim (Hamburg: Felix Meiner, 1989). Translations: *The Older Sophists*, ed. Rosamond K. Sprague (Columbia, S.C.: Univ. of South Carolina Press, 1972), 30–67; *Helen* in *Readings from Classical Rhetoric*, ed. Patricia P. Matsen, Philip Rollinson, and Marion Sousa (Carbondale: Southern Illinois Univ. Press, 1990), 34–36.

HERMOGENES was born around A.D. 161 in Tarsus in southern Asia Minor. A famous anecdote has him visited at the age of fifteen by the emperor Marcus Aurelius, who came to see the boy in response to reports of his astonishing oratorical precociousness. This ability, however, soon deserted H., and for the rest of his life he was an undistinguished speaker (Philost. *Lives of the Sophists* 2.577). H. was perhaps the most influential Greek rhetorician during late antiquity, Byzantine times, and the Renaissance. Five works have come down in his name: *PROGYMNASMATA, ON STASEIS (PERI TÔN STASEÔN), ON INVENTION (PERI HEURESEÔS), ON TYPES OF STYLE (PERI IDEÔN)*, and *ON THE METHOD OF FORCE (PERI METHODOU DEINOTÊTOS)*. Of these, only *ON STASEIS* and *ON TYPES OF STYLE* are certainly genuine; *ON THE METHOD OF FORCE* is spurious without a doubt, and *PROGYMNASMATA* and *ON INVENTION* are doubtful. For simplicity, H. will be referred to here as the author of all the works except *ON THE METHOD OF FORCE*. The five works are illustrated throughout, generally in exhaustive detail, by numerous examples, usually taken from Demosthenes but also from other speakers and writers.

The *PROGYMNASMATA* treats twelve exercises with no introduction or conclusion. The first *progymnasma* is fable (*mythos*). Fables take their name from their inventors: for example, Cyprian, Libyan, etc. Fables may be based on untruth and should be plausible; they are sometimes concise, sometimes expanded by the use of direct speech. The diction of a fable should be unperiodic and possess sweetness (*glykytês*). The moral may be put first or last (1).

Next is narrative (*diêgêma*), which H. defines as the exposition of something having happened, or as if it had happened. It differs from narration (*diêgêsis*) in the same way that a poem (*poiêma*) does from an entire poetical work (*poiêsis*). There are four kinds of narrative: mythical (*mythikon*), dramatic (*plasmatikon* or *dramatikon*), historical (*historikon*), and political (*politikon*). There are five forms (*schêmata*): direct declarative (*orthon apophantikon*), indirect declarative (*apophantikon engkeklimenon*), interrogative (*elengktikon*), unconnected (*asyndeton*), and comparative (*syngkritikon*). H. says that the direct form is suited to stories (*historiai*), the indirect to disputes (*agônes*), the interrogative to refutation (*elenchos*), and the unconnected to epilogues, since this form produces emotion (2).

Chreia (*chreia*) is defined as the concise exposition of some word or deed or both, generally for some useful purpose. The chreia differs from the memorial (*apomnêmoneuma*) mainly in length; the memorial may be long, but the chreia must be concise. It differs from the aphorism (*gnômê*) in that the aphorism is a bare statement, but the *chreia* is often produced by question and answer; the aphorism is based only on words, while the chreia may be based on deeds; and the aphorism has no reference to a particular person, while the chreia does. There are three types: declarative (*apophantikê*), interrogative (*erôtêmatikê*), and investigative (*pysmatikê*). The working out (*ergasia*) of a chreia is: brief encomium of the speaker or doer; paraphrase (*paraphrasis*) of the chreia itself; proof (*aitia*), which may be direct, from the contrary, by illustration (*parabolê*), by example (*paradeigma*), or by authority (*krisis*); and exhortation (*paraklêsis*, 3).

The fourth exercise is the aphorism (*gnômê*), which H. defines as a general statement that dissuades from something, persuades toward something, or shows the nature of something. Aphorisms can be true, plausible, simple, compound, or exaggerated. The working out of the aphorism is similar to that of the chreia: brief encomium; direct exposition of the proverb; proof, which may be from the contrary, by enthymeme, by illustration, by example, or by authority; and exhortation (4).

Next is refutation (*anaskeuê*) and confirmation (*kataskeuê*). H. says that these do not apply to fictitious things, but only to things open to argument. A refutation is conducted by showing that something is unclear, implausible, impossible, inconsistent or contrary, inappropriate, inexpedient. Confirmation is conducted by the opposites of these (5).

The commonplace (*koinos topos*) is an amplification of a demonstrated fact. It proceeds by the following: introduction; examination of the contrary; the deed itself; comparison; aphorism; attack of past life based on present behavior; rejection of pity by sketch (*hypotypôsis*) of the deed itself and by the final (*telika*) headings (the lawful, just, expedient, possible, suitable, and description of the crime); and exhortation (6).

The seventh *progymnasma* is encomium (*engkômion*), which H. defines as the exposition of good qualities belonging to someone in general or in particular. There may also be encomia of things, animals, plants, rivers, etc. Encomium differs in general from praise (*epainos*) in that the former is lengthy while the latter may be brief. After saying that invective is a type of encomium, H. points out the difference between encomium and commonplace: the former aims at nothing more than the recognition of excellence, while the latter aims at a reward. The topics of encomia may be ethnicity (*ethnos*), city, family (*genos*), birth, upbringing (*trophê*), training (*agôgê*), nature of the body (under the headings beauty, size, speed, and strength), nature of the soul (under the headings justice, temperance, wisdom, and manliness), pursuits (*epitêdeumata*), externalities (family, friends, wealth, etc.), time, manner and aftermath of death, and comparison. H. says that encomia of animals, things, plants, etc. should be conducted similarly, and that an encomium of a god is called a hymn (*hymnos*, 7).

Comparison (*synkrisis*) has the same topics as encomium: city, ethnicity, upbringing, pursuits, etc. We may compare things as equals, praise two things but show that one is better than the other, praise one thing and censure another, etc. (8).

The next exercise is characterization (*êthopoiia*), which H. defines as the representation of the character of an actual person. He distinguishes it from personification (*prosôpopoiia*), in which both the person and character are invented, and from *eidôlopoiia*, in which words are attributed to a dead person. Characterization may involve definite or indefinite persons, single when a person speaks by himself, double when he speaks to others. It may also pertain to character (*êthikai*), to emotion (*pathêtikai*), or be a mixture of both. Examples are given. The working out involves the three times: past, present, and future. The figures and diction should be appropriate to the character of the subject (9).

The tenth *progymnasma* is vivid description (*ekphrasis*), which is a detailed account involving persons, actions, times, places, seasons, etc. Ecphrasis of an action should include what happened before, during, and after. Topics of vivid description of places, seasons, and persons should include the beautiful, useful, and their opposites. Clarity (*saphêneia*) and distinctness (*enargeia*) are important, and the diction should correspond to the subject. According to H., it does not seem absolutely necessary to have a separate exercise for ecphrasis, since its features are covered in other *progymnasmata* (10).

Then to thesis, which H. defines as debate about a matter without attendant circumstance. It differs from hypothesis in that the former does not refer to particular persons or situations, while the latter does. Some are political, or practical, and involve common questions, and others are unpolitical, or theoretical, and involve specialized, more arcane questions. The thesis differs from the commonplace in that the former involves something in doubt, while the latter involves something agreed upon. Theses may be simple, in reference to something, or double. They are divided by the final (*telika*) headings: the just, expedient, possible, and appropriate, or their opposites. The thesis should conclude with exhortation and discussion of the typical habits (*ethê*) of mankind (11).

The final *progymnasma* is introduction of a law (*nomou eisphora*). H. says that in deliberation (*pragmatikê*) there is attendant circumstance, while in an exercise (*gymnasma*), there is not. The divisions are the evident, just, lawful, expedient, possible, and appropriate (12).

ON STASEIS proposes to divide political questions (*politika zêtêmata*) into headings. A political question is a reasoned debate concerning persons or actions, judged in terms of the justice, honor, expediency, etc. of prevailing laws or customs (1.1–3). Actions open to judgment are first, those for which a person is accused of committing a crime; second, those for which a person is accused on account of another's actions; third, a mixture of the two. Actions that are equal are not open to judgment (1.4–5).

Questions are capable of being contested (*systatic*) or not (*asystatic*). The latter are one-sided (*monomerês*), in which there are strong arguments, but only on one side; completely equal (*isazon*); reversible (*antistrephon*); unanswerable (*aporon*), in which there is no solution or finality; implausible (*apithanon*); impossible (*adynaton*); dishonorable (*adoxon*); and without explanatory circumstances (*aperistaton*). There are other questions that are close to being *asystatic* but declaimed nonetheless. These are considerably one-sided (*heterorrepes*), ill-conceived (*kakoplaston*), and prejudged (*proeilêmmenon*, 1.5–8).

After a general discussion of the division of a speech (1.8–10) H. discusses contested questions. First is the stasis of conjecture (*stochasmos*), which occurs if the question is doubtful (*asaphes*) rather than obvious (*phaneron*). If the question is obvious, then it is either perfect (*teleion*) or imperfect (*ateles*). If imperfect, the stasis is definitive (*horikê*), which comprises an investigation into the name for an act. If the question is both obvious and perfect, there is an investigation into the quality (*poiotês*) of the act, which involves some deed or statement in writing (*rhêton*). If about a statement, the stasis is legal (*nomikê*); if about an act, the stasis is rational (*logikê*, 2.10–12). If rational, it involves something in the future or in the past. If the future, the stasis is deliberative (*pragmatikê*), if the past, forensic (*dikaiologia*). This, too, is a stasis of quality. For the forensic stasis H. discusses possible pleas and counterpleas (2.12–13).

He then returns to legal stases, where there are questions about the wording and intent (*rhêton kai dianoia*) of laws, wills, decrees, etc. An inference (*syllogismos*) from comparing an act not specifically mentioned in the law to one that is may also be involved (2.13–14). A conflict of laws (*antinomia*) may occur, as well as ambiguity (*amphibolia*) about the precise sense (2.15–16). Then to the stasis of objection (*metalêpsis*), which involves the validity of the suit itself. Here there is no question of conjecture, or definition, or quality, but only whether it is necessary to inquire into any of these (2.16–17).

Next H. gives a fuller treatment of the main stasis of conjecture. When it involves both persons and actions, conjecture is divided into objection to the indictment (*paragraphikon*), demand for evidence (*elengchôn apaitêsis*), will (*boulêsis*), ability (*dynamis*), "from beginning to end" (*ta ap' archês achri telous*), plea of justification (*antilêpsis*), counterplea (*metalêpsis*), alternative motive (*metathesis aitias*), plausible defense (*pithanê apologia*), and common quality (*koinê poiotês*, 3.17–18). All these aspects of conjecture are discussed in minute detail (3.18–27).

H. says that thus far he has discussed the perfect and single stasis of fact. An imperfect single stasis can be based on actions alone, when the person is not in dispute; it is not based on persons alone. Perfect dual stasis occurs when two acts and two persons are on trial, and imperfect dual stasis is based on action when only actions are on trial but based on persons when only persons are on trial (3.28–30). There are three further types of the dual stasis of fact: 1) concomitant (*empiptôn*), when in the use of alternative motive some other question has to be divided; 2) previous (*prokataskeuazomenos*), when it is necessary to examine another question as to fact; and 3) cumulative (*synkataskeuazomenos*), when the questions at issue are supported by the same signs. H. adds the stasis from intention (*gnômê*), when the act and person are known and only the intention is in question (3.30–32).

H. divides the major stasis of definition (*horos*) into presentation of the case (*probolê*), which comprises the things from beginning to end; definition, which distinguishes the act and arises from things passed over in from beginning to end; counterdefinition (*anthorismos*), which arises from the result achieved; inference (*syllogismos*), which draws together the definition and counterdefinition; intention of the lawmaker (*gnômê tou nomothetou*), which each party examines to its own benefit; magnitude (*pêlikotês*), which shows that what has happened is serious; comparison (*pros ti*), which shows that it is greater to do something this way than another way; and sometimes one of the stases of counterproposition (*antithesis*). If that happens, counterplea or objection (*metalêpsis*) and plea of justification will follow immediately, then common quality—which is taken up from the attributes of the person, depending on whether they are definite, indefinite but able to be guessed at, or completely indefinite—and intention (4.32–34).

The dual definitive stasis has numerous types (4.35–38). The plea of justification is divided into presentation of the case, which occurs as in definitive stasis; elements of right (*moria dikaiou*), which involves whether someone can be charged for acts not outlawed; person; definition; then the headings that follow definition up to comparison—those that H. discussed in the previous section on definitive stasis; plea of justification itself; counterplea; counterproposition; another counterplea; thesis (*thesis*), quality in common; and intention (5.38–40). The elements of the plea of justification are reviewed (5.40–44) and then the stasis of counterproposition (*antithetikê*, 6.44–46). H. says that efforts to distinguish between different types of counterproposition are not very useful, nor are the efforts precisely to distinguish plea for pardon from transferral of blame (6.46–48).

Then to the stasis of deliberation (*pragmatikê*), under these divisions: the lawful (*nomimon*), just (*dikaion*), expedient (*sympheron*), possible (*dynaton*), honorable (*endoxon*), and projected outcome (*ekbêsomenon*). The deliberation can be written, where the question arises from the wording, or unwritten, where behavior (*ethos*) must be examined as the lawful heading. In the written type, the lawful heading is divided according to the legal stases (7.48–51).

The stasis of objection (*metalêpsis*) can also be written or unwritten. The written is a perfect objection (*teleia paragraphê*) to the admissibility of the suit, and the first inquiry involves one of the legal stases, or sometimes one of the definitive stases. Then there is further inquiry by some other of the rational stases. The unwritten is divided into presentation of the case; objection to the admissibility of the suit on the basis of the wording; counterargument (*metalêpsis*); inference; definition; counter proposition; a secondcounter argument; plea of justification; thesis; common quality; and intention (8.52–54).

The stasis of wording and intent is divided into presentation of the case based on the wording; intent (*dianoia*) of both the lawmaker and the person on trial; prohibition against additional information (*to mê prosdiôristhai*); the contrary intent (*palin dianoia*) of the lawmaker; inference; definition; counter proposition; counterargument; comparison; forced definition; thesis; second counterargument; plea of justification; common quality; and intention (9.54–56).

The stasis of conflict of laws (*antinomia*) is divided into presentation of the case according to the wording; intent; a second presentation of the case based on the letter; a second intent. Some of the headings that follow—prohibition against a second definition, the other intent of the lawmaker, inference, and the definition opposed to inference—are omitted because they are equally balanced for both sides. But a heading peculiar to conflict of laws asks which of the written laws includes, and which is included; that is, which of the two maintains the validity of both laws (10.56–60).

Then to the stasis of inference, which is divided into presentation of the case based on the act; the wording of the law; inference; definition; intention of the lawmaker; magnitude; forced definition; comparison; and sometimes counter proposition—if so, counterargument, plea of justification, common quality, and intention will follow. This stasis generally corresponds to the division of stasis of definition (11.60–61). Stases of inference are based on the equal (*apo tou isou*); the greater (*apo tou meizonos*); the opposite (*apo tou enantiou*); or the lesser (*apo tou elattonos*), according to that which results from the lesser (11.61–62).

Finally, H. discusses the stasis of ambiguity (*amphibolia*), which is divided into presentation of the case based on the wording; a second presentation of the case based on the letter, in reference to ambiguity; intent of the lawmaker; the law including and the law included; counter proposition; counterargument; thesis; common quality; and intention. The stasis of ambiguity is only useful if the ambiguity concerns not all, but part, of the question. Ambiguity is found in all questions involving oracles (12.62–64). The work ends abruptly here.

ON INVENTION examines selected parts of the oration. The explanations and definitions are often unclear, but are almost always accompanied by examples, usually from Demosthenes.

Book 1 begins with a discussion of introductions (*prooimia*). The first section is on introductions from impression (*hypolêpsis*), which involve persons and actions (1.1). Next are introductions from amplification through subdivision (*hypodiairesis*). H. calls these clever and sharp, and identifies three types: involving two crimes of equal severity; when other prejudices (*hypolêpseis*) against a person can be adduced; and when punishment is rendered not only for the present crime but also for possible crimes in the future (1.2). Then introductions from abundance (*periousia*), when the accused could be punished for another crime as well as the one with which he is charged (1.3). The introduction from advantage (*kairos*) is powerful. Here the speaker shows that the claim (*axiôsis*) brought forth has already been granted (1.4). Book 1 closes with a discussion of the parts of the introduction, which consist of a proposition (*protasis*); reasoning (*kataskeuê*); explanation (*apodosis*), which is the claim; and position (*basis*), which ties together the *protasis* and *apodosis* (1.5).

In Book 2 H. discusses narration (*diêgêsis*). He begins with the introductory statement of a case (*prokatastasis* or *prodiêgêsis*). In general, the speaker in every introductory statement should inquire into and cite older events or circumstances as well as those useful for the claim or judgment (*krisis*) at hand (2.1). These introductions should be framed in terms of their application to various situations, involving a change of cities (*metoikoi*, 2.2); the introduction of new laws (*nomôn eisphora*) with attendant circumstance (*peristasis*), and rebuttals (*lysai*) of existing laws with attendant circumstance (2.3); proposals for war or the cessation of war, and how to go from the introductory statement to the narration proper (2.4); impiety (*asebeia*)—when accusing, inquire into past events (2.5); and crimes against the state (*demosia adikêmata*, 2.6).

H. concludes Book 2 with a discussion of the development of narration, which allows for much more expansiveness than the introduction, and where repetition and embellishment are desirable. Style (*tropos*) embellishes the narrative. There are three types: simple (*haplous*), ornate (*engkataskeuos*), and highly wrought (*endiaskeuos*). When the evidence is overwhelmingly favorable, use the simple narration. If the narration is concise and political (*politikê*), use the ornate type, and if concise and rather brilliant (*phaidrotera*), the highly wrought type. Most narrations combine all three styles. The climax (*akmê*) of the narration is tripartite, consisting of the deed, the claim, and the reason for the claim (2.7).

Book 3 is addressed to a certain Julius Marcus. H. says that he will discuss the introduction of the headings (*kephalaia*) of stasis theory, their types, and their sources. He will also discuss solutions to problems (*lysai*), epicheiremes, and the working out (*ergasiai*) of epicheiremes and enthymemes (3.1). But before doing so H. analyzes the preface to the proof (*prokataskeuê*), which sets forth the headings and questions in a case (3.2). The headings are then examined in more detail. [At this point, as elsewhere in the work, editors including Spengel and Rabe have rearranged the chapters in the manuscripts to arrive at a more logical order. Their arrangement is followed here.] A heading, depending on whether the speaker is accusing or defending, needs confirmation (*kataskeuê*) or rebuttal (*lysis*), and epicheiremes perform either task. H. says that he will succeed where many have failed: he will clearly explain the invention of an epicheireme, which confirms the heading or the solution (*lysis*), and the invention of a working out (*ergasia*), which confirms the epicheireme, and the invention of the enthymeme, which confirms the working out.

If the speaker introduces the heading, all that is required is a simple statement (*thesis*) and a confirmation of this with epicheiremes and a premise (*protasis*). But if the opponent first establishes the heading and the speaker then introduces it, he must arrange the heading more fully with 1) the opponent's premise, 2) the opponent's reason (*hypophora*), 3) the speaker's response to the premise (*antiprotasis*), 4) the supporting reason (*anthypophora* or *lysis*), which needs epicheiremes for proof. H. goes on to note that sometimes these parts are omitted without appreciable damage to the thought (3.4).

There are two types of solution to a problem (*lysis*): direct (*enstasis*) and indirect refutation (*antiparastasis*). These should be confirmed with epicheiremes (3.6). A third type of solution to a problem is forceful (*biaion*), which involves turning the words of the opponent to one's advantage (3.3).

Next H. discusses epicheiremes and their sources. Epicheiremes are found in circumstances (*peristasis*), words, actions, trials (*dikai*), cases (*hypotheseis*), and life. There are epicheiremes from place, time, manner, person, cause, and act. Some, H. says, add a seventh type, material (*hylê*). He then reviews examples of the use of epicheiremes in confirming or rebutting various headings. In the ensuing examples H. mentions another type of epicheireme, from the critical time (*kairos*, 3.5).

A section on the working out (*ergasia*) of epicheiremes follows: from comparison (*parabolê*), example (*paradeigma*), the lesser, the greater, the equal, and the opposite. Just as more than one epicheireme may be used to confirm or rebut a heading, so there are multiple ways of working out an epicheireme (3.7).

Enthymemes confirm the working out and add sharpness (*drimytês*). Enthymemes have the same six sources as epicheiremes, and multiple enthymemes can be used, but the sharpness can become too much if multiple supporting reasons, epicheiremes, workings out, and enthymemes are employed (3.8). H. also briefly discusses the enthymeme that reinforces another enthymeme (*epenthymêma*, 3.9).

Then to the technique, "from beginning to end" (*ap' archês achri telous*), which has its own type of epicheireme called *hypodiairesis* (amplification through subdivision). This technique may also be embellished by figures (*schêmata*). The subdivision may involve the act itself, from the greater or lesser, or be derived from similarity (3.10). Another device that is often used after "from beginning to end" is the hypothetical (*to plaston*) epicheireme, though H. takes issue with the name, saying that every subdivision is hypothetical (3.11). H. goes on to say that it is difficult to rebut "from beginning to end." A defendant should use the antithetical forms of stasis, but other forms may also help (3.12).

The arrangement of epicheiremes is twofold. One is to put epicheiremes affording absolute proof (*apodeiktika*) first, then move to the more panegyrical. This is more pleasing than arranging them in the opposite order. The second, which, according to H., is more clever, is to place epicheiremes calling forth the next heading (*proklêtika*) at the end, so that the speech becomes a single, coherent body (3.13).

H. also discusses methods for handling stases of definition (*horos*) and inference (*syllogismos*, 3.14), and he concludes Book 3 with a section on elaboration (*diaskeuê*), defined as the vivid description (*diatypôsis*) of a case. This is derived from the past, present, and future. Elaboration lends the case a poetical quality. Periodic constructions should be avoided. H. goes on to discuss techniques of vivid description, including the use of subdivision (*hypomerismos*) and topoi (*chôria*).

Book 4 begins with a general discussion of forms of style, or figures of speech (*schêmata logou*). If the epicheiremes and *ergasiai* are political (*politika*) and afford absolute proof (*apodeiktika*), the style of the speech should be compact, and should include antithesis and periodic sentences. If the epicheiremes and and workings out (*ergasiai*) are panegyrical, the sentences should be stretched out, delivered vigorously but still in one breath (*pneumatikôs*) (4.1). Antithesis has the effect of "doubling" the thought, and can be stretched out into a long sentence (*pneuma*) by the addition of *kôla*. It can also be formed rhythmically and become a period. Antithesis is so worthy of admiration that it can embellish every aspect of the thought of a speech (4.2).

A fuller discussion follows of the period, which H. defines as resolution and completion of a whole epicheireme, often by enthymemes. He also discusses the relationship between the *protasis* and *apodosis* in the period, and says that periods may have *kôla* of equal or unequal length. They may be constructed from one, two, three, or four *kôla;* the *kôlon* is defined as a completed thought (*apêrtismenê dianoia*). The period also lends itself to the use of chiasmus (4.3).

H. now examines the *pneuma* in detail; it is defined as a complex sentence measured in *kôla* and *kommata* that is complete in thought and can be delivered in one breath. The *komma* has up to six syllables, the *kôlon* is from seven syllables up to the length of a line of hexameter, and a sentence longer than that is described as stretched out (*schoinotenes*) and is especially useful in proemia. The *pneuma* takes two forms: the expression of one thought by many *kôla* or the expression of several things, one per *kôlon*. *Pneumata* may be declarative (*apophantika*), questioning (*kat' erôtêsin*), refutative (*elengtika*), declarative (*deiktika*), repudiative (*arnêtika*), or dissuasive (*apagoreutika*). H. makes it clear that the *pneuma* has many variations and discusses in particular climax (*akmê*), which is either a change of figures within a *pneuma* or the exposition of thoughts in successive *pneumata* (4.4).

A brief discussion is added of tension (*tasis*), which is a *pneuma* too long to be delivered in one breath (4.5). Then to a series of figures: *dilêmmaton* (4.6); *parêchêsis,* the use of several words or phrases with similar sound but different meaning (4.7); *kyklos* (circle), beginning and ending a period with the same noun or verb (4.8); *epiphônêma,* additional statement (4.9); *tropos* (turn), any word used out of its normal context (4.10); *semnos logos,* solemn speech (4.11), and *kakozêlon,* affected style (4.12). H. then considers figured problems (*eschêmatismena problêmata*), of which there are three types: contrary (*enantion*); indirect (*plagion*); and emphatic (*kata emphasin*), H.'s own invention (4.13).

Book 4 concludes with the comparative problem (*synkritikon problêma*), which is explained only by example, as in "for this reason, it is not reasonable that I wanted to do this, but for the same reason, it is reasonable that you wanted to do it" (4.14).

Book 1 of the lengthy treatise *ON TYPES OF STYLE* begins by saying that it is essential for the orator to understand the types (*ideai*) of style, for in this way even the mediocre speaker can be successful. The treatise, H. says, will focus on style as practiced by

Demosthenes (with ample illustrations from his speeches), for he more than any other mastered the various styles of political oratory (189–93). There are seven principal types of Demosthenic style: clarity (*saphêneia*), grandeur (*megethos*), beauty (*kallos*), rapidity (*gorgotês*), character (*êthos*), sincerity (*alêtheia*), and forcefulness (*deinotês*). Elements common to all types of style include thought (*ennoia*), approach (*methodos*) to the thought, and diction (*lexis*) appropriate to these. Diction can be divided into figures (*schêmata*), clauses (*kôla*), word order (*synthesis*), cadence (*anapausis*), and rhythm (*rhythmos*), which is produced by word order and cadence (193–95). The introduction closes with elaboration on these general elements of the types of style (195–201).

Clarity, the first principal type, is produced from distinctness (*eukrineia*) and purity (*katharotês*). Purity is produced by all the elements discussed above (thought, approach, etc., 202). The thoughts contributing to purity are common, not at all obscure. The proper approach is narration of bare facts without amplification (202–04)). The proper diction is common, neither obscure nor harsh, and the proper figure is straightforward with the noun in the nominative case, for use of the oblique cases necessarily involves amplification. The clauses should be short, one per sentence. As for word order, cadence, and rhythm, the sentences should be metrical to some extent. It is better to use iambs and trochees than dactyls and anapests, and avoidance of hiatus should be only a small concern (205–10). Distinctness primarily concerns the approach of the speech; it involves the arrangement of the speech—what the speaker will say first, second, etc. Thoughts providing background also produce distinctness, as do thoughts giving the speech a clear outline and arrangement. The necessary diction is that used for purity (210–17).

Grandeur, the second main type, includes bulk (*ongkos*) and dignity (*axiôma*) and is necessary to prevent clarity from degenerating into the mundane and common. It has six subtypes or species: solemnity (*semnotês*), harshness (*trachytês*), vehemence (*sphodrotês*), brilliance (*lamprotês*), florescence (*akmê*), and abundance (*peribolê*, 217–18). Solemn thoughts are about the gods, about matters actually divine (natural phenomena, etc.), about matters divine but involving men (immortality of the soul, justice, etc.), and about human affairs that are great and glorious. Solemnity is produced by generality, not particularity, and it includes declaration without hesitation, allegorical speech, and hinting at solemn thoughts (219–24). H. recommends broad sounds that open the mouth wide, including long vowels; restrained use of metaphor (very bold metaphors are vulgar); nouns and pronouns, or verbs acting as nouns; and the avoidance of verbs. The proper figures are those that contribute to purity, producing straightforward statements. Hesitation is damaging to solemnity, as are direct address (*apostrophê*) and parenthesis (*hypostrophê*), which break up the flow of the expression (224–29). The clauses proper to solemnity are the same as those contributing to purity, that is, short ones. As for word order, cadence, and rhythm, H. recommends the dactyl, anapest, paeon, iamb, spondee, and epitrite, but not the trochee or ionic measures. Each sentence must end on a foot proper to solemnity (229–32).

H. then proceeds to harshness, the second species of grandeur, whose opposite is sweetness. The thoughts that contribute to harshness involve open censure of a greater person by a lesser person. H. remarks that examples of pure harshness are extremely rare in Demosthenes. The only approach that creates harshness is to censure boldly and openly. The proper diction is metaphorical and severe (232–36). The figures most proper to harshness are those involving commands and questions; the clauses should be brief—phrases (*kommata*), actually, rather than clauses. Word order, cadence, and rhythm should create an unmetrical, disjointed, unpleasant effect (236–39).

Next is vehemence, whose thoughts, like those of harshness, involve censure and refutation. But vehemence is directed against lesser persons, and thus the censure is almost abusive. H. says that superiors can be attacked with harshness, but not with vehemence, because the latter is stronger than the former. Vehemence and harshness have essentially the same approach and similar diction (239–41). The figures proper to vehemence include direct address, question (*erôtêsis*), and demonstrative (*deiktikon*) expressions. The proper clauses, or rather phrases, are perhaps even shorter than those proper to harshness, while the word order, cadence, and rhythm should be the same as those of harshness (241–43).

Then to brilliance, the fourth species of grandeur. It is found in distinguished acts and is marked by direct, confident speech, expressing honorable thoughts honorably (243–47). The diction that creates brilliance is the same as that which produces solemnity; the proper figures are *anairesis* (denial), *apostasis* (departure), and asyndeton. Brilliance may also be created by introducing sentences with subordinate constructions that expand the thought. Clauses contributing to brilliance should be long; word order, cadence, and rhythm should be the same as those proper to solemnity (247–49).

Florescence, the fifth species, generally arises from the subtypes already examined. The thoughts, approaches, and diction characteristic of it are the same as those proper to harshness and vehemence. The figures that create florescence are those proper to brilliance and vehemence, with the addition of parenthesis (*epembolê*). The clauses, word order, cadence, and rhythm are the same as those that create brilliance (249–52). H. goes on to discuss the difference between florescence and the other subtypes and makes the point that florescence always has brilliance, but brilliance does not have florescence. The mixture of harshness, vehemence, and brilliance, which can each exist on its own, creates florescence (252–58).

Last of the subtypes contributing to grandeur is abundance, i.e., amplification. Thoughts involving abundance occur when something extraneous is added to the speech. These additions also pertain to distinctness, which may seem paradoxical since abundance and distinctness seem to be opposites. But many subtypes can coexist, and, in fact, mixing them is one of the most difficult parts of oratory. Abundance does not have a characteristic diction, except perhaps the use of parallel constructions. Delay (*epimonê*), or the use of synonyms, should be added to the approaches proper to abundance (264–67). The figures of abundance are in general those that lead to second and even third thoughts, such as enumeration (*aparithmêsis*); repetition (*epanalêpsis*); listing things in order of importance (*kata protimêsin*); the use of hypothetical argument, especially with division (*merismos*); and the use of subordinate clauses (*plagiasmos*). Demosthenes, in his desire to create grandeur, used abundance everywhere (268–71). H. then mentions again the use of subordination and particularly reexamines division (271–74). Aside from those figures that lead to second or third thoughts, figures of negation and affirmation, copulative constructions of negation ("not only this but also that"), and dense constructions (*kata systrophên*) also produce abundance. Finally, all types of clause, word order, cadence, and rhythm produce abundance (274–77).

H. next discusses beauty, the third principal type of style, along with its counterpart elegance (*epimeleia*). Beauty lends harmony and symmetry to a speech, giving it a good, consistent quality throughout, which some call the complexion (*chrôma*) of the speech (277–80). No thoughts per se, or approaches, are characteristic of beauty. The diction proper to beauty is the same as that which creates purity. Generally, short words contribute to beauty. The figures that create beauty are those providing embellishment, such as balanced clauses (*parisôsis*), although H. cautions that this sort of balance can make the speech less persuasive (280–84). Others are repetition at the beginning of the clause (*epanaphora*) and at the end (*antistrophê*). Things florescent are usually brilliant and beautiful, but things can be beautiful without being florescent and brilliant. Another figure creating beauty is to begin a clause with the word that ended the preceding clause (*epanastrophê*, 284–86). Then there is climax, which H. defines as repeated anastrophe, balanced clauses with paired thoughts, transposition (*hyperbaton*), transposition with parenthesis, novel turns of phrase (*kainoprepê schêmata*), double negative, and the use of many cases (*polyptôton*). All these contribute to beauty (286–90). Word order is also important; it must be somewhat metrical, with words of varying syllables and quantities and with no hiatus. Stately (*bebêkuiai*) cadences should be avoided in trying to create beauty, but suspended and disconnected cadences and rhythms are desirable (290–94).

H. begins Book 2 with rapidity, the fourth of the seven principal types of the Demosthenic style. There is really no thought proper to rapidity, and only one approach, to use rapid and short answers and objections. H. discusses those figures that can help to counteract flatness (*hyptiotês*), the opposite of rapidity. These include parenthesis (*hypostrophê*), sometimes called interweaving (*kataplokê*), and overrunning (*to epitrechon schêma*) (295–98). Then to figures that are concise and rapid, including asyndeton, variation (*exallagê*), short divisions with second clauses, repetition (*epanaphora*) and repetition at the end of clauses (*antistrophê*) with short phrases, and frequent, brief interweaving (*symplokê*, 298–302). Any sort of diction can contribute to rapidity, but short words and clauses are best. The proper word order avoids hiatus; the rhythm should be based on the trochee, and the proper cadence ends with a trochee and is not stately (302–03).

Next is character (*êthos*), the fifth basic type of style. The principal stylistic contributors to character are simplicity (*apheleia*) and modesty (*epieikeia*), as well as a truthful and unaffected (*endiatheton*) manner and, to a lesser extent, indignation (*barytês*, 303–04). H. examines simplicity first; the thoughts proper to it are the same as those that create purity, that is, simple and common thoughts, as well as those that tend toward the trivial. Epicheiremes made from comparisons with animals and plants also produce simplicity, as do some but not all oaths (305–09). The approaches characteristic of simplicity are the same as those that create purity, and the same is generally true of the diction, except that certain words especially lend themselves to simplicity. The figures and clauses are, again, the same as those of purity, but simplicity requires a consistent, stately rhythm and cadence (309–13).

H. turns now to sweetness, which he considers a factor contributing to simplicity. Sweet thoughts involve myth, or things akin to myth, or things that share something with myth but are more believable (these in order of decreasing importance). In addition, descriptions of sensually pleasing and even shameful things produce sweetness, as do erotic thoughts and praise of ourselves or those related to us (313–16). Finally, H. dwells at length on how the endowment of inanimate objects or animals with human qualities is characteristic of sweetness (317–19). The approaches proper to sweetness are the same as those that create purity and simplicity, and the proper diction is that of simplicity, that is, pure and poetical. The use of epithets and subtlety (this will be discussed later) also creates sweetness. The proper figures are those that create simplicity, purity, and beauty, and the proper word order is that which creates beauty and is almost metrical. The cadences and rhythm should be solemn and stately (319–22). Also contributing to sweetness, and hence to simplicity and thus character, are sharpness (*drimytês*) and pointedness (*oxytês*). These involve the use of striking speech and the use of words in unusual ways (323–25), as well as three kinds of sharpness that, according to H., are not found in Demosthenes: the use of words that are different in meaning but sound similar; the use of a word first in the usual sense and then in an unusual sense (*paronomasia*); and the use of a mild metaphor followed by a strong one, which softens the force of the latter metaphor (325–28).

Modesty is the other major contributor to character. It is produced when the speaker deliberately shows himself to be less than he is, or equal to the average person, and also when he asserts that he comes to court only under compulsion (328–31). Modesty is created by various forms of omission (*paraleipsis*) and speaking simply. H. says that the diction, figures, word order, cadences, and rhythms that produce modesty are the same as those that create purity and simplicity (331–36).

H. now turns to the sixth principal type of style, sincerity. Simple thoughts are typical of this style, those that are unaffected (*endiathetai*) and clear. The proper approaches are ones involving clarity and ease of comprehension, but H. stresses that they are also difficult to describe. Use of unaffected expression, particularly to indicate wonder, is one approach, as is to answer questions rapidly (336–41). Other good approaches are to say something without introduction and connectives, to interrupt the natural flow of the sentence in indicating emotion, to use abusive language without indicating it beforehand, and to say something that seems to come to mind on the spot (341–44). The diction should be rough and violent, and coined words should be used. If pity is the object, however, purity and simplicity and sweetness must be employed. The figures typical of sincerity are the same as those that produce vehemence, such as direct address, question, and demonstrative expressions (344–46). Others include perplexity (*diaporêsis*), stopping a sentence (*aposiôpêsis*), judgments (*epikriseis*), correction of a previous statement (*epidiorthôsis*), and incomplete division (*apolytos merismos*), in which the second half of a division is suppressed in order to emphasize the obviousness of the first part. The proper clauses, word order, cadence, and rhythm are similar to those that produce harshness; but when pity is the object, those typical of simplicity should be used (346–49).

A subtype of sincerity is indignation (barytês). No thoughts by themselves create indignation; irony, which is the approach proper to indignation, creates indignation, since the speaker says the opposite of what he means. Irony is strongest when used in reference to the speaker himself or the jurors, far less so when used in reference to the opponent (349–51). Perplexity, as well as hesitation (endoiasis) combined with judgment (epikrisis), also involve indignation. No particular diction nor any of the other stylistic elements are characteristic of indignation (2.8.351-53).

H. now comes to the last of the principal types of style, force. He considers it simply to be the proper use of the other types and subtypes of style and of everything else that a speech comprises. H. argues that his use of the word *forceful* (deinos) is not necessarily incompatible with its common meaning of "terrible" or "fearful" (354–57). There are three variations of forceful speech. One is forceful and appears to be so; another is forceful and does not seem so; and the third seems to be forceful but is not. The first is created by the thought and other stylistic elements, the second by the approach, and the third by the diction. The thoughts characteristic of the first kind of forceful speech are paradoxical, profound, cunningly contrived, etc., as are the approaches. But the approaches and diction that are proper to grandeur also contribute to this kind of force (358–60). The proper figures, clauses, word order, cadences, and rhythm are the same as those that create solemnity, florescence, brilliance, and abundance. A particularly good figure for this purpose is the use of dense constructions (kata systrophên). The second kind of forceful speech, as H. has already said, is created by the approach. In this type, the speech is natural and simple, and the diction, figures, clauses, etc. should be relaxed (361–62). The third kind of forceful speech, again as H. has already mentioned, is created primarily by the diction, which is rough, vehement, and even solemn and used to express superficial and common thoughts. H. concludes by referring to his own more comprehensive treatment of this subject in a separate treatise, *ON THE METHOD OF FORCE*.

The next topic of the present treatise is political oratory and the best of the famous orators (362–65). Political oratory (politikos logos) is created by combining all the types of style. The best practitioner of political oratory is Demosthenes. In political oratory clarity, character, and sincerity are most important, followed by rapidity, then abundance, purity, and distinctness. Next in importance would be harshness and vehemence, then florescence, solemnity, and brilliance. Grandeur is also necessary to an extent, as is force, especially the kind that is but does not seem forceful, less so the kind that is and seems forceful, and not at all the kind that is not but seems to be. H. says that political oratory always requires beauty, which helps to prevent triviality (*euteleia*) and stiffness (*sklêrotês*, 366–69).

H. posits three kinds of political oratory: deliberative (*symbouleutikos*), judicial (*dikanikos*), and panegyric (*panêgyrikos*). The best deliberative speeches have grandeur, force, and character. The true judicial speech is the opposite of a deliberative speech; it should possess character, modesty, and simplicity, as well as grandeur produced primarily by abundance (370–71). In discussing panegyric, H. says he mostly means panegyric apart from political affairs, which perhaps should not be considered a part of political oratory at all. Plato is the best practitioner of this nonpolitical panegyric. It is created by all the subtypes making up grandeur, except roughness and vehemence, with an equal amount of simplicity usually thrown in. Sweetness and elegance are desirable, as is the kind of force created by the approach, though never the kind created by diction. Rapidity is to be avoided in this kind of panegyric. As for political panegyric, it requires almost the same elements as deliberative speech, though with more brilliance and solemnity (372–74).

Poetry is the most panegyric of all the branches of literature. All poetry is panegyric, and Homer is the best poet, for he is the master of every style (374–76). Panegyric oratory in poetry has all the features of panegyric oratory in prose, with the overt addition of poetic elements. These elements are far more subdued in panegyric in prose, and rare in deliberative and judicial oratory. The thoughts characteristic of poetry involve myth, marvels, metamorphoses, and personification, and the proper approaches include those that produce panegyric oratory, with the addition of the use of divine invocation (376–78). H. says that the diction proper to poetry is obvious, and that no figures are particularly typical of poetry; it uses the same ones as panegyric oratory. The meter and various aims of the author determine the proper clauses, word order, rhythms, and cadences (378–80).

H. says that he will discuss second- and third-rate orators and will do so first in the context of what he calls purely political oratory, which is to be distinguished from the Demosthenic kind (380). Purely political oratory is created by the same types of style that produce clarity and modesty and simplicity of character, as well as sincerity, for these lend a speech persuasiveness. H. then discusses individual orators (the "canon" of Attic orators, with Critias added in place of Demosthenes) in terms of the types and subtypes of style: Lysias, moderately elegant and rapid; Isaeus, elegant, highly rapid; Hyperides, elegant, with excessive grandeur; Isocrates, pure, distinct, highly elegant and beautiful, no rapidity at all; Dinarchus, clear and sincere but also harsh and vehement; Aeschines, overwrought but grand and beautiful; two Antiphons, one sincere, grand, and elegant, the other solemn, grand, and abundant; Critias, solemn and sincere; Lycurgus, rough, vehement, and unelegant; and Andocides, abundant and indistinct (380–90).

H. proceeds to purely panegyric oratory (*haplos panegyrikos*), which is to be distinguished from the kind that Plato practiced. Purely panegyric oratory should have grandeur, clarity, and embellishment, which can be found in both poetry and prose, and especially in history. After critiques of Xenophon, Aeschines, Nicostratus, Herodotus, Thucydides, and Hecataeus (390–96), H. concludes the treatise by saying that discussion of the poets that rank below Homer is too large a topic for the scope of this work (396–401).

ON THE METHOD OF FORCE has short discussions of various aspects of style and content, which are illustrated with passages from Demosthenes, Homer, Plato, Thucydides, and other writers. The first subject is the relationship between the parts of a speech and the thought (1). Next, three methods of invention of prose style are proposed: foreign (*ethnikê*), legal (*nomikê*) and technical (*technikê*, 2). There are two mistakes of style, impropriety (*akyria*) and corruption (*paraphthora*, 3). Use monotony (*tautotês*) of speech, or a single word, when that word is most clear, but use diversity (*poikilia*) of speech, or more than one word, when those words are equally good choices and still clear (4). Superfluity (*perittotês*) has two forms: according to style (*kata lexin*), arising through dwelling on the point (*diatribê*) and use of different words with similar meanings (*plethos*), and according to thought (*kata gnômên*), arising through pointlessly corroborating enthymemes and the use of common words to clarify unusual words (5).

There are two remedies for willful (*authadê*) and reckless (*tolmera*) thoughts: a brief qualification (*prosthêkê*) or admission of recklessness (6). Omission (*paraleipsis*) and becoming silent (*aposiôpêsis*) increase the suspicion of the audience. Omission is used when the matters at hand are trivial (*mikra*), well--known (*gnôrima*), or disturbing (*epachthê*, 7). Some criticize circumlocution (*periplokê*), but it is appropriate for three occasions: when the subject matter is shameful (*aischra*), distressing (*lypêra*) to the audience, or disturbing (*epachthê*) to the speaker (8). Repetition (*epanalêpsis*) occurs in three ways: for instruction in something, for commendation or censure of a person, and for the establishment of character (*êthous bebaiôsis*, 9). Question (*peusis*) is an irrefutable (*anantirrhêton*) figure. It involves either things agreed upon by nature or proven beforehand by logic. Both types are equally forceful (10). Lack of connectives (*asyndeton*) is ethical (*ethikon*), and the use of connectives is pragmatic (*pragmatikon*, 11). Introduction (*proekthesis* or *hyposchesis*) is a prefatory statement with headings, while summary (*anakephalaiôsis* or *epanodos*) is a recapitulation of the speech (12).

The so-called "equal figures" (*isa schêmata*) pertain to debate (*agônistika*), display (*epideiktika*), and sophistry (*sophistika*, 13). They are *hyperbaton* (transposition), placing the reason for what is said in the middle of the statement (14); antithesis, opposing one idea to another (15); and *parison* (almost equal), the same word, with the addition of one or two syllables, indicating a different idea (16). When should the orator pretend to speak extemporaneously? In deliberative (*symbouleutikê*) oratory he should should admit to careful thought beforehand, but in forensic (*dikanikê*) the speaker should pretend to speak extemporaneously, even if he has prepared beforehand, so that the judges will not suspect trickery by a clever orator. In encomiastic oratory, either method may be used (17). Amplification (*auxêsis*) should be used in lawsuits (*dikai*) and proofs (*apodeixeis*) when the case is overlooked or the person on trial is honorable (18). The orator should speak a falsehood acknowledged by the audience if it benefits the audience (19). Swear oaths not on deeds, but on character (*êthos*, 20). Private advocates (*synêgoroi*) should be assigned to women, the aged, children, slaves, and those charged on specious grounds (*euprepeia*, 21). Conveying the opposite of what one wants to have happen without appearing to do so is accomplished by saying things that are easy to refute, contrary, and reversed (22). There are further comments on the prosecutor's anticipation of the defense's arguments (23), how to make assertions without appearing to do so (24), and three ways for the speaker to praise himself without being offensive (25).

Random thoughts follow on two forensic tricks used by Demosthenes (26); the types of second or responding speeches (*deuterologiai*, 27); two techniques for narration (*diêgêsis*, 28); the writers of old appropriating common ideas by admitting their commonality (29); the use of poetry in prose and parody (30); the preferability of encouraging rather than fighting against the prevailing emotions of the audience (31); admission (*homologia*) and defense (*apologia*) for generally acknowledged wrongs (32); the brief treatment of great matters to create a tragic effect and expansive treatment of small and trivial matters for a comic effect (33–34); and the lack of true ambiguity in the works of the writers of old (35). Next come brief remarks on deliberative oratory (*dêmêgoria*), dialogue, comedy, tragedy, and the Socratic symposium (36). The treatise ends on the use of denial (*apophasis*) as opposed to affirmation (*kataphasis*, 37).

Text: *Hermogenis Opera*, ed. Hugo Rabe (Leipzig: Teubner, 1913). Translations: of the *Progymnasmata* in Charles S. Baldwin, *Medieval Rhetoric and Poetic (to 1400) Interpreted from Representative Works* (New York: Macmillan, 1928), 23–68; Ray Nadeau, "Hermogenes' *On Stases*: A Translation with an Introduction and Notes," *Speech Monographs* 31 (1964): 361–424; *Hermogenes' On Types of Style*, trans. Cecil W. Wooten (Chapel Hill: Univ. of North Carolina Press, 1987); *Hermogenes On Issues: Strategies of Argument in Later Greek Rhetoric*, trans. Malcolm Heath (Oxford: Clarendon Press, 1995).

ISOCRATES, one of the most famous and influential Greek orators, lived from 436 to 338 B.C. Twenty-one of the sixty orations extant under his name in Roman times survive today. There are also nine extant letters. A central figure in Athenian politics and education, I. also put forth views on rhetorical theory, though these remain somewhat obscure, largely because his handbook on rhetoric (*technê*) has not survived.

There are a number of references to the handbook in ancient writers. Quintilian says that both I. and Aristotle left textbooks of rhetoric, and that Aristotle's was the larger (3.1.14). Plutarch (*Dem.* 5.7) claims that Demosthenes secretly obtained the handbooks of I. and Alcidamas, while Cicero (*De Inv.* 2.2.7) remarks that he has not actually seen I.' handbook but has discovered many precepts of his pupils (cf. Diog. Laert. 24.2; Cic. *Brut.* 12.48; for further references, see Radermacher, *Artium scriptores* [Vienna, 1951] pp. 153–87). Quintilian (2.15.4) says that I. called rhetoric the "worker of persuasion" (*peithous dêmiourgos*), while elsewhere it is claimed that he called it the "science of persuasion" (*epistêmê peithous*, Sextus Empiricus, *Against the Professors* 2.62). I. thought that all oratory had elements of praise (*laus*) and blame (*vituperatio*); the narration (*narratio*), according to members of the Isocratean school, should be lucid, brief, and plausible (*Quint.* 3.4.11; 4.2.31). Comments on style preserved by several late writers (Radermacher, pp. 157–58) indicate that I.'s handbook had a section on the purities (*katharai*) of style. Among its recommendations were the avoidance of hiatus, of ending one word and beginning the next with the same syllable, and of putting the same conjunctions close together. Words may be metaphors and elaborate, sometimes coined or common; diction should have various rhythms, and events should be narrated in proper order.

I.'s views on rhetoric and rhetorical education are also indicated by two speeches, *AGAINST THE SOPHISTS* (*KATA TÔN SOPHISTÔN*) and *ANTIDOSIS*. In the former I. attacks sophists in general for their pretension and greed (1–8), as well as those who profess to teach political oratory (*politikos logos*). These so-called teachers impart inflexible rules and ignore the importance of native ability (9–15). I.'s own view is that anyone, with the proper effort, can gain knowledge (*epistêmê*) of the elements (*ideai*) of discourse, learn to choose subjects, arrange them properly, fit them to the occasion, and embellish the whole speech with striking thoughts (*enthymêmata*) and rhythmical and musical words. The student must have ability and determination, and the teacher must be exact and serve as a model, so that the student will speak more gracefully (*anthêroteron*) and charmingly (*chariesteron*) than others (16–18). The speech concludes with an attack on earlier writers of rhetorical handbooks (19–22).

In the lengthy *ANTIDOSIS*, written in his old age, Isocrates defends his career and educational methods. Near the end of the speech he puts forth a theory of rhetorical education. No art can implant virtue in depraved people, but it is possible to improve morally if one learns to speak well and persuade one's listeners. Anyone who wishes to deliver speeches worthy of praise will, of course, support causes that are good and honorable. From the actions of men he will select the most illustrious examples and will himself be influenced and improved by them. The speaker wishing to persuade will take pains to cultivate an upright character and to become esteemed among his fellow citizens (274–78).

Text and translation: Isocrates, *On the Peace, Areopagiticus, Against the Sophists, Antidosis,* trans. George Norlin (Cambridge, Mass.: Harvard Univ. Press, 1985).

LONGINUS has traditionally been considered the author of the fragmentary text *ON THE SUBLIME* (*PERI HYPSOUS*), but there is doubt about his authorship and, indeed, about the time of composition. The manuscripts give the author as "Dionysius Longinus" or "Dionysius or Longinus," and until the early nineteenth century Cassius Longinus of Palmyra, who lived in the third century A.D., was thought to be the author. But internal evidence points to a date of composition in the first century A.D. (for instance, the treatise mentions no literature written after that date). In any case, the author is almost certainly not Dionysius of Halicarnassus. Whoever the author was (for simplicity, he will be referred to here as Longinus) and whenever he wrote, *ON THE SUBLIME*, of which about two-thirds survives, is a work of great importance. L. transcends rigid rhetorical rules and categories and, by analyzing selected poetic passages, offers a discussion of what makes literature pleasurable, forceful, and great, that is, sublime.

L. begins by telling his addressee, one Postumius Terentianus, that he hopes that his own observations concerning the sublime will prove to be more useful than those of the Sicilian rhetorician Caecilius of Calacte (first century B.C.), whose treatise on the sublime he considers sketchy and unsatisfactory. L. defines the sublime as the highest excellence (*akrotês*) and distinction (*exochê*) of discourse, which alone is responsible for literary fame. Supreme literary skill produces not persuasion in the hearer but ecstasy (*ekstasis*), and what inspires wonder is always superior to the merely persuasive and pleasurable (1.1–4). While it is said that genius is born, not taught, nonetheless there is an art of sublimity that can be subjected to systematic rules (2.1–3). After a gap in the text we find L. analyzing faults that often arise in the attempt to achieve sublimity. These are tumidity (*to oidoun*, 3.1-4); puerility (*to meirakiôdes*), which results in overelaboration or frigidity (*psychrotês*, 3.4); false emotion, sometimes called *parenthyrson* (3.5); and frigidity (4.1–7). L. declares the truly sublime to be that which pleases all the people all the time, something devoid of empty externalities that leaves a permanent impression and holds up under repeated scrutiny (7.1–4).

Next come the five sources of sublimity. Two are natural: the power to conceive great thoughts and strong and inspired emotion. Three involve art; they are figures (*schêmata*) of thought (*noêsis*) and figures of speech (*lexis*); noble diction (two components: choice of words and the use of metaphorical and artificial language); and grandeur. L. says that he will proceed to discuss these sources one by one and remarks, by way of a preface, that Caecilius left out emotion, mistakenly thinking that sublimity and emotion were the same thing or not noticing that emotion sometimes contributes to sublimity (8.1--4).

The first source, the power to conceive great thoughts, is most important (9.1-4). Then, after a substantial gap in the text, we find L. discussing Homer's superiority to Hesiod in representing the gods and in depicting heroic greatness (9.5--11). This discussion leads to a comparison of the *Iliad* and *Odyssey*, by which L. attempts to illustrate the decline of Homer's genius from the former to the latter work (9.11–15).

L. then asks whether anything else contributes to the sublime and points to the selection and organization of material. Examples follow (10.1--7). Next L. adds amplification (*auxêsis*), which he defines as the accumulation of all the details and topics inherent in a situation. Sublimity may also be found in a single idea, but amplification always involves quantity and a degree of redundance (11–12.2). Another gap in the text follows, after which L. is discussing grandeur (*megethos*) and comparing that of Plato, Demosthenes, and Cicero (12.3–13.1). L. goes on to discuss another factor, the imitation of earlier great writers (13.2–14), and then on to visualization or imagination (*phantasia*), which is defined as the vivid representation of emotion and enthusiasm. Examples from both poetry and oratory follow (15.1–12).

Next are figures (*schêmata*); L. gives an example of the proper use of figures by discussing the Marathon oath, or apostrophe, used by Demosthenes in *On the Crown* (16). Figures must be subtle if they are to contribute to sublimity (17). Then, giving examples from literature, L. discusses other figures: rhetorical questions (18); asyndeton (19); following another gap in the text, asyndeton combined with repetition (*anaphora*) and vivid description (*diatypôsis*, 20); use of connectives (21); transposition (*hyperbaton*), which is the arrangement of words out of the normal sequence and marks great emotion (22); accumulation (*athroismos*), variation (*metabolê*), and climax, as well as changes of case, tense, person, number, and gender (23–24);

vivid use of the present tense for the past (25); variation of person (26); change to direct speech (27); and periphrasis, which must be used with moderation (28–29.1). All figures help to increase emotion, which is an essential part of sublimity (29.2).

After some comments on diction (30.1–2) and another gap in the text we find L. discussing the use of familiar language (31), then proceeding to metaphors, with examples of their use in literature. Metaphors contribute to sublimity and should be used in emotional and descriptive passages. But again, there is the danger of overuse (32.1–7). Next L. digresses at length on his view that mediocre writers (e.g. Apollonius, Theocritus, Bacchylides, Ion), even when flawless in execution, are inferior to geniuses (e.g. Homer, Pindar, Sophocles), even when the latter make mistakes (32.8–36). Returning to metaphors, L. begins to discuss comparisons (*parabolai*) and similes (*eikones*) (37), but there is another gap in the text. After that L. is on the topic of hyperbole, which adds intensity but must be used with care and subtlety (38).

Next is the proper arrangement of words, the only remaining of the five factors that at the beginning L. said contribute to sublimity. Under this heading are rhythm and sentence structure (39.1–4), then a few of the things damaging to sublimity: poor rhythm, phrases that are too closely knit or chopped up, excessive brevity, and vulgar vocabulary (41–43.6). The work ends with a discussion of the decay of literature. In response to a question posed to him by a philosopher, L. argues that the decay is caused by vices such as avarice and sloth. He concludes by saying that the topic of his next treatise will be emotion, an important factor in the sublime (44).

Text and translation: Aristotle, *Poetics*, trans. Stephen Halliwell; Longinus, *On the Sublime*, trans. W. Hamiklton Fyfe, rev. Donald A. Russell; Demetrius, *On Style*, trans. Doreen C. Innes based on trans. by W. Rhys Roberts (Cambridge, Mass.: Harvard Univ. Press, 1995).

LUCIAN was born in Samosata in Syria around 120 and died about 180. He practiced sophistic rhetoric and then went over to philosophy, proceeding to develop the diatribes and satiric dialogues for which he is famous. Two of his approximately eighty works give good indications of his rhetorical thought: *HOW TO WRITE HISTORY (PÔS DEI HISTORIAN SYNGRAPHEIN)* and the ironic *A PROFESSOR OF PUBLIC SPEAKING (RHÊTORÔN DIDASKALOS)*.

HOW TO WRITE HISTORY is addressed to a certain Philo, to whom L. will offer advice on historiography, which is a difficult branch of literature (1–5). L. discusses common faults first. Most writers of history do not properly distinguish it from encomium (*engkômion*), which may involve lies, while history does not. History must also be kept separate from poetry and, seldom have praise (*epainos*). The goal of history is what is useful (*to chrêsimon*), which comes from the truth alone. Pleasure (*to terpnon*) is a by-product, not to be pursued (6–13). The main problems with historical writing are overt poeticism (14–23), outright error, lack of judgment in assembling material, prolixity, and overcompression (24–33). The good writer of history has political understanding (*synesis politikê*), which is innate, and power of expression (*dynamis hermêneutikê*), which can be acquired. He must be objective and impartial, as Thucydides was (34–42). The historian's style (*lexis*) should be clear (*saphês*), with ordinary vocabulary and figures (*schêmata*). He should research carefully, arrange events well, and present them vividly. An introduction (*prooimion*) may be omitted, but if used it should make only two points, not three as it does in the orators (43–54). The transition from introduction to narrative (*diêgêsis*) should be gentle, and the narrative itself should be smooth and clear. Rapidity (*tachos*) is useful, but too much topographical description should be avoided. Speeches should be appropriate to the speakers but are also an opportunity for the historian to display his eloquence. Praise and invective (*psogos*) must be reasonable and supported by evidence. Historians should write with an eye to posterity (55–63).

L. addresses *A PROFESSOR OF PUBLIC SPEAKING* to a student wishing to be a public speaker. The occupation requires hard work but is well worth it. L. will show the young man an easy way to success (1–6). There are two paths, one narrow and rough, the other level and flowery. A muscular, rugged man will greet the student at the rough road and guide him, pointing out the footprints, now indistinct, of Demosthenes, Plato, and others (6–10). At the easy road will be a handsome, clever dandy, who will order the student to obey his every command, telling him to bring shamelessness, brashness, a loud voice, elaborate clothes, and a retinue (11–15). Though appearance is most important, sprinkling speeches with fifteen or twenty Attic words lends credibility. In general, use obscure and unfamiliar words, for then people will think that you are smart. Read contemporary speeches and declamations (*meletai,* 16–17). Do not worry about arrangement, never stop talking, and make historical allusions. Turn everything into song. Begin with Troy or the beginning of the world and plant friends in the crowd (18–21). Laugh at the other speakers, lie, be shameless and jealous, and slander; then you will be famous (22). Live a private life filled with vice and be sure to use depilatories (23). The speaker concludes by remarking that he has been unsucessful in court but very notorious, and that is the important thing (24–25).

Text and translation: Lucian, *Anacharsis or Athletics, Menippus or The Descent into Hades, On Funerals, A Professor of Public Speaking, Alexander the False Prophet,* etc., trans. A. M. Harmon (Cambridge, Mass.: Harvard Univ. Press, 1925); *How to Write History, The Dipsads, Saturnalia,* etc., trans. K. Kilburn (Cambridge, Mass.: Harvard Univ. Press, 1959).

MARTIANUS CAPELLA (5ifth century A.D.) wrote a compendium of the seven liberal arts, *THE MARRIAGE OF MERCURY AND PHILOLOGY* (*DE NUPTIIS MERCURII ET PHILOLOGIAE*), which was highly popular and influential during the Latin Middle Ages. An elaborate mythological and allegorical framework is developed in Books 1 and 2, where the virgin Philology is betrothed to the god of eloquence, Mercury. The marriage ceremony is held in heaven before the Olympian deities. The seven liberal arts serve as bridesmaids. Each is introduced in the subsequent seven books and gives a technical and reasonably comprehensive survey of her discipline—Book 3 on grammar, 4 on dialectic, 5 on rhetoric, 6 on geometry, 7 on arithmetic, 8 on astronomy, and 9 on harmony. Each of the trivial arts (grammar, dialectic, and rhetoric) must be stopped before she has finished: the gods become bored with grammar; Athena rebukes dialectic for fallacies and prevents her from reviewing them—dialectic agrees reluctantly with her own biting rejoinder to an insulting comment made by Bacchus before she had begun her disquisition; and rhetoric is signalled by Mercury that her time is up, appropriately after she has reviewed the topoi of the conclusion of a speech.

Book 5 on rhetoric is a syncretic compilation of many sources, including Greek ones, with which M.C. is obviously conversant. The length is about 40 percent of the *Rhetorica ad Herennium,* and the treatment is reminiscent of *RAH,* a major exception being the extensive use of Cicero's speeches as sources of exemplary illustrations (Cicero is singled out for special praise in the prefatory section because he excelled not only in the practice of rhetoric but also in rhetorical theory, 436). The long allegorical preface, which describes the personified rhetoric, cleverly alludes to the basics of rhetorical instruction (three kinds of speech, levels of style, three kinds of arguments, etc., 427–37) before introducing and naming her (438).

Rhetoric defines herself from the points of view of her duty (*officium*) and her purpose (*finis*), as Cicero had in his *De Inventione* (1.5), and gives a brief overview of the subject: the question (*quaestio*), limited (*finita*) or unlimited (*infinita*); the five parts of instruction (her duty); and the two kinds of questions, principal and incidental (439–43). M.C. then begins with the issues (*status* or *constitutiones*). He has three: conjectural, definitional, and qualitative; and he claims

that Hermagoras's fourth is part of the qualitative issue (444–46).
M.C. intrudes a discussion of the three different audiences appropriate to the three kinds of speech (forensic, deliberative, and epideictic)
and relates the issues to all three, not just, as in Cicero, to forensic
(447–49, 454, and 467–68). The basic discussion of the issues is clear
and illuminating (450–60), but the subsequent treatment of judgment about the issues (461–65) is confusing as it blends back into a
review of the limited question (466) and the issues of deliberative
and demonstrative speeches (467–68). The nature of the case or cause
(*natura causae*, 469) is briefly reviewed, and a much fuller discussion
follows of how to proceed with our case ("the direction of the case,"
Stahl, *ductus causae*, 470–505), an interesting prescriptive outline of
the mental procedures in approaching the case. Five types are
discussed: the simple, subtle, figured, oblique, and mixed. These
procedures of intellectual organization appropriately lead to a
briefer review of organization or arrangement (*ordo rerum* or *dispositio*), the second traditional part of rhetorical instruction (506–07).
M.C. has seven parts of the speech: introduction (*principium*),
narration (*narratio*), division (*partitio*), proposition (*propositio*), argumentation (*argumentatio*), conclusion (*conclusio*), and epilogue
(*epilogus*).

Style (*elocutio* or *eloquentia*) follows (508–37). Four general traits
(from Cicero) are praised: proper Latinity, clarity, copiousness, and
ornateness (508). Literal and metaphorical language, including
coined and borrowed words and comparisons, begin the discussion
(509–13), followed by an interesting examination of sentence structure, including the rhythms to be used in ending clauses and sentences (*compositio*, 514–22). There is an abrupt shift to figurative
language (523–25), beginning with irony, apostrophe, hesitation
(*diaporêsis*), accumulation (*erôtêma*), multiple answers implied
(*pysma*), appearance (*diatypôsis*), introduction of a contrary case
(*anteisagôgê*), ridicule (*diasyrmos*), and transference (*metastasis*),
which M.C. identifies as figures of thought or expression (*figurae
sententiarum*, 526). After briefly pausing to finish the earlier discussion of sentence structure, on sentence parts of various size and
complexity (526), M.C. continues on figures of speech (*figurae
elocutionum*), which are distinguished from figures of thought in that
figures of speech depend on the actual order of the words, whereas

figures of thought do not (530). These figures of speech serve only to embellish: *antithesis, isokôlon, parison, homoioptôton, homoioteleuton, paronomasia, plokê, palillogia, epanalêpsis, anadiplôsis, prosapodosis, epanaphora, antistrophê, symplokê, polyptôton, synônymia, tautologia, klimax, asyndeton, diezeugmenon, antezeugmenon, pleonasmos,* and *elleipsis* (531–37).

The brief treatment of memory (538–39) stresses that order and sequence are the keys to memory and, in support of that view, mentions the famous anecdote about the poet Simonides, who remembered the seating arrangement at a banquet after the building collapsed and so was able to identify the dead buried in the rubble (538). The section on delivery (*actio, pronuntiato*) is not much longer (540–43). M.C. then returns to a full discussion of the (now) five parts of a speech (544): the introduction (*exordium*); narration (*narratio*); proposition (*propositio*); argumentation (*argumentatio*); and conclusion (*peroratio*). In the subsequent, topically oriented treatment of each part (545–65), prescriptively reminiscent of *RAH,* the proposition is not mentioned, but the division or overview (*partitio,* 556) and recapitulation at the end of the argumentation (*anakephalaiôsis* or *enumeratio,* 564) are. The conclusion here is also identified as the *epilogus* (565). Rhetoric then concludes with a loud kiss on Philology's forehead (565)—she is (appropriately) always calling attention to herself, and in the introductory part of Book 5 Roman orators seem to be (in a difficult passage) noted for being loud (432).

Text: *Martianus Capella,* ed. Adolfus Dick (Stuttgart: Teubner, 1969). Translation: *Martianus Capella and the Seven Liberal Arts,* trans. William Harris Stahl and Richard Johnson, with E. L. Burge, 2 vols. (New York: Columbia Univ. Press, 1977).

MENANDER RHETOR, who lived in Laodicea in Asia Minor in the third century A.D., is traditionally considered the author of two treatises, *DIVISION OF EPIDEICTIC SPEECHES (DIAIRESIS TÔN EPIDEIKTIKÔN)* and *ON EPIDEICTIC (PERI EPIDEIK-TIKÔN)*. He was known as an expert on epideictic rhetoric in Byzantine times and wrote commentaries on Hermogenes and on Minucianus's *Progymnasmata*, but it is doubtful that he is the author of these treatises and, indeed, whether both were written by the same person. There is little doubt, however, that both belong to the late third or early fourth century A.D. The order of the chapters in the second treatise, *ON EPIDEICTIC*, is disputed, but here the traditional order is followed.

Book 1 of *DIVISION OF EPIDEICTIC SPEECHES* begins with the division of rhetoric into three parts: speeches in law courts, speeches in assemblies or councils, and epideictic speeches (*epideiktikoi logoi*), which are either encomiastic (*engkômiastikoi*) or invective (*psektikoi*). Epideictic speeches have the headings of blame (*psogos*) and praise (*epainos*). If to gods, the praises are called hymns and divided according to the name of the god, e.g., hymns to Apollo are called paeans and *hyporchêmata*, those to Dionysius dithyrambs. If to mortals, the praise is either of cities and countries or men and animals (331–32).

M. then discusses hymns to the gods in more detail. Hymns are those containing invocations (*klêtikoi*) or involving departures (*apopemptikoi*); scientific (*physikoi*) or mythical (*mythikoi*); genealogical (*genealogikoi*) or fictitious (*peplasmenoi;* using personification); and precatory (*euktikoi*) or deprecatory (*apeuktikoi*). In hymns of invocation the poet has greater license than the prose writer because he is allowed to describe in greater detail the places from which the gods are summoned. The style (*hermêneia*) should display freshness (*hôra*) and splendor (*kosmos*). The rare hymn of divine departure is found only in poetry. It involves the places from which the god departs and to which he goes. The style should give pleasure (*hêdonê*). Scientific hymns should be lively (*empsychoteroi*) and grand (*megalonousteroi*), and are especially suited to poets. An example is identifying Apollo with the sun and discussing the nature of the sun. Some go into great detail, some do not, according to the audience (333–37). Mythical hymns are similar to genealogical hymns, but all genealogical hymns involve myth, whereas not all mythical hymns involve genealogy. Mythical hymns must not involve science; they are better suited to poets, who can clothe the myth in adornment—bare myth inspires tedium and disgust—by arrangement (*harmonia*) and figures (*schêmata*). Genealogical hymns, if combined with other forms, may be long or short. The style should have purity (*katharotês*) and freedom from excess (*to aproskores*). Fictitious hymns, i.e., mythopoeic, must naturally involve lesser-known gods. They should be continuous, polished (*glaphyrôs*) and not unpleasing, corroborated by fact, and internally consistent. If the subject is not supernatural, e.g., poverty, the style should be simpler (*aphelestera*), if divine, more solemn (*semnotera*). Precatory and deprecatory hymns may stand alone or in combination with other hymns. Prayers should be simple and brief (338–44).

In Book 2 M. discusses how to praise a country. This involves nature, characteristics, or location. Praise of a country is made in terms of pleasure and utility. Examples are given. M. adds that some encomia are honorable (*endoxa*), some ambivalent (*amphidoxa*), and others, e.g., that of a barren country, are paradoxical (*paradoxa*, 344-46). Next is praise of a city, which involves position as well as origin, accomplishments (*epitêdeuseis*), and actions (*praxeis*). M. goes into detail, then digresses on how to praise harbors, bays, and citadels (346–53). Returning to cities, he examines the second main heading, origin, with examples (353–59).

Book 3 turns to the third main heading for cities, how to praise them for accomplishments, which divides into those relating to politics, science, art, and abilities (*dynameis*). Three political systems are good (kingdom, aristocracy, and democracy), three bad (tyranny, oligarchy or plutocracy, and what M. calls laocracy, goverment by the rabble). M. advises that if the city to be praised is a tyranny, it should be represented as a kingdom, etc. (359–61).

The fourth main heading for cities is actions, which are judged in terms of the virtues—justice, temperance, prudence, and courage—and their parts. Justice is considered under three parts: piety, fairness, and reverence. Temperance involves either public life (education, rules for marriage, etc.), or private (adultery, other bad behaviors). Prudence also involves public (the accurate codification of laws, etc.) and private (whether there are many esteemed rhetors, sophists, geometers, etc.). Courage divides into peace (behavior when confronted with earthquakes, famine, drought, etc.) and war (361–65).

In general, praises of cities may be for all time or for a specific occasion (festival speeches, etc.). Assemblies and festivals are praised on either common (the benefits of festivals for men) or specific grounds, relating to particular times, places, etc. (365–67).

ON EPIDEICTIC begins with a discussion of the imperial oration (*basilikos logos*), an encomium of the emperor. The introduction (*prooimion*), of which there may be more than one, should emphasize the emperor's good qualities. M. offers several model introductions. After the introductions comes the topic of the emperor's city (*patris*) and nation (*ethnos*), if famous. If not, try his family (*genos*), or begin with the emperor himself. Next come his birth (*genesis*), his nature (*physis*), upbringing (*anatrophê*), education (*paideia*), accomplishments (*epitêdeumata*), and actions (*praxeis*). There should be a new introduction for each heading treated. The actions praised should always be divided into the four virtues: courage, justice, temperance, and wisdom. Also mention the brilliance of the emperor's fortune (*tychê*) and make a detailed comparison between his reign and those that preceded him. Then comes the epilogue and, finally, a prayer for the emperor's health (368–77).

The speech of arrival (*epibatêrios*) involves an address to 1) one's native city on returning from a trip, 2) a visited city, or 3) a visiting governor. M. treats the third situation first. The introduction should naturally convey joy, then move to the governor's subjects, according to whether their previous circumstances were good or bad. Then to praise of the emperor, which should be brief. The epilogue should greet the governor as a godsend. The same scheme, with only slight modification, works for a governor who has visited the city before (377–81). After a brief discussion of the difference between the arrival speech and the speech of address (*prosphônêtikos*) M. turns to the first and second situations, speeches to cities. Material for these should be derived from the speaker's love for the city (its beauty, history, etc.), which leads to an encomium of the founder, if he was good. After the introduction based on joy there should follow amplification based on the contrast between present joy and previous sadness, then the encomium of the founder and praise of the position, nurture (*anatrophê*), and accomplishments of the city, with expressions of enthusiasm preceding each of these sections. Here M. adds that the arrival speech and patriotic speech (*patrios logos*) are similar except that the latter does not have the expression of joy. Following the accomplishments of the city should be its actions, under the four virtues mentioned above, with comparisons for each virtue. The epilogue should describe the layout and special features of the city. Then to advice on how to construct a Trojan oration (*Trôikos logos*), which involves praise of the country, its history, the city, etc. (382–88).

Next is the talk (*lalia*), which is useful in various forms of deliberative and epideictic speech. M. gives an example of an encomium of a governor in talk form. Agreeable examples and stories should be interspersed, for the talk requires sweetness (*glykytês*) and pleasantness (*hêdonê*). Herodotus and Xenophon are among the models for this technique. It is also useful to invent a dream or to claim to have heard a report. The talk is good for advice on concord and on taking interest in oratory and for satirizing and preparing the audience. The talk allows for a lack of organization; in fact, disorder is desirable. It is also a useful form for speeches of arrival. Plutarch's *Lives* are an excellent source for the talk, as are poets and works on metamorphosis. The style should be simple (*haplous*); brevity and proportion are also important. Others forms of the talk are those involving departure (*syntaktikê lalia*), in which grief is expressed, and arrival (*epibatêrios lalia*), in which joy is expressed (388–94).

The propemptic talk (*propemptikê lalia*) is a speech sending a traveler off with praise and love. It requires delicacy (*habrotês*) and charming narrative content. One type admits advice, when a superior sends off an inferior (e.g., teacher and pupil). A second type involves affection (*êthos erôtikon*) directed from one equal to another, a third an encomium directed from an inferior to a superior. Then to an analysis of an example of the second type, a young man seeing off a friend (395–99).

The epithalamium (*epithalamios*), called by some the wedding speech (*gamêlios*), is a hymn to marriage and all that it involves. The epithalamium has two types, one more formal (*syntonos*), which is similar to actual oratory, one less so (*syngraphikôteros*). M. discusses introductions for each type, then general material common to both types, e.g., marriage's place in mythology, stories of union between rivers, animals, trees, etc. Then to encomia of the families and the bride and bridegroom and a description of the bridal chamber. Finally, there should be mention of the prospect of children and a concluding prayer. Sometimes detailed descriptions of marriage and love can be incorporated into the speech (399–405).

The bedroom speech (*kateunastikos logos*) is an exhortation to intercourse after marriage and should be brief. There should be an encomium of the bride and encouragement of the bridegroom, but the latter must not be vulgar. There should also be comparison to an athletic event and description of the beauty of the bridal chamber and bride. The bridegroom should be advised to pray to certain of the gods, and the speaker should pray for the couple's happiness and fertility. There are special topics for speakers who are relatives, married men, or strangers, and material based on the season in which the intercourse is to take place. Mythological parallels may be used, as well. M. cautions that only one or two of these suggestions will suffice for any given occasion and adds that although there is no set division for this type of speech, the following is suggested: brief proemium; exhortation to the man; the time; exhortation based on the past, particularly the courtship; the seasons; examples from myth and history; beauty of the bride, etc.; the gods of marriage; the advantage of marriage; prayer for happiness and children. Charm and freshness (*hôra*) are paramount. The speech should be simple and similar to the talk (405–12).

The birthday speech (*genethliakos logos*) consists of introductions, praise of the day, encomium of the family, encomium of the person according to the normal divisions, and praise of the day again. There are also suggestions for the birthday speech for a very young man [this chapter appears to be incomplete] (412–13).

The consolatory speech (*paramythêtikos*) laments the deceased and amplifies the significance of the event. It is based on the same material as the monody [explained below]. After amplifying the lamentation as much as possible the speaker should proceed to consolatory topics, such as the advantages of death over life; the inevitability of death; the death of cities and nations; the deceased's satiety, if his life was good, and relief, if it was a bane; his afterlife in the Elysian Fields or with the gods. The speech should be of moderate length and, like the epithalamium, has formal and less formal types (413-14).

The address (*prosphônêtikos logos*) is a speech spoken in praise of a governor. It is an incomplete encomium based on the actions of its subject. It divides into introduction, brief praise of the emperor (under the headings of war and peace), and praise of the governor based on his actions and family. The actions should be divided into the four virtues. M. suggests historical and legendary exemplars for each virtue. Comparisons, optional praise of the city, and epilogue follow (414-18).

The funeral speech (*epitaphios*) was originally delivered by Athenians over the war dead and was a lament. But now, because in most cases there is a long interval between death and the speech, it is generally an encomium. It should be divided according to the headings of encomium (family, birth, nature, upbringing, education, accomplishments) and spoken with great emotion (*pathos*) with an element of lamentation in each part. There should also be mention of actions and fortune, and comparisons. Then to lamentation, consolation to the family, and advice to wife and children. Finally, praise of the family for not neglecting the funeral, and prayer (418-22).

The crown speech (*stephanôtikos*) consists of an introduction based on the emperor's glory and the gift to him of a crown. If appropriate, an encomium of his family follows. If not, the next topic is fortune. Then to education, virtues (courage in war and deeds in peace), remarks on gratitude, and reading of the honorary decree. This speech should be no more than two hundred lines long (422-23).

The ambassador's speech (*presbeutikos*), spoken on behalf of a city in distress, should be similar to the crown speech, but at every point there should be amplification of the emperor's humanity. There should also be glorification of the city and vivid description (*diatypôsis*) of its present woes, with piteous mention of the monuments, etc. that have fallen down. After an appeal for mercy, the emperor should be asked to receive the decree (423-24).

The speech of invitation (*klêtikos*) may be delivered when inviting a governor to a festival. The introduction should state the reason for the invitation, then encomia of the festival (which is the primary subject), city, and governor should follow. Then to the introduction of the festival and comparison of it with others, making clear the importance of the governor's acceptance. If the invitation is not to a festival but simply to the city, the introduction may mention the speaker's prestige, avoiding vulgarity. Then to encomia of the city, based on its actions alone, and the governor. If this is his first visit, the country, city, and achievements of the people should be described. After comparison with other cities describe the journey and city, and mention in the epilogue the city's readiness to greet the governor. If the governor has seen the city before, there should be an introduction, encomia of the city and governor, and remarks on the position and beauty of the city. After that, proceed as if this were his first visit. If the city has no prestige, substitute the position of the country or city for the encomium. Another method for this type of speech is to juxtapose the governor and city, then treat the rest normally (424–30).

The speech of departure (*syntaktikos*) obviously involves distress, real or feigned. Odysseus's departure from Alcinous and Arete is the model. There should be an encomium of the city from which the speaker departs, remarks on the destination, a prayer for those left behind and for the speaker himself. If the speaker is departing fom his own city, he should express love and distress and praise his destination. The speech ought to be simple and display sweetness by descriptions, historical exempla, etc. The city being addressed should always be praised first. If it is in talk form it must be brief, and if it is the speaker's only speech of the day it may be somewhat informally delivered and be no more than three hundred lines long (430–34).

The monody (*monôdia*) has Homeric antecedents. Its purpose is to express lamentation and pity. If the speaker is not a close relative of the deceased he should mix encomium with the lament. If closely related he should also lament his own bereavement. If the deceased is a leader there should be an encomium of the city; and if he was young, much should be made of that. The speaker should always begin by railing against the gods. The monody should be divided into present, past, and future, all in reference to the deceased. Then to mention of his place in the city, the funeral, and his physical beauty. M. adds that monodies are generally delivered only over young people but may be delivered by a husband over his wife. Monodies should be no more than 150 lines in length, and the style should be relaxed (*anetos,* 434–37).

The Sminthiac oration (*Sminthiakos*), in praise of Apollo, has two introductions. The first should state that gratitude is due to the god. In the second the speaker should say that others (e.g., Homer and Pindar) have praised Apollo, that this is his humble effort to do the same, and that he begs for strength. Then to a hymn to the god himself. The speaker should ask where he should begin, then discuss Apollo's origins. After this discussion, there should be an encomium of the country and remarks on Apollo's support of it. Then to his powers, which are archery, prophecy, music, and medicine. Each of these sections should be preceded by an introduction. After discussing these in detail M. prescribes a section on the city (Alexandria), its foundation by Alexander, and its great festivals. Then to a section on the festival, and the idea of festivals in general. M. adds that each subject (e.g., music) should have a general, prefatory section stating that it is a good thing. Finally, there should be a section on the temple and statue of Apollo, and a concluding appeal to to the god, using his many names (437–46).

Text and translation: *Menander Rhetor,* ed. and trans. D. A. Russell and N. G. Wilson (Oxford: Clarendon Press, 1981).

MINOR LATIN WRITERS ON RHETORIC (RHETORES LAT-INI MINORES) is a collection of late classical and early medieval treatises on rhetoric, edited by Karl Halm and published in 1863. The first section contains writers on figures of thought and style (*SCRIPTORES DE FIGURIS SENTIARUM ET ELOCUTIONIS*). RUTILIUS LUPUS treats 41 schemes or rhetorical figures in two books (pp. 3–21). The Greek name of each figure is given, followed by a definition and examples in Latin. Most of the examples are Latin translations of portions of speeches from Greek sources. AQUILA ROMANUS follows with essentially the same procedure, except that he adds an introduction and most of his examples are from Latin sources, especially Cicero (pp. 22–37). JULIUS RUFINIANUS begins by adding 38 more figures to Romanus, starting with irony, a species of allegory (pp. 38–47) and then follows with a book on 44 figures of style (pp. 48–58), and a book on figures of thought (pp. 59–62). Most of Rufinianus's examples are from Virgil.

The next item in Halm is in verse: *VERSE ON FIGURES OR SCHEMES (CARMEN DE FIGURIS VEL SCHEMATIBUS*, pp. 63–70). Here again the terms are in Greek and the explanations in Latin. After a series of basic descriptions of syntactical units (beginning with *komma*) in three lines of verse, 58 schematic arrangements of words are defined, again with three lines of verse for each entry. They are organized alphabetically until the final 12. Another anonymous prose treatise follows on figures of thought, *SCHEMATA DIANOEAS QUAE AD RHETORES PERTINENT* (pp. 71–77). Sixty-three figures (all but two with Greek names) are listed and defined in Latin, but citations to Quintilian are substituted for definitions in the final 17.

The next two pieces in Halm were important sources of knowledge about rhetoric during the Middle Ages. The first is the *ART OF RHETORIC (ARTIS RHETORICAE LIBRI III)* of Fortunatianus, a fifth-century authority (pp. 81–134). This is a compendium, written in a question-and-answer form, based essentially on Quintilian, Cicero, and especially the *Rhetorica ad Herennium*—its prescriptive, formulaic rules read very much like an abridged version of the *RAH*. Greek terms are generally used throughout, sometimes with Latin transliterations. After some brief basic definitions (of rhetoric, the orator, etc.) the first book takes up invention, using Hermagorean issues (*status*). Book 2 finishes that consideration (2.1–11) and then turns to the four parts of a speech: introduction (*principia*), narrative (*narratio*), argumentation (*argumentatio*), and conclusion (*peroratio*, 2.12–31). Book 3 briefly reviews arrangement (*dispositio*, 3.1–2), style (*elocutio*, 3–12), memory (*memoria*, 13–14), and delivery (*pronuntiatio*, 15–23). The second work, *DE RHETORICA*, was always linked with Fortunatianus. It is a brief overview of rhetoric and rhetorical invention purportedly by St. Augustine (pp. 137–51). It is also explicitly Hermagorean in approach. A translation appears in Miller.

The next work in Halm is the longest, a commentary on Cicero's *De Inventione* titled *EXPLANATIONUM IN RHETORICAM M. TULLII CICERONIS LIBRI DUO*, by Victorinus (pp. 155–304). Its prolix treatment, however, is generally more confusing than illuminating. Halm appends to it some further brief, anonymous comments on the *De Inventione* (pp. 305–10).

Next is the *INSTITUTIONES ORATORIAE* of Sulpitius Victor (pp. 313–52). After a brief overview of the parts of rhetoric, parts of a speech, etc. (1–23), the remainder and bulk of the work considers the Hermagorean issues (*status*, 24–62). Most of the briefer compendium that follows, *PRAECEPTA ARTIS RHETORICAE* by Severianus (pp. 355–70), also treats invention within a Hermagorean framework, as does the subsequent much longer work on invention by C. Julius Victor, *ARS RHETORICA HERMAGORAE, CICERONIS, QUINTILIANI, AQUILI, MARCOMANNI, TATIANI* (pp. 373–448), which claims in this title to be a compilation of a number of earlier authorities.

MARTIANUS CAPELLA (pp. 451–92), for whom there is a separate entry herein (q.v.), is followed by two of the three most influential encyclopedic treatments of rhetoric in the Middle Ages (the third is that by Martianus himself), those by CASSIODORUS (pp. 495–504) and ISIDORE (pp. 507–22). Another medieval and explicitly Christian work follows by Master Albinus, who is joined in a dialogue about rhetoric by King Karl. The king asks appropriately leading questions, which are answered by Albinus (pp. 525–50). Priscian's *PRAEEXERCITAMINA*, for which there is also a separate entry (q.v.), follows (pp. 551–61).

Then there are four brief essays by Emporius (pp. 561–74): *ON ETHOPOEIA* (trans. in Miller); *THE RULE FOR COMMONPLACES; THE RULE FOR DEMONSTRATIVE SUBJECTS;* and *THE RULE FOR DELIBERATIVE.* Next is *VERSES OF THE FAMOUS SCHOLAR, RUFINUS, ON WORD ARRANGEMENT AND METRES IN ORATORY* (pp. 575–84). It is also translated in Miller, as is the final entry in Halm, Bede's *CONCERNING FIGURES AND TROPES* (pp. 607–18). In between Emporius and Bede are an anonymous excerpt (pp. 585–89) with an interesting section on history (pp. 588–89); an even briefer excerpt on the issues by Clodian (pp. 590–92); and two excerpts commenting on Cicero's *De Inventione,* one anonymous (pp. 593–95) and the other by one Grillius (pp. 596–606).

Text: *Rhetores Latini Minores,* ed. Carolus Halm (Leipzig: Teubner, 1863). Select translations: *Readings in Medieval Rhetoric,* ed. Joseph. H. Miller, Michael H. Prosser, and Thomas W. Benson (Bloomington: Indiana Univ. Press, 1973).

NICOLAUS was born in southern Asia Minor probably in 410 or 412 A.D. (although some propose a date as late as 430), studied in Athens, and taught rhetoric in Constantinople in the reign of the emperor Leo (457–474). He published declamations and an art of rhetoric, which are lost, as well as the handbook of *PROGYMNAS-MATA* that survives today.

N. has an introduction in which he defines a *progymnasma* as a preliminary training in each of the parts and types of rhetoric. Certain *progymnasmata* are useful for particular types of rhetoric, of which there are three: forensic, deliberative, and panegyric (Spengel, 3:449). The end of forensic is justice; of deliberative, expediency; and of encomium and censure, the beautiful. N. goes on to identify and define five parts of the political speech—introduction, narration (*diêgêsis*), antithesis, rebuttal (*lysis*), and conclusion (*epilogos*)—and observes that certain *progymnasmata* are useful to each. The purpose of rhetoric itself is not to persuade but to speak persuasively (450–51).

The first *progymnasma* is fable (*mythos*). Fables take their names from certain places or persons; for example, Aesopian, Lydian, Phrygian, and Libyan. Fable belongs to the deliberative type of rhetoric, since it is used to persuade or dissuade (452), and it is part of the narration. Fables are untrue stories that approximate the truth by being persuasive. They are composed from places (a story about elephants must be geographically accurate, 453); proper times (a story about the song of the nightingale must take place in spring or summer, not winter); words (one must attribute guileless speech to sheep, coarse speech to wolves, etc.); and facts (one must not say that a lion was revived by the smell of cheese). The diction of a fable should be simple and straightforward. Fable differs, among other ways, from *chreia* and aphorism (*gnômê*) in that it is based on untruth, *chreia* and aphorism on truth (453–54).

The next training exercise is narrative (*diêgêma*). For the definition of narrative N. refers the reader to Apthonius but says that according to most the difference between narration (*diêgêsis*) and narrative is that the former is more general and the latter more particular. There are three types of narrative: told (*aphêgêmatika*), acted (*dramatika*), and mixed (455). Further, narratives can be fabulous (*mythika*), historical (*historika*), pragmatic (*pragmatika*), and dramatic (*plasmatika*). Narratives have six elements: the person acting, the matter being accomplished, the place, the time, the cause, and the manner. Sometimes the material (*hylê*), a seventh element, is added (455–56). After identifying and giving examples of five stylistic approaches to narrative (457) N. lists five virtues: conciseness (*syntomia*), clarity (*saphêneia*), persuasiveness (*pithanotês*), pleasure (*hêdonê*), and grandeur (*megaloprepeia*). Narrative provides training in all three types of rhetoric (457–58).

Next is chreia (*chreia*), a word or action, well-aimed and concise, referring to some person and being undertaken for the revision of something in life (459). The reference to a person distinguishes it from the aphorism. N. identifies and gives examples of three main types: logical (pertaining to words), practical (pertaining to deeds), and mixed; they may also be witty (459–60). Some reveal how things are, some how they should be. The chreia is especially advantageous for deliberative oratory, since it either encourages toward something useful or discourages from something evil (461). It is divided into eight headings: encomiastic, paraphrastic, probable, true, by example, by comparison, from the judgment of others, and with a brief exhortation (462).

The fourth exercise is aphorism (*gnômê*), which is a general expression conveying advice and exhortation toward something useful in life. The differences between the aphorism and the chreia are: whereas the chreia involves both words and actions, the aphorism only involves words; the aphorism does not refer to a specific person, while the chreia does; the chreia is composed from some surrounding circumstance, the aphorism usually from words; and the aphorism entirely concerns desire for good or flight from evil, but the *chreia* may also be introduced for purposes of wit (463–64). Aphorisms can be true, persuasive, simple, double, without cause, and with cause; some show how things are, others how they should be (464–65). Aphorism offers the same training for the types and parts of rhetoric as the chreia does and is divided into the same eight headings (465–66).

Next is refutation (*anaskeuê*), which is discourse likely to refute something put forth persuasively; its counterpart is confirmation (*kataskeuê*). We may properly refute and then confirm or confirm and then refute (466). Refutation is normally divided into these headings: unpersuasive, powerless, indecent, inexpedient, and disputatious. Further, there are the headings falling under parts that pertain to critical circumstances: place, time, person, or others. N. sets forth for refutation a problem concerning Daphne (466–67). Practice in refutation is particularly useful for judicial oratory, and it will also contribute to all the parts of political oratory except the epilogue (468). The proper tone must be adopted to fit the circumstances (469). Confirmation (*kataskeuê*) is discourse that confirms something put forth persuasively (469). The arrangement, headings, and division are the same as those of refutation (470).

Commonplace (*koinos topos*) follows. N. defines it as amplification of and attack upon what is agreed to be unjust (470). Invective (*psogos*) differs from commonplace in that the latter encourages judges to punish the wrongdoer, but the former involves mere slander and engenders only hatred toward the the particular person attacked (and no particular person is attacked in commonplace, 471). Commonplaces may be simple (e.g., against a thief), or double (e.g., against a thief-murderer). They are appropriate for the epilogue and the proemium (472). The proemium must be aimed not at a definite person but at the type of problem in general (473). After the proemium, the headings of the commonplace are from the contrary; explanation of the case, not in detail, but with exaggeration and intensification; the heading of extent (*periochê*); comparison (474–75); before the case; and the final (*telika*) headings, which are the expedient, just, lawful, practicable, honorable, necessary, and easy (475–76). A final heading is outline (*hypotypôsis*), which involves description of the case. Finally, commonplace provides training in judicial oratory (476–77).

Next is encomium, a detailed praise of a defined person or problem in reference to things agreed to be good. N. says that each of the exercises has been invented to train students in the three types of rhetoric, judicial, deliberative, and panegyric. Since panegyric is encomiastic and is complete in and of itself, the *progymnasma*, encomium, is either part of a speech or a whole speech (477–78). It differs from praise (*epainos*) in that encomium is comprehensive and lengthy, while praise is specific and brief. The end of encomium is the beautiful. Encomium is traditionally divided into things concerning the soul (prudence, justice, temperance, and courage), the body (beauty, strength, stature, and speed), and externals (birth, friends, wealth, etc., 479). But N. prefers his own division, with the headings from class (subdivided into nation, from city, and ancestry), from birth, from upbringing, then deeds and comparisons (480–81).

The ninth *progymnasma* is invective (*psogos*), which has the same headings as encomium, with contrary enthymemes and epicheiremes. Both praise and invective are encomia (482). Then to a reiteration of the difference between commonplace and invective and a lengthy digression on whether the division of rhetoric into three types only is sufficient (482–84). Encomia demand polished and theatrical diction, just as deliberative oratory needs weight and honor, and judicial oratory needs vehemence (485).

N. discusses comparison (*synkrisis*) next, explaining why it is necessary that it be a separate *progymnasma* when there is already suitable practice for it in both commonplace and encomium (485–86). He defines comparison as a side-by-side examination of good or base persons or circumstances by which we attempt to show that both things are equal or that one is superior to the other. It is used either as a part (as with encomia and commonplaces) or as a whole speech (486–87). The division is the same as in encomium, but the headings are doubled, for each side of the comparison (487). Diction should be showy and theatrical, though not without dignity. Comparison provides training for all five parts of the speech (487–88).

The eleventh exercise is characterization (*êthopoiia*), defined as discourse fitting the parties concerned, displaying character (*êthos*) or emotion (*pathos*) or both together. Character refers to behavior in general, emotion to behavior in specific circumstances. Characterizations can be ethical, pathetic, or mixed (489). After discussing the views of others on the distinction between characterization and personification (*prosôpopoiia*), N. says that characterization is divided into three times: past, present, and future. The proper procedure is to have the speaker begin from the present, refer to the past, come back to the present, then go to the future. N.'s example is "What would Peleus say upon hearing of the death of Achilles?" Characterization is useful for all three types of rhetoric and also provides training in the epistolary style (489–91).

N. proceeds to vivid description (*ekphrasis*) and defines it as a narratival composition bringing places, times, persons, festivals, or circumstances distinctly to view (490–92). It differs from narration (*diêgêsis*) in that the former examines things in a general manner, the latter in a particular manner. After a discussion of the particular problems posed by describing statues, portraits, and the like, N. observes that this exercise trains the student especially for the narrative part of a speech and that it is useful for all three types of rhetoric (492–93).

Next is thesis, defined as a problem admitting logical inquiry, without definite persons and all other attendant circumstances (493). Thesis differs from hypothesis in that the former lacks attendant circumstances (e.g., should one marry?), while the latter has them (e.g., should a man with three children, having left his wife who can no longer bear children, marry?). N. decides that thesis is of the deliberative type, but of panegyrical material and division (494–96). Thesis provides training in panegyric and deliberative oratory and in all the parts of the speech (496). N. concludes by saying that some theses refer to physical matters and others to political (497).

The fourteenth and final *progymnasma* is introduction of a law (*nomou eisphora*). Some laws are common (e.g., those concerning the affairs of the city in general), others private (e.g., those concerning contracts between citizens). Some laws provide for rewards, others for punishments. A decree (*psêphisma*) differs from a law in that the former is time-specific, the latter for all time. Introduction of a law is divided by the final headings (*telika*), which are written or unwritten (497–98). Written is from law, unwritten from custom. N. says that introduction of a law chiefly concerns judicial oratory but also has some connection to deliberative and panegyrical. It provides training in all the parts of oratory except narration (498).

Text: *Rhetores Graeci*, ed. Leonardi Spengel (1853–56; rpt. Frankfurt: Minerva, 1966), 3:447–98.

PHILODEMUS was a pupil of Zeno of Sidon, a famous Epicurean philosopher who taught at Athens in the latter part of the second and early part of the first century B.C. He was born in Gadara in Syria around 110 B.C. and lived in Italy from about 75 to his death in approximately 40. Under the patronage of Lucius Calpurnius Piso, P. taught Epicurean philosophy to young Romans. *ON RHETORIC (PERI RHETORIKÊS)* and an earlier, and much shorter *HANDBOOK ON RHETORIC (PERI RHETORIKÊS HYPOMNÊMATIKON)* were written sometime in the middle of the first century. The remains, some of which have been lost and now exist only as copies, were preserved on charred and fragmentary papyri found at Herculaneum in what was perhaps P.'s personal library. Because of the condition of the text, any reconstruction is speculative and imprecise.

ON RHETORIC is written to a certain Gaius. The surviving fragments begin with the latter part of Book 1, where P. discusses the relationships among science (*epistêmê*), art (*technê*), natural ability (*physis*), and training (*askêsis*). The goal of rhetoric is to persuade in a speech. Sophistic rhetoric (*sophistikê rhetorikê*) is an art (Sudhaus 1.1–12 = Suppl. 3–8).

In Book 2 the main topic is whether rhetoric itself is an art. P. discusses the arguments of others for and against and also examines Epicurean views on rhetoric. He then advances his own theories. P. says that sophistic rhetoric is only the art of epideictic oratory. The "sophists," to P., are professional rhetoricians who teach sophistic. They call it rhetoric and claim that it trains students in deliberative and forensic rhetoric and is an art. But P. says that the ability to persuade in deliberative or judicial oratory is the result of talent and practice; rules for it cannot be set down, and so it cannot be called an art. It produces its results regularly and not at random. Sophistic is not an art of politics. Deliberative and forensic are practical forms of rhetoric. An art has certain elementary principles that generally apply and must be learned and practiced and cannot be conjectured. According to Epicurean doctrine sophistic is an art, politics is not (1.13–18; 19–23 = Suppl.11–61; 123–36;136–37 = Suppl.61–62;137–46; 2.65–130).

Book 3 is lost. In its full form Book 4 was a criticism of rhetoric. Only the treatments of style (*lexis* or *phrasis*) and delivery (*hypokrisis*) survive, along with a brief discussion of the orator's sphere of activity. In the context of what constitutes a beautiful style (*kalê lexis*) P. discusses solecism (*to soloikizein*), barbarism (*to barbarizein*), obscurity (*asapheia*) that arises from lack of mastery of the subject, improper use of periods, and the overuse of *hyperbaton*. Style (*phrasis*) has tropes (*tropoi*), figures such as metaphor, allegory, etc.; rhetorical shaping (*schêmata*), periods, *kôla*, *kommata*, and combinations thereof; and formations (*plasmata*), which seem to refer to levels of style, i.e., the plain, middle, grand, and elegant. Allegory is subdivided into the riddle (*ainigma*), proverb (*paroimion*), and irony (*eirôneia*). The sections on rhetorical shaping and stylistic formation are lost. Rhetoric does not teach people to avoid faults of speech, nor does it teach delivery, nor the possible arguments for any given subject. Sophists misuse oratory of praise and censure by praising bad things or by praising and censuring the same person, and so forth. In summary, P. claims that rhetoric is not the mother of the arts and sciences (1.147–225).

Book 5 contrasts the unfortunate rhetor and fortunate philosopher. Philosophers employ strict logic, while rhetoricians use only probabilities and guesswork, which cannot answer moral questions. P. says that rhetors harm many, while philosophers are beloved for assisting people in their troubles. Sophistic style is suited to epideictic oratory and written works but not to deliberative and forensic speech. Lack of rhetoric actually plays better with a jury than forensic training. Rhetoric is not bad per se, but it is often misused. Philosophy, the path to a happy life, is more profitable than epideictic, especially that practiced by the sophists, who are stupid and unreasonable. The art of rhetoric contributes nothing to the happy life. Even if a man is virtuous otherwise, he is thought a scoundrel because he is a rhetor (2.131–67; 1.225–70).

Book 6 attacks schools of philosophy that support the teaching of rhetoric. The extant portion first discusses Nausiphanes, a natural philosopher of the latter part of the fourth century B.C. who was a pupil of Democritus and the teacher of Epicurus. P. objects to his position that a study of natural philosophy is the best training for an orator. P. also attacks Aristotle for supporting rhetoric to the detriment of philosophy, as well as Aristotle's reasons for studying rhetoric and politics. He objects to what are, according to him, three

Aristotelian positions: that rhetoric makes people and governments friendly to you; that it produces a stable government encouraging the study of philosophy; and that current statesmen are inadequate. P. reiterates earlier claims that the study of rhetoric is not compatible with happiness and is generally useless (1.270–325, revised in 2.1–64).

Book 7 attacks the Stoics, Aristotle, and other works on rhetoric and ends with another comparison of rhetoric and philosophy. It repeats many familiar themes. The only use for rhetoric is public, and in public rhetors get in the way. Philosophy is private and leads to happiness away from the bustle of politics (1.325–85).

In the *HANDBOOK ON RHETORIC* P. uses the technique of refuting the comments of others, beginning, apparently, with Diogenes. He says that sophistic rhetoric does not include the study of politics and is not political science. The rhetorical schools do not produce political acumen or train statesmen for practical speaking. Rhetoric is not politics, and the rhetor is neither a statesman nor a public speaker. People hire sophists because they marvel at complicated, elaborate speech and think that they will be successful if they emulate it. But rhetorical training leads students to find that if their speeches are successful they are suspected of misleading the jury, but if the speeches fail they are angry about having paid money for their training. Most who study rhetoric are poor public speakers, and many who do not study it are good ones. Good speakers who have rhetorical training are outnumbered by good speakers without it. The latter have ability, desire, knowledge acquired from study, and a disputatious spirit (2.196–303).

Text: *Volumina Rhetorica,* ed. S. Sudhaus, 2 vols. + suppl. (Leipzig: Teubner, 1892–96). Translation: Harry M. Hubbell, "The Rhetorica of Philodemus," *Transactions of the Connecticut Academy of Arts and Sciences* 23 (1920): 243–382.

PLATO (c. 429–347 B.C.) takes up sophistry and rhetoric in five of his *Dialogues*. The *PROTAGORAS* and *THEAETETUS* provide a full account of the skeptical, relativistic basis of sophistry as philosophy in the context of the specific teachings of Protagoras. *THE SOPHIST* attacks the venality of the teachers and their distinctive teaching, eristic (*antilogikê technê*, 232). Sophists only treat conjectual, apparent wisdom (233) and teach a method of arguing on any side of any position. Like the painter, then, they only imitate true knowledge, creating images, fantasies, or resemblances of the truth (239–40). Finally they are hypocritical dissemblers, either publicly as popular orators or privately in disputation, where their specialty is getting their opponents to contradict themselves (268).

In the *GORGIAS* P. imagines a lengthy exchange between Socrates and the famous visiting rhetorician, Gorgias (whose manner is parodied in Agathon's speech in the *Symposium*). As is customary in such exchanges, Socrates in effect cross-examines Gorgias, who identifies himself as a rhetorician and teacher of rhetoric (449) and claims that rhetoric is the creator of persuasion (*peithous dêmiourgos*, 452–53). Socrates initially responds by observing that rhetoric only persuades by creating belief, not knowledge, about right and wrong (455). The implications of Gorgias's triumphant rejoinder, that rhetoric works, that it succeeds (456–57), become the framework for the rest of the dialogue, a discussion marked by Gorgias's inability to counter the attacks and radical assertions made by Socrates.

To the Socratic objection that rhetoricians do not need to know anything but must only appear knowledgeable, Gorgias counters that the orator must be instructed in many other disciplines and must be a good man (460)—paradoxically, since he concedes that the powers of rhetoric may be misused and abused (457). Socrates then develops an elaborate parallelism that attacks rhetoric by analogy (463–65). Rhetoric, he says, is not an art (*technê*) but only an experience or knack that fakes reality. In society both man's soul and his body are attended to. Exercise and medicine (in the broadest sense, including diet) help the body; legislation and the judicial processes help the soul. There are four counterfeit perversions of each of these four aids to humanity. On the body's side, dressing to advantage, putting on makeup, etc. merely fake the results of exercise, while the preparation of food to make it taste good is merely a sham of a good, healthful regimen, which should be based not on taste but true nutritional value. On the soul's side, sophistry is sham legislation, and rhetoric is pseudo-justice [here we see the origins of judicial rhetoric's domination of rhetorical theory in antiquity].

P. does not allow Gorgias or any of the other interlocutors in this dialogue to give the obvious answer to this attack, that it is predicated on false dichotomies. No one in the dialogue notes that Socrates has turned eristic against its practitioners by using one of the basic argumentative tools of the sophists, the dilemma, in which an opponent is forced to accept one of two equally unacceptable conclusions. Food is not either tasteless and healthful or tasteful and of no value. One can exercise regularly, be extremely healthy, *and* wear beautiful clothes and makeup. Similarly, one is not either a persuasive counterfeiter of real knowledge or an unpersuasive purveyor of the truth. The opposite of both is clearly possible. One can be the essence of integrity and knowledge *and* be a persuasive speaker, and lies can be proposed in the most unpersuasive ways imaginable.

The same kind of false dichotomy underlies Socrates' radical teaching that it is better to suffer evil unjustly than to be unjust and avoid punishment. No one in the dialogue is allowed to point out that it is still better, and possible, to be just and not suffer wrongly. The perverse notion that success is rhetorical and bad and that virtue should customarily take its beatings without defending itself is never countered. Socrates concludes with unusually harsh views: that the only acceptable use of rhetoric is in legal prosecution (480 and 504); that rhetoric, flute playing, dithyrambic poetry, and tragedy all aim only at pleasure and gratification and are, therefore, unacceptable flattery (501–02); and that, given a choice, even sophistry is preferable to rhetoric (520).

This apparent Socratic severity is considerably abated in the other dialogue that considers rhetoric, the *PHAEDRUS*. Here Socrates is asked to critique a clever speech by Lysias that paradoxically argues that the nonlover makes a better lover than one truly in love (230c–34c). Socrates reveals his own deep familiarity with rhetoric when he criticizes the speech for being repetitive and using trite commonplaces, while commenting on the concepts of invention and arrangement (235–36). Ultimately Socrates rejects the speech's trivialization of the subject matter and delivers his own replacement speech, praising the divinity of eros (237a–41d). He goes on to rebuke himself for including criticism of love and produces a second oration in praise of love (244–57b). The discussion then returns to the written compositions of rhetoricians and politicians (258). Socrates objects to the effects of writing—for, among other things, ruining the memory—and rejects the current practices of rhetoric for his own practice of dialectic, which seeks the truth. He closes with an appeal for a higher rhetoric combined with dialectic that will be committed to persuading people of the truth and predicts that Isocrates, who writes speeches for others and himself, will bring rhetoric to that higher plane.

Neither the *PHAEDRUS* nor, especially, the *GORGIAS* can be understood without reference to basic Platonic interests and assumptions. P. is deeply suspicious of the influence on human beings of the flesh, the material world, and the constraints of everyday life. He believes that these are less true and less real than the immaterial worlds of the soul and of ideas and that the best life is led by freeing oneself from the selfish, flesh-centered pursuit of success in this materially constrained world. Such an attitude is intrinsically and necessarily inimical to rhetoric, which is designed to provide individual success in the practices of the everyday, material world—a world of opinion, plausibilities, and probabilities. And this success gratifies the individual ego. A considerable part of the Socratic hostility to rhetoric in the *GORGIAS* stems from the fact that rhetoric, fundamentally, is a means of pleasing the self. For Socrates such pleasure is meretricious and essentially sham or false, like doctoring up food or cosmetically doctoring up one's appearance. And so, as many twentieth-century scholars have observed, the obvious logical fallacies and superficial absurdities of the stern Socratic position in the *GORGIAS* are probably indicators of a desire to call the readers's attention in the most dramatic way to the need for transcending the normal goals of personal aggrandizement, for which—as Callicles and Polus, two other interlocutors in the dialogue, are made to point out so emphatically—rhetoric is probably the best tool. Socrates wants human beings to exercise another and different tool, the disinterested dialectic that aims to arrive at truth.

Texts and translations: Plato, *Euthyphro, Apology, Crito, Phaedrus,* trans. H. N. Fowler (Cambridge, Mass.: Harvard Univ. Press, 1914); *Laches, Protagoras, Meno, Euthydemus,* trans. W. R. M. Lamb (Cambridge, Mass.: Harvard Univ. Press, 1924); *Lysis, Symposium, Gorgias,* trans. H. N. Fowler (Cambridge, Mass.: Harvard Univ. Press, 1925); *Theaetetus, Sophist,* trans. H. N. Fowler (Cambridge, Mass.: Harvard Univ. Press, 1921).

PRISCIAN (c. 500 A.D.) was an influential grammarian. His massive *Institutiones grammaticae* is the most comprehensive of all the extant Latin grammars and was a standard authority in Western Europe down into the Renaissance. His free adaptation, with the Latin title *PRAEEXERCITAMINA,* of the Greek text of Hermogenes' *Progymnasmata* provided the only Latin text of a separate treatise on this subject in Western Europe until the texts of Aphthonius and Hermogenes were translated and printed during the Renaissance. Consequently, this little treatise is of the greatest importance for the knowledge and transmission of the *progymnasmata* throughout the Middle Ages and early Renaissance. Twelve exercises are treated separately, with no introduction or conclusion: story or fable (*fabula*); narrative (*narratio*); application (*usus*); aphorism (*sententia*); refutation (*refutatio*); commonplace (*locus communis*); praise (*laus*); comparison (*comparatio*); address (*allocutio*); description (*descriptio*); thesis (*positio*); and proposing a law (*legis latio*). Each exercise is defined and then discussed with interspersed examples.

Fable, P. says, is "a fictitious speaking with a verisimilar arrangement exhibiting an image of the truth" (1). He identifies important writers of fables and three kinds from the names of their authors (Cyprian, Libyan, and Sybaritic) but subsumes all under the name of Aesop. P. explains that fables say things about real life by analogy, e.g., about beauty by reference to the peacock, about cunning by reference to a little fox, etc. Fables can range from brief analagous references all the way to well-developed story-analogies that may or may not rely on dialogue. An example about apes is given. P. recommends an informal style and the avoidance of circumlocutions. The moral (*epimythion* in Greek or *affabulatio* in Latin) is placed at the beginning or, more normally, at the end of the fable (1–4).

Narrative may be fabulous (*fabularis*), fictitious (*fictilis*), historical (*historica*), or legal (*civilis*). Having already discussed fabulous narration, P. points out that the fictitious is used in tragedies and comedies [interesting, since another common use of the term *fabula* in Latin grammatical and rhetorical tradition is for the plot in dramatic plays], historical to tell about things that really happened, and legal for orators in presenting cases (5). P. then discusses and exemplifies various verbal modes of presenting the story of Medea: direct statement (best for history); oblique statement (best for rhetorical contests); reproachful statement (best for proving or possibly for fictitious narrating); statement without connectives, i.e., using asyndeton (best for perorations); and comparative statement (6-7).

Application, P. says, is called *chreia* in Greek and succinctly matches words or deeds to give some lesson about people or situations—"Plato said that the muses live in the souls of geniuses" (8). Application involves words alone, narrative of actions alone, or a mixture of both. It is distinguished from the memoir (*commemoratio*) by its relative brevity and from the aphorism in several respects. First, aphorism is always directly put, while application may involve questions and answers. Application is also usually found in action, while aphorism is always verbal. Finally, application always involves a specific person [as Plato, above], while aphorism does not. The kinds of application in antiquity are the direct (*indicativus*) and the questioning (*interrogativus*) [Halm accepts an emendation adding a third, *percontativus*, which is translated "argumentative" in Miller—but *percontativus* has essentially the same meaning as *interrogativus*, i.e., "interrogating" or "investigating"]. P. recommends and gives examples of the following arrangements: 1) praise of the person on whom the application is based, 2) exposition of the application itself, and 3) a fuller elaboration of what it means (9–10).

Aphorisms are general pronouncements that 1) urge us to do something, 2) urge us not to do something, or 3) explain the nature of something (11). They are true or like true, simple or complex, or hyperbolic. They work just like the application. First praise the sources of the aphorism, then develop it, and finally elaborate on it (12–14).

Refutation disproves a proposition, while confirmation adduces additional proofs (15). You may work from uncertainty, incredibility, impossibility, failure to follow logically, impropriety, and inconvenience.

Commonplace merely amplifies something already proven or assumed to be true and so emphasizes one's point and accomplishes conviction (16). P. offers the example of someone who perpetrates some sacrilegious act, noting that the reason we call this process of amplification commonplace is that it will apply to any and all perpetrators of sacrilege. P. recommends the following process of arrangement: review the opposite of the act in question; go over the act itself; follow with a comparison and an aphorism; speculate about the background of the perpetrator; and close with an appeal to the emotions of the audience by vividly describing (*demonstratio*) in all its gory details exactly what the perpetrator did (16–19).

Praise is general (e.g., of man) or particular (of Socrates). Animals, plants, ideas, anything can be praised; the opposite is blame. Praise and blame are similar to commonplace [since they essentially magnify or amplify points]. The difference is in the purpose. Commonplace has a goal of achieving some result [conviction about the sacrilegious act, etc.], while praise has no specific goal at all other than to praise (20–21). P. outlines the topoi to be taken up in the praise of humans, animals, plants, and places (21–24).

Comparison brings together things like, unlike, greater to lesser, or lesser to greater (25). P. briefly follows the topoi he has just developed for praise to illustrate like comparisons (25–26).

Address creates a fictitious imitation of the speech of characters and traits, e.g., composing what Andromache might have said over dead Hector (27). This becomes personification (*conformatio*), Greek *prosôpopoiia*, when speech is given contrary to nature. Greek *eidôlopoiia* is giving speech to the dead. Address is either specific, by a particular character (e.g., Andromache), or generic and typical (any grieving widow). Simple address is interior monologue. Double address imagines an audience. It is of the greatest importance to maintain the propriety of the speech to the character, time, situation, circumstances, etc. (28).

Description collects and vividly presents people, events, times, situations, places, etc. (29). P. reviews some details (29–30). He then emphasizes the most important traits of description: directness and immediacy (*planities et praesentia*). Finally, the description should match or suit what is described (30).

Thesis treats some general question, e.g., whether marriage is good or not (31). Should the focus change to the specific, e.g., to a particular person and situation (e.g., whether so-and-so should marry), the thesis becomes a supposition or hypothetical issue more suitable for disputation. Theses are either civil (questions of public good, etc.) or private (i.e., mainly philosophical, 32). Some are simple (one issue); others are double (two issues related to each other). The topoi of theses indicate sections or boundaries of consideration: the just, the useful, the possible, and the suitable (33).

Proposing a law is either actual or a rhetorical exercise (34). Proposed laws can be argued on the grounds of obviousness, legality, justice, utility, possibility, and suitability (34).

Text: *Grammatici Latini,* ed.Heinrich Keil, 8 vols. (1857–70; rpt. George Olms, 1961), 3:430–40. Translation: *Readings in Medieval Rhetoric,* ed. Joseph M. Miller, Michael H. Prosser, and Thomas W. Benson (Bloomington: Indiana Univ. Press, 1973), 52–68.

QUINTILIAN (first century A.D.) was born in Spain sometime in the 30s and died before 100. He received the best grammatical and rhetorical training and achieved great success as a practitioner and teacher of rhetoric. Brought to Rome in 68, he established a famous school, similar to that of Isocrates centuries before in Greece. His *INSTITUTIO ORATORIA* is the longest and most comprehensive work on rhetoric from classical antiquity.

The preface (*Proemium*) to Book 1 begins by asserting that the complete orator must be a good man (*vir bonus,* Pr. 9). He should also be a true philosopher (Pr. 18). Q. then reviews the outline of his work: Book 1 on education prior to rhetorical training; Book 2 on the definition of rhetoric and basic rhetorical education; Books 3–7 on invention (*inventio*), under which he includes arrangement (*dispositio*); Books 8–11 on style (*elocutio*), under which are included memory (*memoria*) and delivery (*pronuntiatio*); and Book 12 on the resulting orator (Pr. 21–22). He closes with the observation that it is a waste of time to educate students with no talent (Pr. 26).

The child's education begins with the influence of what and whom he first hears. Consequently, it is important to have a nurse who speaks Latin correctly (1.1.4–5), and it is equally desirable to have well-educated and well-spoken parents (1.6). Since the student will pick up correct Latin from his environment, linguistic education should begin with Greek, which is the basis of Latin learning anyway (1.12 and 4.1). Q. recommends encouraging children to learn their alphabet by playing with block letters made from ivory (1.26). That exercise leads to practice in writing, which is of the utmost importance (1.28). Q again insists that only a good man can be a good orator (1.2.3) and, consequently, emphasizes the importance of the moral education of children, while recommending public, group education as opposed to private education at home (2.4–21). Group education will allow the instructor to appeal to students' ambition in competing with each other (2.22–23). The first job of the teacher is to assess each child's talents and character. Memory is the most important natural skill (1.3.1), but in general, children with precocious intellects do not turn out well (3.3). Q. opposes corporal punishment in education (3.13–14). He then reviews in detail the kind of reading to be done in grammatical education (1.4). Then he turns to the basic lessons about style (1.5).

There are three virtues of speech (*oratio*): correctness (*emendata*), lucidity (*dilucida*), and ornateness (*ornata*, 1.5.1). Q. gives a detailed review of correct and incorrect usage (5.2–70), ending with brief remarks about the literal (*propria*) and figurative or metaphorical (*translata*) uses of words (5.71–72). He then turns to language (*sermo*) for speaking and writing (1.6); a long discussion of etymology (1.6.28–38) includes treatment of phony or pseudo etymologies (6.36–38). Archaic words add majesty but must be used sparingly (6.39–41). This section concludes with a discussion of correct usage (6.43–45), which Q. defines as the usage agreed on by educated men in actual speaking (6.45). Orthography is the subject of the next section(1.7), and comments on reading (*lectio*) and interpretation (*enarratio*) follow (1.8–9), as well as a discussion of what students should read: fables (*fabellae*, 1.9. 2), aphorisms (*sententiae*, 9.3), and statements of moral application (*chriae*, 9.4–6). Other areas of education necessary before going to technical instruction in rhetoric are music (10.9–33), geometry (10.34–49), comic acting for delivery (1.11.1–14), and gymnastics (11.15–19). The concluding section discusses children's learning capabilities (1.12).

Book 2 begins with the question of the boundaries between grammar and rhetoric and with Q.'s assertion that teachers of rhetoric (*rhetores*) and teachers of literature (*grammatici*) need to better define and stick to their proper provinces of education (2.1). The next two sections (2.2 and 3) are also introductory. The first examines the makeup of classes, with a particular focus on separating students by ages so as not to expose younger students to older ones, apparently in the context of sexual misbehavior (2.2.14–15). The second takes up the question of how soon students should be exposed to the best possible teachers (2.3). Q. then reviews the first things to teach the student of rhetoric, i.e., the early exercises (2.4; he does not use the term, *progymnasmata*). Instruction should start with writing prose narratives; fables (*fabulae*), fiction (*argumentum*), and history (*historia*) are mentioned (2.4.2). Historical narration provides the best practice (4.2–18). Next, students should practice confirming or refuting the credibility of historical events (4.18–19); then praising famous men and denouncing evil men (4.20–21). Commonplaces (*communes loci*) are general attacks on vices or types of viciousness and may praise or defend, as well (4.23). Theses compare and contrast and treat such questions as whether town life or country life is better, whether being a lawyer or a soldier is better, etc. (4.24–25). Then students can examine motives—these are a kind of *chria* (4.26). Finally, there is practice in praising or denouncing laws (4.33–40). In addition to written exercises, early education should involve close analyses and critiques of historical writing and speeches (2.5), good and bad (2.5.10). Q. briefly gives his opinion on how heavily to use topoi in instruction (2.6). Students should not memorize their own compositions (2.7). Teachers should adapt techniques to the strengths and weaknesses of their students (2.8), who, in turn, should regard their teachers as their parents (2.9). At this point students should begin practice declamations (*declamationes*) on deliberative and forensic subjects (2.10). Q. says that most instructors of rhetoric mistakenly begin here (2.11), although he concedes that students lacking the basic training that he advocates are usually more forceful speakers (2.12.1). Teaching students by reductive, slavish reliance on rules [i.e., excessive use of topical instruction] should be avoided; flexibility and adaptability are more important (2.12–13). It is best to treat rhetoric under three heads: the art, the artist, and the work (2.14.5). Q. surveys previous definitions of rhetoric (2.15) and defines it himself as the science of the good man speaking well (2.15.33–34). Rhetoric is useful (2.16). Then to the question of whether rhetoric is an art (2.17). After reviewing earlier opinions, Q. decides that the art of rhetoric is realized in action, not in the product (2.17.25–26), and concludes this section with his own proof that it is an art (17.41–43). Some arts are theoretical, others practical, and still others productive (2.18.1–2). The art of rhetoric is mainly concerned with action and, hence, is practical, even though when speeches are written down, they appear to be a productive art (18.2–5). On the question of the relative significance of nature (*natura*) or instruction (*doctrina*) in the creation of an orator (2.19), the average orator owes more to nature, the complete one more to training (19.2). There are two kinds of speech (*oratio*): continuous (*perpetua*), i.e., rhetorical, and concise (*concisa*), i.e., dialectical; Zeno compared the latter to the closed fist and the former to the open hand (2.20.7). The matter (*materia*) of rhetoric is everything that can be the subject of a speech (2.21.4).

Book 3 opens with a review of the early rhetorical theorists (3.1.8–21). Q. claims not to be an adherent of any particular school (1.22). After discussing the origins of rhetoric (3.2), he turns to its parts: invention, arrangement, style, memory, and delivery (*inventio, dispositio, elocutio, memoria, pronuntiatio*, 3.3). There are three kinds of oratory: epideictic or demonstrative (*demonstrativum*), deliberative (*deliberativum*), and judicial (*iudiciale*, 3.4), with three kinds of audiences having three different expectations: to be pleased, receive advice, and make a judgment (3.4.6). Every speech has matter and words (*res* and *verba*), and the faculty of speaking is achieved by nature (*natura*), art (*ars*), and practice (*exercitatio*, 3.5.1). The orator ought to do three things: teach, i.e., communicate information (*docere*), move (*movere*), and delight (*delectare*, 5.2). Indefinite and definite questions (*quaestiones infinitae et finitae*), specific questions, and various kinds of causes are reviewed (5.5–18). A long discussion of the issues (*status*) follows, including their relationship to questions and causes (3.6). There is no agreement on the precise number of them (3.6.22). Aristotle's logical categories are included (6.23–28). There are three kinds of causes (6.104). The first concerns praise and blame; Q. reviews the topoi for praising gods, men, cities, public works, etc. (3.7). Deliberative causes are covered next (3.8). They should not be limited (as some authorities assert) to questions of expediency (*utilitas*); Q. prefers Cicero's view that the primary concern in deliberative rhetoric is what is honorable (*dignitas*, 3.8.1). Deliberative speeches do not always need an introduction (8.6); what carries the greatest weight in such speeches is the authority of the speaker himself (8.12)—*êthos* thus becomes inartificial, i.e., not, as in Aristotle and most subsequent authorities, an argument or proof constructed by the art of rhetoric (see 6.2.18). The three areas of study here are the subject being discussed, the audience being advised, and the speaker giving the advice (8.15–16). Q. discusses the exercise of impersonation (*prosopopoeia*) on deliberative themes and considers it very difficult (8.49–55). The judicial kind of speech is considered next (3.9). It has five parts (3.9.1): introduction (*proemium*), statement of facts (*narratio*), proof (*probatio*), refutation (*refutatio*), and conclusion (*peroratio*). Partition (*partitio*) is properly an aspect of arrangement and so not a part of a whole speech (as some authorities say) but part of each individual question taken up (9.2–3).

Every cause is either simple, with one point of controversy, or complex, with more than one (3.10.1–2). A third kind involves comparison (10.3). After these points are determined in a judicial controversy, we need to consider the following (3.11): what the question (*quaestio*) is, the rationale for our case (*ratio*), the judgment (*iudicatio*), and the central point or foundation of the case (*continens* or *firmamentum*).

Book 4 continues with an explanation of the order of judicial causes (Pr.6). The introduction's only purpose (4.1.1–5) is to prepare the audience to be well-disposed toward the speaker (the artificial part of *êthos*), to pay attention to what he says, and to be teachable (*dociles*). Q. rejects the division by some of the introduction into two parts (1.42) and points out that what the particular needs will be for a particular audience and a particular cause cannot be taught ahead of time (1.43–44); improvisation itself appears better anyway to the audience (1.54). He then discusses the transition to the statement of facts (*narratio*, 1.78–79), which is considered next (4.2). Length and complexity will vary, and occasionally the statement of facts can be left out (4.2.9). The purpose of it is not merely to inform the judge but also to influence him on our behalf (2.21), i.e., to put our own spin on the facts of the case and scatter anticipations here and there of our subsequent proof (2.50–51). Q. does not agree that the order of the statement of facts should always follow the actual order of the events narrated (2.83). Nor are emotional appeals (pathetic proofs) to be avoided (as some urge)—if opportunities arise, use them (2.111). The proof (*confirmatio)* follows (4.3–5.12). Q. rejects the theory of digression between the statement of facts and the proof (3.1–3). First in the proof is the proposition (*propositio*, 4.4), which states the main question and the essential arguments (Greek *epicheirêmata*). The partition (*partitio*) is the ordering and listing of propositions, ours and our adversaries', as appropriate (4.5.1).

Book 5 follows Aristotle's division of proofs into the artificial and inartificial (5.1). Inartificial proofs are legal precedents (5.2); hearsay (5.3); results extracted by torture (5.4); the evidence of documents (5.5); oaths (5.6); and evidence, written or spoken, provided by witnesses (5.7). Artificial proofs are designed by the orator's art to create conviction (*fides*), are inevitably about things or people, and are always either necessary, credible, or not impossible (5.8).

Every artificial proof (*probatio*) consists of signs (*signa*, 5.9), artificial because they must be construed or interpreted; arguments (*argumenta*, 5.10); and examples (*exempla*, 5.11). Arguments include what the Greeks identify as *enthymêmata, epicheirêmata,* and *apodeixeis*—which mean basically the same thing (5.10.1). Q. discusses disagreements over precisely what these terms refer to (10.1–8). Latin *probatio* (proof) best translates Greek *pistis* (10.8). Q. then turns to the places where arguments are found, the topoi (10.20). He reviews arguments from people (10.23–31) and things (10.32–99), including definition (10.54–64), division (10.65–72), similarities (10.73–94), and hypothetical arguments (10.95–99). Examples may be drawn from history (5.11.15), from fictitious literature (11.16), from fables (11.19–20), or from proverbs which amount to brief fables (11.21). The comparison or simile (*similitudo*) works like the example (11.22–35). External authorities, i.e. commonly held views, as, for example, expressed in aphorisms, can also be used (11.36–42). Q. next takes up the ordering of proofs (5.12). The best arguments should be treated individually, while the weaker ones may be lumped together (5.12.4). The particulars of each case will show us whether to put our strongest argument first or last [implying that the order of treatment will be suggested by the content itself, i.e., that an intrinsic relationship exists between form and content]. The only firm rule is never to go in descending order from strongest to weakest (12.14). The popular kind of topical instruction that tries to anticipate every circumstance and situation is unnecessary and actually impossible (12.15–16). The refutation (*refutatio,* 5.13) must rebut our opponent's proofs (5.13.1) and must not simply ignore even what may seem indefensible (13.9). The opponent's weak arguments should be rebutted together, the good ones individually (13.11–14), but every single thing our opponent says should not be attacked point by point (13.37). Use ad hominem arguments where appropriate and workable (13.39). Do not over elaborate, work your points to death, or protest too much (13.51). Q. ends on the use of proofs in framing conclusions (13.60) before turning to the enthymeme and epicheireme (5.14). Enthymeme is sometimes used to refer to an incomplete syllogism (5.14.2). Epicheireme has three parts: major and minor premise (first and second *confirmatio*) and conclusion (14.5–7) and so is really just like a syllogism, except it treats credible [i.e., probable], not true statements (14.14). Some call the enthymeme a rhetorical syllogism, because it conveys its proof without stating it explicitly (14.24). Epicheiremes and enthymemes should be used sparingly (14.27).

Book 6 opens with a lament for the death of Q.'s son (subsequent to the death of his wife) and then goes to the conclusion (*peroratio*) of a speech. There are two kinds; one recapitulates, and the other appeals to the emotions (6.1). Q. reviews the topoi for arousing the judge's emotions by the prosecution (6.1.9–20) and for the defence's muting them, including impersonation (*prosopopoeia*) and even actions (1.21–35). The peroration is so important that it demands all the orator's powers (1.51–52). It is, in fact, the most important part of a judicial cause (6.2.1). Emotional power sways the court and is indeed the life and soul of rhetorical work (2.4–7). Q. claims to treat the conclusion the traditional way, with two species: emotion (*adfectus* for Greek *pathos*) and moral character (Greek *êthos* has no real Latin equivalent, but *mores,* Q. explains, is customarily used). The former is more violent, and the latter calmer (2.8–17). To be effective, *êthos* demands that the speaker actually be of good character (2.18). Pathos enables the speaker to make the facts seem worse than they are and hence is a crucial kind of amplification (2.20–24). The best way to stir up emotions in others is to have them yourself. The speaker should vividly imagine the causes of them and be able to pass that vivid representation on to the court (2.25–31). That results in what the Greeks call *enargeia*—a vivid re-creation of the scene (2.32–36). Q. now turns to the rhetorical problem of the defense in dispelling these strong emotions that may have been aroused in the judge by the prosecution (6.3). Inducing laughter is the best method. Q. refers to the publication (perhaps by Tiro) of three books of jests by Cicero, who was noted for his wit (6.3.3–6), and gives an extensive review of humor and its bases. There should be no off-color jokes or obscenities (3.29). Brevity is praised (3.45). Most effective humor is light and easy to understand (3.93). Q. then considers the disputation or debate (*altercatio*), which involves brief arguments pro and con (6.4), and concludes with a brief review of judgment (*iudicium,* 6.5).

Book 7 takes up arrangement (*dispositio*). Q. reviews his definitions of division of things into individual entities (*divisio*), separation of entities into parts (*partitio*), the proper organization into sequential coherence (*ordo*), and the distribution of things and parts according to the particular demands of the case (*dispositio*, 7.1.1-3). He then uses the issues (*status* or *constitutiones*) as the bases for arranging arguments with reference to both *ordo* and *dispositio*. This long discussion is filled with examples. First is conjecture, which treats the past and involves people, causes, and intentions (*consilia*)—i.e., questions of who, why, and the motivation (7.2). Next is definition—i.e., what category or term is to be applied to the subject of the dispute (7.3). The order (*ordo*) of treatment here is invariable: first find out what a thing is and then whether it is the subject of the litigation (7.3.19). Next is quality (*qualitas*)—i.e., what kind of thing is involved (7.4). The best defense is to argue that the thing done is actually virtuous (*honestum*, 4.4). If the quality of the act cannot be defended, either plead ignorance (4.14) or ask for mercy (4.17-18). Quantity (*quantitas*) should be included under quality (4.41). Q. then takes up explicitly legal aspects (7.5), which have to do with the letter and spirit of laws, their meaning (7.6), and contradictory laws (7.7). The syllogism is a deductive tool to draw conclusions from the literal sense of laws (7.8). Questions of ambiguity can come anywhere (7.9). Q. concludes with a general review of the issues and their organization (7.10).

The preface to Book 8 summarizes what has been covered so far (Pr. 6-12), and then begins on style (Greek *phrasis*, Latin *elocutio*), which is the most importat aspect of rhetoric, because it demands the most assistance from the rules of art (Pr.16). At the same time style is inherently associated with content, and the best stylistic devices will be suggested naturally by the subject (Pr.21-22), words having been invented to express things (Pr.32). Style involves either individual words or words in combination (8.1.1). Single words should be in correct Latin, clear, ornate, and create the desired effect. Words in combination should be correct, properly put together, and figured. Clarity (*perspicuitas*, 8.2) involves propriety of reference, avoids obscurity (8.2.12) and ambiguity (2.16), and is essential (2.22). Ornament (*ornatus*, 8.3) must be virile, bold, chaste, and not effeminate (8.3.6). True beauty and utility always go together (3.11). There are three categories of invididual words: words used in their ordinary, proper sense (3.24-30); newly invented words (3.30-37); and words used metaphorically (3.38–39), which is proper only to words in combination. Words in combination must avoid these faults: Greek *kakemphaton*, the possibility of inadvertent double entendre (3.44–47); *tapeinôsis*, indecency or meanness (3.48–49); *elleipsis*, inadequacy to express what we mean (3.50–51); *homoeideia*, sameness (3.52–55); *cacozelon*, wrong affectation (3.56–58); *anoikonomêton*, wrong arrangement; *aschêmatiston*, wrong use of figuring; *kakosyntheton*, wrong putting together of words; and *sardismos*, mixing of dialects (3.59–60). The process involves three stages: clearly imagine what you want to say, express it accurately and adequately, and then add brilliance and lustre (3.61). Consequently, vivid representation (*enargeia*) is an accomplishment of style (3.61–71). So are similes (3.72–82), which should avoid obscurity in reference (3.73). Emphasis either means more than it says or something it does not say (3.83–86). Other necessary characteristics are Greek *apheleia*, chaste beauty; Latin *copia*, copiousness; and *vis*, force. Force is subdivided into Greek *deinôsis*, sublimity; *phantasia*, imagination; *exergasia*, finish; *epexergasia*, intensity; and *energeia*, vigor (3.87–89). Bitterness and pungency may also be of use (89). Amplification and minimization (8.4) stylistically control meaning by either exaggerating or minimizing the meaning and hence emphasize our points. There are four kinds: incremental, which rises to a climax (8.4.3–9); comparison, which rises from the lesser to a greater (4.9–14); suggested inference (*ratiocinatio*, 4.15–26); and repetition or accumulation (*congeries*, 4.26–27). Minimization works the same four ways (4.28). Hyperbole will be treated later under tropes (4.29). Now to the wise saying or expression, aphorism (*sententia* or Greek *gnômê*, 8.5). Sometimes the aphorism is part of an enthymeme or the major premise of an epicheireme (5.4). Sometimes the enthymeme is purely ornamental (5.10). *Noema* is any implied conception (5.12). In tropes (8.6) the proper or ordinary meanings of words are changed to other meanings (8.6.1). The commonest trope is the Greek *metaphora* (Latin *translatio*, 6.4–18). A continuous series becomes allegorical or riddling (6.14). Metaphors may be far-fetched (6.17). Then come synecdoche (6.19–22), metonymy or hypallage (6.23–28), antonomasia or substitution for a name (6.29–30), and onomatopoeia (6.32–33), which does not now involve new creations. [The text becomes garbled.] Catechresis (Latin *abusio*) uses a term nearest to something for which no term exists (6.34–36). Finally to metalepsis (Latin *transumptio*), the rarely used transition from one trope to another (6.37–38). The remaining tropes do not change meaning but merely enhance and adorn speech (6.40). Epithet (*epitheton*) is an example (6.40–43). Allegory (Latin *inversio*) may involve a series of metaphors (6.44–45) or no metaphors at all as in pastoral, biographical allegory (6.46–47). Mixed allegory mixes metaphorical and literal references (6.48–50). Allusions, "unexplained examples," are allegorical (6.52). If too obscure, allegory becomes riddling (6.52–53). Another kind of allegory is ironic, called *illusio* (6.54–55); allegory may also involve mockery or taunts (6.56–57), sarcasm, wit, contradiction, and proverbs (6.58). Then the Greeks add disguised mockery (*mykterismos*, 6.59). Next are periphrasis or circumlocution (6.59–61), hyperbaton, the transposition of words (anastrophe, when the transposition involves just two words, 6.62–66), and hyperbole (6.67–76).

Book 9 treats figures (*figurae*, Greek *schêmata*), which involve any reshaping of speech out of the ordinary or obvious (9.1.4). A figure is any artistic new form of speaking (1.14). There are two modes. In one the expression (*sententia*) itself is reshaped (1.10). In the other, the special sense of reshaping, we have a positional change in sense or speech (1.11). It is generally agreed that there are two parts: figures of expression (*sententia*) or thought (Greek *dianoia*) and figures of words (*verba*) or speech (Greek *lexis*, 1.16–17). Q. quotes at length from Cicero on figures of thought (1.26–45). He begins his own discussion of these figures (9.2) with reshapings of questions (9.2.6–16). Then come suggestion (*suggestio*) or anticipation (Greek *prolêpsis*, 2.16–20); hesitation (*dubitatio*, 2.19–20); communication (*communicatio*, 2.20–22); suspension (*sustentatio*, 2.22–23); surprise (*inopinatus*, Greek *paradoxos*, 2.23–24); concession (*permissio*, 2.25); feigning (*simulatio*, 2.26); exclamation (*exclamatio*, 2.27–28); impersonation (*fictio personae*, Greek *prosôpopoiia*, 2.29–37; apostrophe (*aversus*, 2.38–39); vivid representation (*evidentia*, 2.40–44); sustained and other forms of irony (2.44–50), and figures related to irony (2.51–53); interruption (*reticentia*, *obticentia*, or *interruptio*, Greek *aposiôpêsis*, 2.54–57); imitation of other people's traits (*imitatio morum alienorum*, Greek *êthopoiia* or *mimêsis*, 2.58–63); emphasis, involving something latent (2.64); and indirection or unambiguous ambiguity (*suspicio*, 2.65–99), necessary when it is unsafe to speak openly, when speaking plainly involves indecency, or just for the sake of adding elegance to our speaking. Q. concludes with a brief review of additional categories of figures from other authorities—Cicero, Rutilius, Celsus, etc. (2.102–07). There are two kinds of figures of speech (*figurae verborum*, 9.3): one involves the way we speak, the other the actual arrangement of words (9.3.2). In this treatment Q. frequently avoids giving the term for a particular figure and occasionally points derisive asides at previous authorities who have minutely classified and given names to these techniques (e.g., 3.25). The first kind of figure involves what amount to deliberate errors or breaks with normal usage (3.2–26), e.g., using the wrong gender, putting a plural where a singular properly belongs, using the comparative for the positive, etc. In the second kind of figure we add, omit, or change the normal order of words (3.27–65), e.g., repetition (*adiectio*), asyndeton (Latin *dissolutio*), polysyndeton, and climax (*gradatio*, Greek *klimax*). Q. adds a third kind of figure, which involves similitude, sameness, or contrast of expressions (3.66–86). In this category are various kinds of puns; similar words, similar or identical endings of clauses (Greek *homoioteleuton*), similar cases (Greek *homoioptôton*), and similar or equal clauses themselves (Greek *isokôlon*); and antithesis. Again Q. reviews other figures identified by other authorities (3.87–99). The final section of this book (9.4) discusses the syntax of rhythmical prose. In general, Q. agrees with Cicero (9.4.1–2) and decides that rhythmic structure (*compositio*) is necessary (4.9). There are basically two kinds of speech: the closely knit and the looser (appropriate to dialogues and letters). The closely knit has three forms: the phrase (Greek *komma*), the clause (Greek *kôlon*), and the complete, rounded sentence (Greek *periodos*). In every rhythmic structure there are three necessary ingredients: order (4.23–33), connection (4.32–44), and number or rhythm (4.45–147). Rhythm is measured by metrical feet (4.52 and 4.79ff), although rhetorical rhythm is not bound, like poetry, to fixed rules (4.56). Rhythm is particularly important in the conclusion of sentences (4.57). Various rhythms are discussed for phrases, clauses, and sentences and for various parts of the speech, particularly the introduction, statement of facts, and conclusion. Continual practice in writing rhythmical prose will enable the orator to improvise rhythms when speaking extemporaneously (4.114). The best judge of rhythm is the ear (4.116). In conclusion Q. notes that rhythm should be appropriate to delivery (4.138).

Book 10 points out that these precepts for speaking are not enough. The oratorical powers must become second nature in what the Greeks call ingrained habit (*hexis*), and this is achieved by practice in writing, reading, and speaking, which finish off the preparation of the orator (10.1.1–7). Vocabulary and expressions will be gained by reading the best writers and orators (1.8). In addition to orators (1.9–26), read poets (1.27–30), historians (1.31–34), and philosophers (1.35–36). Q. reviews Greek authors, beginning with Homer, in these generic categories: epic, pastoral, elegiac, iambic, lyric, comedy, tragedy, history, oratory, and philosophy (1.46–84). Then to Roman writers of epic, elegiac, satire, iambic, lyric, tragedy, comedy, history, oratory, and philosophy (1.85–131). In the last category, the style of Seneca is praised but also extensively criticized for epigrammatic brevity and other vices (1.125–31). Q. next turns to the imitation of authors and the use of models as a means of training (10.2), and then to writing (10.3), which is the foundation of all eloquence (3.3). Practice writing as much as possible. The importance of prewriting is emphasized (3.5 and 18). Q. opposes dictation and the popular use of scribal secretaries (3.19–22). Correction and revision (10.4) follow, and then exercises in translation and paraphrase (10.5). Prethinking, the mental process (*cogitatio*) of figuring out what we are going to say and in what order (10.6), stands between writing and extemporaneous speaking (6.1). With cultivation this practice will produce results equal to memorization of a carefully written speech (10.6.4). Finally, Q. turns to speaking extemporaneously (10.7), the crown and highest reward of rhetorical training (10.7.1). The subsequent parts of the improvised speech must be thought out ahead of time even as the earlier parts are being spoken (7.10–18). Q. discusses the common habit of busy pleaders (e.g., Cicero) of writing out the most important parts of their speeches ahead of time and improvising the rest in court with the assistance of prepared notes (7.30–33).

Book 11 opens with a discussion of propriety or decorum, the appropriate harmonizing of style with subject matter, occasion, the speaker, etc. (11.1). Then to memory (11.2). Q. rejects the method of associating words with a series of related images or symbols as a useful or realistic means of memorizing a speech (2.17–26) but does favor the simpler use of images to recall sections of speeches (2.29). He has a few specific suggestions, e.g., memorizing from one's own written version of the speech (2.32) and memorizing aloud to gain the added assistance of the ear (2.33), but points out that ultimately there is no substitute for hard work augmented by a lot of practice (2.40). Although verbatim memorization is preferred, if possible (2.44–45), the actual delivery should make it seem that the speech is being delivered extemporaneously, because that is more impressive to judges (2.47). Delivery (*pronuntiatio* or *actio,* 11.3) is, as Demosthenes said, everything, because it is the crucial mediation between what we have to say and the audience we are trying to influence (11.3.2–6). Hortensius achieved his great success mainly from his skillful delivery, which apparently far exceeded his rather mediocre abilities in writing speeches (3.8). A detailed discussion of control of the voice (3.14–65) and gesture (3.65–149) follows, including body language (3.66 and 122); dozens of humorous anecdotes and observations are made along the way, which give the modern reader a revealing glimpse into Roman dress and behavior. Q. then continues with the decorum of delivery (3.150–84), including the general characteristics of delivery (3.154–60), the kinds of delivery most appropriate for certain parts of the speech (3.161–74), and the relationship of delivery to subject matter (3.174–76) and to different speakers themselves (3.177–84).

Book 12 defines the ideal orator and his duties (Pr.4). Most important is the moral character of the speaker (12.1–2). Q. endorses Marcus Cato's definition of the orator as "a good man skilled in speaking" (*vir bonus dicendi peritus,* 12.1.1) and argues extensively why the orator must be a good man—e.g., a bad man is a fool, and no orator can be a fool (1.4); evil preoccupies the mind, and the orator cannot be preoccupied (1.7). To insure the proper development of that character, the orator must carefully study right living in all the branches of learning, in natural, moral, and rational philosophy (12.2). He must not be a philosopher per se, since the philosopher removes himself from practical living, but he must be wise in a Roman sense, i.e., practically, as a true citizen and statesman (2.6–8). He will not belong to any particular philosophic school but will pick and choose from them all what is best and most useful for him and his vocation (2.23–28). Finally, he must be familiar with all the best examples of character and actions to be found in history (2.29–31). The ideal orator must also have a thorough knowledge of the law, civil and religious (12.3), as well as a rich storehouse of examples ready to use, not just from history, but from mythology, poetry, and oral tradition (12.4). With these weapons, the perfect orator will also need a lofty, confident spirit (12.5). He will begin pleading in court whenever he is ready, not prematurely and not too late (12.6). In actual practice (12.7–9) he will prefer defense to prosecution (12.7.1–7). As for fees (7.8–12), the orator will charge selectively and judiciously but only according to his needs, and he will regard any fee that he does need to charge not as a payment but as the return of one good deed for another (7.12). In treating cases (12.8) the orator should become thoroughly familiar with every aspect, testing and examining everything and being particularly skeptical about what his clients tell him. Additional points about the actual practice of pleading (12.9) include the admonitions not to sacrifice our client's case for the sake of the applause of the audience aimed at us (12.9.1–7) and not to make a habit, as some do, of pointlessly attacking the character and wisdom of our opponents (9.8–12). Q. then turns to the kinds of speech to be used by the ideal orator (12.10). Just as painters and sculptors have different styles, so do orators—except for Cicero, who was a master of all of them (12.10.12). Q. reviews the controversy over Asiatic, Attic, and Rhodian rhetoric in the context of Cicero (10.12–26), concluding that it is better simply to consider the term *Attic* to refer to the best kind of speaking (10.26). Q. concedes that the Greek language sounds better than Latin and is more precise (10.27–39), and so Latin should push its strengths of gravity and fullness (10.36). The spoken and written versions of a speech should be identical (10.51), although some things that may be included just for the sake of oral argument before the judges should perhaps be omitted in the written version for posterity (10.55–57). Q. then reviews the three traditional kinds of speaking (10.58–65), giving Latin equivalents of the Greek terms: *subtile* (refined, precise, or plain) for *ischnos* (thin, lean, meager); *grande* and *robustum* for *hadros* (stout, large, strong); and *medium* or *floridum* for *anthêros* (florid). The first of these should generally be used for the statement of facts and proof (10.59), with the middle, and especially the grand—if, like Cicero, one can master it—for the other sections (10.60–62). But these three categories are not adequate descriptors, since there are gradations and variations within them (10.66–68), and, moreover, the ideal orator will use all the styles, depending on the circumstances of the case, the part of the speech, the audience, etc. (10.69–72). The orator should then retire in good time, before his powers fail him, to write, teach, and advise (12.11).

Text and translation: Quintilian, *Institutio Oratoria*, trans. H. E. Butler, 4 vols. (Cambridge, Mass.: Harvard Univ. Press, 1920–22).

The *RHETORICA AD ALEXANDRUM* is a systematic handbook of rhetoric probably written about the same time as Aristotle's *Rhetoric*. The name of the treatise and its preservation with the works of Aristotle result from the preface, which takes the form of a letter supposedly written by Aristotle to Alexander the Great. This letter is universally regarded as a forgery and was probably added to the work at a later date. Scholars have often attributed the work to Anaximenes of Lampsacus (c. 380–320 B.C.), a contemporary of Aristotle, on the basis of a passage in Quintilian (3.4.9) in which it is said that Anaximenes identified the same seven subtypes of oratory that are mentioned in the beginning of the treatise and form the basis for the discussion that follows. Anaximenes is reported to have been a tutor of Alexander and to have accompanied him on the expedition to the East. He wrote a history of Greece and biographies of Philip and Alexander, all now lost.

The *RHETORICA* begins with a classification of speeches into deliberative (*dêmêgorikon*), epideictic, and judicial (*dikanikon*). These are subdivided into exhortation (*protropê*), dissuasion (*apotropê*), encomium, invective (*psogos*), accusation (*katêgoria*), defense (*apologia*), and investigation (*exetasis*). Exhortation and dissuasion are discussed first. In these types one argues that a course of action is or is not just, lawful, expedient, honorable, pleasant, easily practicable, possible, or necessary. Sample lines of argument are given for justice, legality, and expediency (1).

Next the subjects of deliberative speeches are reviewed: religion, law, the constitution, alliances and treaties, war, peace, and finance. Arguments are suggested for each. Views on ideal laws and constitutions for various forms of government are given, along with specific suggestions about arguing for or against legislation. General observations follow on alliances and treaties, war, peace, and finance, along with arguments for and against (2).

Encomium and invective involve amplification and minimization of good and bad qualities. The topics are the just, lawful, expedient, honorable, pleasant, easily practicable, and their opposites. Examples and methods are given (3).

Accusation and defense, which are connected to judicial oratory, are discussed next. Various suggestions for accusation are given and three methods of defense: prove that what is charged was not done;

show that it was lawful, just, and advantageous; or beg forgiveness by admitting error (4).

Then to investigation, which is to show that intentions, actions, or words are inconsistent with one another or with the rest of someone's life. Specific procedures for doing so are suggested (5). Elements common to all seven subtypes of oratory are discussed next. The topics listed above (the just, lawful, etc.), while employed in all subtypes, are especially used in exhortation. Amplification and minimization are especially used in encomium and invective. Proofs (*pisteis*) are most useful in accusation and defense. There are also anticipation (*prokatalêpsis*), request (*aitêma*), recapitulation (*palillogia*), prolixity, moderation in length, brevity, and interpretation (6).

There are two kinds of proof: direct (probabilities, examples, tokens, enthymemes, aphorisms, signs, and refutations) and supplementary (opinion of the speaker, witnesses, evidence given under torture, and oaths). Each type of direct proof is discussed in detail (7–13), and a section on the differences among them follows (14). Supplementary proofs are handled similarly (14–17).

Anticipation is defined as maintaining goodwill by anticipating criticisms of the audience and the arguments of the opponent. Methods are discussed, along with ways of handling interruptions (18). Requests, defined as demands made by the speaker on the audience, are described next (19), followed by recapitulation (20). A brief discussion of the use of irony in recapitulation (21) is followed by remarks on elements of style, including length and diction, framing a double statement, clarity, antithesis, and parallelism of both structure (*parisôsis*) and sound (*paromoiôsis*, 22–28).

Next is a detailed review of the structure of deliberative speeches of exhortation and dissuasion. The introduction consists of a preliminary statement, appeal for attention, and securing of goodwill. (29). Narration (*apangelia*) of past and present events, or forecast of future events, must be clear (in terms of both facts and diction), brief, and convincing (30). The facts of the case should be arranged in different ways, and perhaps even appended to the introduction, depending on how numerous and familiar they are (31). The confirmation (*bebaiôsis*) is based on proofs or on the grounds of the just, lawful, expedient, honorable, pleasant, easily practicable, possible, and necessary (32). The opponent's arguments should be anticipated, followed by a recapitulation (33). The exhortation should create compassion and gratitude; dissuasion, envy and hatred (34).

The structure of encomium and invective is dealt with next. After the introduction, the appropriate topics are things external to virtues (good birth, strength, beauty, and wealth) and virtues themselves (wisdom, justice, courage, and honorable habits). Birth should be taken up first, followed by the subject's achievements, character, and habits as a young man, then by his justice, wisdom, and courage as an adult (35).

Next the structure of judicial oratory, including investigation, is reviewed: the introduction; the narrative of facts, if necessary; the confirmation; the anticipation; the recapitulation; and, finally, the creation of compassion and gratitude for ourselves, envy and hatred for the opponent. In a speech for the defense the introduction is followed by refutation of the charges or, if guilt is admitted, argument that the actions were justified or that they were an error. Response to the prosecution's anticipations is next, and then admissions and denials, followed by recapitulation and creation of compassion and gratitude for ourselves, envy and hatred for the opponent (36).

Then to the structure of investigative oratory, although the treatise cautions that this type is not normally used separately. The introduction should make the investigation appear reasonable. Then the investigation proper, which must be conducted in a mild manner so as to avoid ill will, and, finally, a recapitulation (37). The work ends with miscellaneous observations on arrangement, style, methods of proof, the epilogue, securing goodwill, personal behavior, and political matters (38).

Text and translation: Aristotle, *Problems, Books XXII–XXXVIII*, trans. W. S. Hett; *Rhetorica ad Alexandrum*, trans. H. Rackham (Cambridge, Mass.: Harvard Univ. Press, 1937).

RHETORICA AD HERENNIUM is a Latin technical manual that systematically and concisely treats all aspects of rhetorical instruction. The primary focus is on forensic rhetoric, and the work is characterized by arbitrary schematization and prescriptive formulations on how to do everything down to the last detail. It was written around 85 B.C. and syncretically reflects in Latin terms the entire history of Greek rhetoric, including pre-Aristotelian, Aristotelian, Isocratean, Stoic, and later Hellenistic developments, especially the school on the island of Rhodes. The author is unknown, as is the Herennius to whom it is addressed. The origin of the work is a matter of dispute—whether it is a student's notes framed by original comments, an original treatise incorporating Greek materials, or some other possibility. Part of this question is the close relationship, including identical passages, of the first two of its four books to Cicero's early *De Inventione*. From late antiquity to the Renaissance the *RAH* was thought to have been by Cicero. The last two books, which contain the oldest extant treatment of memory and the first systematic discussion of style in Latin, are extremely significant. The whole work exercised an enormous influence on Western culture throughout the Middle Ages and into the Renaissance.

The brief introduction opening Book 1 emphasizes that artistic precepts should be supplemented by practical exercises (1.1–2). Natural talent is not mentioned here (it is later, in the discussion of memory, 3.28). The three kinds of rhetoric, demonstrative (*demonstrativum*), deliberative (*deliberativum*), and judicial (*iudiciale*), are based on three kinds of causes, and the speaker must have five different skills (the five parts of instruction): invention (*inventio*), disposition (*dispositio*), style (*elocutio*), memory (*memoria*), and delivery (*pronuntiatio*). These skills are obtained from artistic precepts (*ars=praeceptio*), imitation (*imitatio*), and practice (*exercitatio*). Books 1 and 2 then treat invention in judicial rhetoric, which is discussed under the six parts of a speech (1.3): the introduction (*exordium*); narration (*narratio*) of the facts of the case; division (*divisio*) of the case, indicating what is contested and the order of treatment; proof (*confirmatio*); refutation (*confutatio*); and conclusion (*conclusio*).

The teaching of this invention is naturally completely topical, i.e. *RAH* concisely but comprehensively plots the "places" (*loci*) where the speaker will find what to say and when and how to say it. This topical focus never strays from the practical realization of the goals of each part of the speech.

Introductions are either direct or insinuating (1.4–11). The purpose of the introduction is to make our audience "receptive, well-disposed, and attentive" (6; Loeb, p. 13). Receptiveness is created by our incisive grasp of the basics of the case, and attention by promising to bring up some new or as yet unexplored aspect (7). We dispose the audience in our favor by saying nice things about ourselves and bad things about our adversaries, flattering the audience, and praising our own case (8). When our case is an unseemly, bad one, when the audience has already been swayed by the opponent, or when the audience is tired of the subject (9), the insinuating introduction gets the speaker into the speech without directly revealing what his point is or where he stands (9–11). There are three kinds of narration, each of which may be based either on facts or on people (12). Narrative based on facts has three parts (13): the fable (*fabula*), history (*historia*), or fiction (*argumentum*). Narration should be brief (*brevis*), clear (*dilucida*), and verisimilar (*veri similis*). This section (3–16) ends with the remark that only the comments on the insinuating introduction are original and differ from the standard rhetorical authorities (16).

After the division (*divisio*, 17), the subjects of proof and refutation bring up the issues [*staseis* of Hermagoras, *constitutiones* in *RAH*]. These are the bases or foundations of each case, the precise focus of the prosecution and defense (18–25). *RAH* has three of them (instead of the Hermagorean four): conjectural (*coniecturalis*), legal (*legitima*), and juridical (*iuridicalis*). We have the first when the case turns on a question of fact, the second when a law or its interpretation is basic to the case, and juridical when the question concerns the rightness or wrongness of an action. There are six species of the legal and two of the juridical (later six species of the conjectural are discussed, 2.3–12). One of the juridical species itself has four subspecies.

After identifying the particular issue, the justification for the defense and the opposite line of attack for the prosecution must be determined. From these the question to be adjudicated will arise, in relation to which the entire speech will be constructed (26), except for the conjectural issue (27).

Book 2 elaborates on the issues and, specifically, how they are to be used. The conjectural comes first with its six species (2.3–12). Commonplaces (*loci communes*) are defined here as topoi to be used by both sides of a case, prosecution and defense (2.5.9). Then come the species of the legal (13–18) and, finally, the juridical (19–26). *RAH* proceeds to discuss the logical processes of argumentation (27 ff.). A complete argument has five parts (28): the proposition (*propositio*), the reason (*ratio*), proof of the reason (*rationis confirmatio*), embellishment (*exornatio*), and a brief conclusion (*complexio*). Sometimes one or both of the last two parts will be omitted. By far the greatest part of the discussion here takes up defective arguments and fallacies, even of embellishment (31–46). Book 2 ends with a discussion not of the brief conclusion of an argument but of the conclusion of a speech. Three things must occur in the conclusion: a summary review of our speech; amplification; and an appeal to the pity of the audience. There are ten topoi of amplification (given from a prosecutorial point of view and identified as commonplaces, 30.47): reference to authority; who has been affected by the crime; the danger to the state of being lenient; how leniency will encourage other similar crimes; the finality of any judgment and, hence, how important it is that the correct verdict be rendered; premeditation; heinousness of the crime generally; unique or special aspects of heinousness; comparison to other heinous crimes, showing that this one is worse than crimes universally accepted as horrible; and, finally, a vivid description of the actual details of the crime. The topoi of arousing pity in the audience (from a defense point of view) include our present bad fortune, our family background, direct appeals for mercy, etc (47–50).

Book 3 takes the same inventional approach to deliberative (3.2–9) and epideictic (10–15) speeches. Although the customarily prescriptive instruction here is briefer, it uses the previous discussion of the forensic topoi and is remarkably comprehensive. *RAH* then turns to the other four parts of rhetorical instruction. The treatment of arrangement or disposition is brief (16–18), mainly because invention itself intrinsically involves arrangement. For example, the topoi of the introduction are strikingly different from the topoi of the conclusion, and their individual selection also involves sequence within the introduction or conclusion. The brief discussion here is, however, illuminating in its treatment of the most effective sequence of arguments (18) and in its perceptive allowance for variations in the normal sequence of the six parts of a speech, based on the special demands created by the situation, the audience, or the subject (17).

The section on delivery that follows (19–27) is the oldest extant treatment of the subject. It is remarkably prescriptive both in defining the scope of the subject and in its sophistication in detailing different kinds and combinations of kinds of delivery. Each of eight different tones of voice, for example, has its own appropriate gestures and expressions (26–27).

Book 3 ends with memory (28–40). *RAH*'s mnemonic system is based on associating words with places, images, and similitudes that will suggest the words and their sequence. The speaker is to do this himself with the places, images, and similitudes that will work best for him personally, and *RAH* rejects some (now unknown) earlier Greek instructions about memory that devised predetermined systems of associated words and images (38–39). The student is to practice the more difficult word-for-word memorization so as to develop the easier facility for topical memorization of content (39).

The longest book, Book 4, on style, opens with an excursus attacking the alleged practice in the Greek rhetorical manuals of adducing many exemplary passages from a multitude of authors and orators of the past (4.1–10). *RAH* prefers original illustrative examples (although it incorporates many examples from previous writers and speakers, without attribution).

There are three kinds of style: the serious (*gravis*), the middle (*mediocris*), and the attenuated (*adtenuata*). The first is marked by grandeur of diction and sentiment and complex syntax; the last by plain but elegant simplicity, oridinary vocabulary and simpler syntax; and the middle stands, roughly, in between (11–14). The speaker must guard against the degeneration of the serious style into swollen bombast, that of the middle into inconsistent slackness, and that of the attenuated into dry, bloodless meagerness (15–16). All speaking, in whatever style, should have three qualities: elegance (*elegantia*), which includes correct Latinity (*Latinitas*) and lucidity (*explanatio*); proper composition (*compositio*); and distinction (*dignitas*, 17–18).

Under distinction are two kinds of ornamentation, of words or language and of thoughts (18). The former involves embellishment of the language itself; the latter creates distinction through content (*res*), not words (*verba*). Forty-four ornamentations of language are discussed, using Latin terminology in place of the received Greek. The first thirty-four (19–41) correspond to the schemes of the grammarians—i.e., they shape the words without altering the meaning; the last ten (42–46) correspond to tropes, which involve a "turn" or change in the sense of the words themselves.

The first thirty-four ornamentations of words are epanaphora (*repetitio*), antistrophe (*conversio*), interlacing of epanaphora and antistrophe (*complexio*), transplacement (*traductio*) [the ear, *RAH* notes, distinguishes these four], antithesis (*contentio*), apostrophe (*exclamatio*), interrogation (*interrogatio*), reasoning by question and answer (*ratiocinatio*), maxim (*sententia*), opposite reasoning (*contrarium*), clause (*membrum*), phrase (*articulus*), sentence or period (*continuatio*), isocolon (*compar*), homoeoptoton (*cadens exornatio*), homoeoteleuton (*desinens exornatio*), pun (*adnominatio*), hypophora (*subiectio*), climax (*gradatio*), definition (*definitio*), transition (*transitio*), correction (*correctio*), paraleipsis (*occultatio*), disjunction (*disiunctum*), conjunction (*coniunctio*), reduplication (*conduplicatio*), synonymy (*interpretatio*), reciprocation (*commutatio*), surrender (*permissio*), indecision (*dubitatio*), elimination (*expeditio*), asyndeton (*dissolutum*), aposiopesis (*praecisio*), and conclusion (*conclusio*).

The last ten ornamentations of words have this in common: their language departs from ordinary, literal usage of words (42). These ten are onomatopoeia (*nominatio*), antonomasia (*pronominatio*), metonymy (*denominatio*), periphrasis (*circumitio*), hyperbaton (*transgressio*), hyperbole (*superlatio*), synecdoche (*intellectio*), metaphor (*translatio*), and allegory (*permutatio*).

The ornamentations of thought (47–69) are distribution (*distributio*); frankness (*licentia*); understatement (*deminutio*); vivid description (*descriptio*); division (*divisio*); accumulation (*frequentatio*); refining (*expolitio*), which includes dialogue (*sermocinatio*) and arousal (*exsuscitatio*); emphasis (*commoratio*); comparison (*similitudo*), which works by contrast, negation, detailed parallel, or abridgment; exemplification (*exemplum*); simile (*imago*); portrayal (*effictio*), delineation of character (*notatio*); dialogue (*sermocinatio*);

personification (*conformatio*); implication (*significatio*); exaggeration (*exsuperatio*); ambiguity (*ambiguum*); implication (*significatio*) by consequence or aposiopesis or comparison; conciseness (*brevitas*); and ocular demonstration (*demonstratio*).

Text and translation: *[Cicero] ad C. Herennium De Ratione Dicendi (Rhetorica ad Herennium)*, trans. Harry Caplan (Cambridge, Mass.: Harvard Univ. Press, 1954).

SENECA THE ELDER (c. 50 B.C.–c. A.D. 40.), a Spaniard, is our principal source of knowledge about practice declamations (*declamationes*) on set topics that were used in three contexts in the early imperial period. First, teachers of rhetoric (*rhetorici* or *scholastici*) composed them as models for their students to imitate. Second, students themselves wrote and delivered them as integral parts of both the middle and advanced stages of instruction. Third, it is obvious from Seneca that practicing orators themselves delivered such speeches as a form of display (of their talents) and entertainment to audiences that ranged from small, intimate gatherings (such as a poetry reading) to large public groups. It is usually supposed that this development exactly parallels the decline of real and meaningful rhetorical opportunities in the transition from the Roman Republic to the more stifling circumstances of the Empire; later, at the end of the first century A.D., Tacitus (q.v.) discusses this question.

In his old age Seneca reconstructed from memory two collections of such speeches by important speakers that he had heard. The *Controversiae* were speeches arguing legal cases for advanced students. Of the ten books of *Controversiae,* Books 1, 2, 7, 9, and 10 are essentially complete, while Books 3–6 and 8 appear largely in excerpted form. The supposedly memorable examples Seneca has assembled are frequently unrealistic and sophomoric, as are the seven extant speeches in the *Suasoriae,* the second collection of practice deliberative speeches, for less advanced students.

Seneca's reconstruction emphasizes three distincitve aspects of these speeches. First are *sententiae,* pithy, epigrammatic statements of the main points. Then comes the division (*divisio*) of the speech into its essential parts based on the questions or issues to be considered. Finally, the particular rhetorical approach—or, we would say today, spin—on this division is identified as the speeches' *color.*

Text and translation: Seneca the Elder, *Controversiae and Suasoriae,* trans. M. Winterbottom, 2 vols. (Cambridge, Mass.: Harvard University Press, 1974).

SEXTUS EMPIRICUS was a Greek doctor and philosopher who lived around A.D. 200. His surviving works are mainly philosophical. *AGAINST THE RHETORICIANS (PROS RHÊTORAS)* is the second book of *Against the Professors (Pros Mathêmatikous)*, which comprises six books.

The main concern of S.E. throughout *AGAINST THE RHETORICIANS* is to show that rhetoric does not exist. He begins by examining definitions of rhetoric, giving Plato's in the *Gorgias* and those of Xenocrates (a follower of Plato), Stoic philosophers, and Aristotle (1–9). S.E. then sets out to prove the unreality (*to anypostaton*) of rhetoric. He refutes a Stoic definition by arguing that the rules of rhetoric are false and that there are no apprehensions (*katalêpseis*) of false things. Rhetoric is not an art for the following reasons: every art has a stable and fixed end (*telos*), but rhetoric does not; one can make a successful speech without having studied rhetoric; many who have studied rhetoric are incapable of making a decent speech (10–19). In reference to arguments of the Academy, S.E. says that rhetoricians are often hated or expelled from cities, but no one expels the arts (20–25). If rhetoric is an art, it will be useful to its possessors or to cities; but it is not and so is not an art. It is harmful to persons because it fills them with danger and worry, and to cities because it endangers the laws (26–42). S.E. refutes the idea that there are two forms of rhetoric, one used by refined persons, the other by the base, and that the accusations against rhetoric are directed only toward the latter (43–47).

Then to the argument that rhetoric does not exist because it has no subject matter. It is concerned with speech (*logos*), but neither the word (*lexis*) nor the speech composed of words is anything, so rhetoric does not exist. Nor does rhetoric create good style (*kalê lexis*) (48–59). S.E. further argues that rhetoric has no end (*telos*). He mentions the view of others that the end of rhetoric is persuasion (*to peithein*) and makes a detailed argument against this view: the end of rhetoric cannot be the true, the false, or any combination of the two (60–71). Rhetoric is actually opposed to persuasion. Its overelaboration offends people, it is not clear, and it does not inspire goodwill (72–78). The end of rhetoric is not, as others have suggested, to discover suitable words (*to tous endechomenous heurein logous*) or to create a certain impression on the judges. Nor is it to achieve what is advantageous (*to sympheron*) or victory (79–88).

The traditional parts of rhetoric, the judicial (*dikanikon*), deliberative (*symbouleutikon*), and encomiastic (*engkômiastikon*), do not actually exist, either (89–105). S.E. concludes by arguing that proof (*apodeixis*) is nothing (106–13).

Text and translation: Sextus Empiricus, *Against the Professors,* trans. R. G. Bury (Cambridge, Mass.: Harvard Univ. Press, 1949).

TACITUS (c. A.D. 56–115) was an orator, historian, and biographer, who wrote one work on rhetorical theory, *A DIALOGUE ON ORATORS (DIALOGUS DE ORATORIBUS)*. The *DIALOGUE* is dedicated to L. Fabius Justus and takes up the question of whether the current (i.e., late first century A.D.) Roman orators really are inferior to earlier ones (1). T. proposes to answer the question by recalling a discussion he overheard on that very subject as a young man. He remembers the tragic dramatist Curiatus Maternus talking to the orators Julius Secundus and Marcus Aper (2), but this conversation first treats the respective merits of rhetoric and poetry. Aper criticizes Maternus for wasting time on tragedies instead of taking up a career as an orator (3), and Maternus responds briefly (4). Secundus decides that he may not be able to adjudicate between the claims of oratory and poetry because he is a good friend of the epic poet Saleius Bassus (5.1–2). Aper then begins a long praise of rhetoric and the career of the orator (5.3–8) and attacks poetry as being less rewarding than rhetoric (9–10). Rhetoric is praised as a powerful tool (5.5) and an important means of achieving personal distinction. The satisfaction of being able to speak extemporaneously is especially appreciated (6.6). Maternus rebuts Aper (11–13) in part by attacking the venality and corruption of oratory as currently practiced, alluding to the imperial spies and accusers who made a career of attacking the enemies of the state (12.3).

A fourth interlocutor arrives (14): Vipstanus Messalla, who, according to Aper, believes that the practice of rhetoric has declined (15.1). Messalla claims to be interested in the reasons for the decline (15.2). Aper introduces the quibbling objection that Cicero and others of his day should be grouped with contemporary orators (16.4–17) as a means of getting to his main point: that different forms of rhetoric have been fashionable at different times, so changes in rhetorical practice do not necessarily mean changes for the worse (18). Aper then defends current rhetorical practice as being appropriate for his day and just as good in its own way as the different rhetorical practices of previous generations were in theirs (19–23), and his conclusion even suggests that oratory is still evolving for the better in the persons of contemporary orators such as Messalla, Maternus, and Secundus (23.5–6). Maternus observes that earlier orators need no defense and that none of those present would really rank himself equal to Cicero and the others attacked by Aper (24). Messalla follows and dismisses Aper's quibble about chronological categories by accepting any kind of category as long as it is admitted that the orators of earlier days were better than the current speakers (25–26). Maternus interrupts and requests Messalla to explain the reason for the decline (27). Messalla attacks first the education of children, previously the responsibility of their parents but now of servants (28–29). From this shoddy and irresponsible early training at home students are sent directly to a rhetorician for technical instruction (30), when they should first be getting a broad and comprehensive liberal education (31) so that they will be able to speak knowledgeably and convincingly on any subject (30.5). Speakers of the past were thoroughly educated in the law and ethics, while the ignorant speakers of today have style but no substance (32). Maternus interrupts again to change the focus from knowledge and theory to practice and exercises, to which Messalla then turns (33). In the old days, practical training was effected by a system of apprenticeship to actual orators, speaking on real occasions in the courts and assemblies (34). Nowadays, Messalla observes, there is a much less effective system of contrived speeches and declamations (the *suasoriae* and *controversiae*) in the rhetorical schools (35).

A lacuna in the text is followed by Maternus speaking about the fact that rhetorical skills were essential in the turbulent political days of the Republic (36–38)—to such an extant, indeed, that no one could achieve success in politics without rhetorical skills (37.3). Rhetoric needed the freedom of space and dress and the large audiences of Republican days (39–40). Without the occasion, the opportunity, and the need for rhetorical skills there is no oratory, as in ancient Sparta, Macedonia, and Persia (40.2–3). But it is not only the occasions for deliberative rhetoric that have been reduced to almost nothing in imperial Rome; little has been left for forensic oratory, as well (41.1–4). The resolution of the original question of whether rhetoric has declined, then, is that the occasions for and uses of rhetoric have been severely circumscribed in the current times of imperial peace, and rhetoric is doing just about as well as it can under these circumstances (41.5). With that remark Maternus stops, and the dialogue is quickly concluded (42).

Text and translation: Tacitus, *Agricola,* trans. M. Hutton, rev. R. M. Ogilvie; *Germania,* trans. M. Hutton, rev. E. H. Warmington; *Dialogus,* trans. W. Peterson, rev. M. Winterbottom, 2nd ed. (Cambridge, Mass.: Harvard Univ. Press, 1970).

THEON was born in Alexandria and is said to have written a rhetorical handbook; commentaries on Xenophon, Isocrates, and Demosthenes; treatises on rhetorical hypotheses, figures, and composition; and the *PROGYMNASMATA*, which is the only work to have survived. His date is uncertain; he may have been a contemporary of Dionysius of Halicarnassus (first century B.C.), but it is more likely that he lived at the end of the first century A.D. and was known by Quintilian, who mentions a "Stoic Theon" (9.3.76). The *PROGYMNASMATA* are described below in the order in which they appear in the Greek MSS, but internal evidence and the external evidence of an Armenian group of MSS reveal the different original order. The Greek MSS also omit some material from the end. There were five additional chapters on reading (*anagnôsis*), oral presentation (*akroasis*), paraphrase (*paraphrasis*), elaboration (*exergasia*), and rebuttal (*antirrêsis*). In the Greek MSS the original order seems to have been subverted because the work was transformed from a treatment intended for teachers into a school text intended for students. This transformation was modeled on later texts that were more popular: the *progymnasmata* of Hermogenes, Aphthonius, and Nicolaus. The rearrangement occurred after Hermogenes wrote his *Progymnasmata*, which makes reference to the work of Theon, and was likely completed by the beginning of the fifth century, since Nicolaus probably knew Theon's modified text.

In the introduction T. identifies three types of speech: encomiastic (*engkômiastikon*), forensic (*dikanikon*), and deliberative (*symbouleutikon*)—and mentions the five exercises that are not discussed later: reading, oral presentation, paraphrase, elaboration, and rebuttal (145–57). He then outlines the order in which he will discuss the *progymnasmata*, observing that reading, oral presentation, and paraphrase should be used from the start, but elaboration and rebuttal only with the acquisition of greater skill (157–58).

A section follows titled "On the Education of Young Students" (*Peri Tês Tôn Neôn Agôgês*). The teacher must have students memorize examples from ancient writers for each *progymnasma* (158–67). The *progymnasmata* are useful not only for those wishing to be orators but also for budding writers or poets and are the foundation stones (*themelia*) of every form of communication. The teacher must encourage recitation (*apangelia*), then teach arrangement and make clear the character (*êthos*) of the problem. Attention must be paid to meter and rhythm, and the expression (*hermêneia*) should be clear and vivid. At first the teacher should take care not to be excessively harsh by correcting all errors but should correct only the most basic. Have the ancient writers themselves correct the students when possible. Delivery (*hypokrisis*) is important in all types of speech (167–72).

Fable (*mythos*), the first exercise, is defined as a false story that depicts the truth. T. limits his treatment only to those fables that have morals, called Aesopic, Libyan, Phrygian, etc. Those not indicating a special class are called Aesopic, not because Aesop was the first writer of fables but because he used them more extensively and skillfully. Some call fables tales (*ainoi*), because they give useful advice. The exercise is to recite the fable, with a simple and clear interpretation; inflect it; combine it with a narrative (*diêgêma*); expand and condense it; add some saying to it, or add a fable appropriate to a saying; and refute and confirm it. T. explains these steps in some detail (172–79). The introduction (*prooimion*) should be appropriate to the fable. Then come the fable (although it is sometimes excluded), the argument (*epicheirêsis*), the refutation of each statement in detail, and the epilogue (179–81).

Narrative (*diêgêma*), the second exercise, is defined as an explanatory account of matters having occurred or as if having occurred. The narrative must have six elements to be complete: the person(s) involved, the act done, the place where it occurred, the time of the act, the manner (*tropos*), and the reason (*aitia*) for it (182–83). The narrative should be clear, concise, and plausible. A detailed examination follows of what contributes to each element, using an example from Thucydides (182–92). The exercise with narrative involves recitation, inflection, combination with a fable, condensation and expansion, changing the order of the principle events in the recitation, varying the way the utterance is expressed when keeping the same order, supplementing each part of the narrative with a proverb, combining two or three narratives together (192–201), and, finally, refutation and confirmation, with a detailed review of their topics (216–222).

Then to chreia (*chreia*), which T. defines as a concise, well-aimed statement (*apophasis*) or action (*praxis*) that refers to a particular person or to something analogous to a person. The aphorism (*gnômê*) and the reminiscence (*apomnêmoneuma*), which is an action or saying that is useful for living (*biopheles*), are related to the chreia. Every concise aphorism, if it refers to a person, produces a chreia, but the aphorism and chreia differ in that the chreia always refers to a person, while the aphorism never does; the chreia sometimes makes a general statement, sometimes a specific one, while the aphorism always makes a general one; the chreia is witty, and sometimes has nothing useful for living, while the aphorism always concerns what is useful in life; the chreia is an action or saying, while the aphorism is only a saying. The reminiscence differs from the chreia in that the chreia is concise, the reminiscence sometimes drawn out; the chreia refers to some person, but the reminiscence is also told by itself. T. says that it is called *chreia* because of its excellence (201–02). There are three main kinds: logical (*logikai*), which make their point through words without action; practical (*praktikai*); and 3) mixed, which share elements of both the logical and practical but make their point with the action (202–06). They may be expressed in the manner of a proverb, in the manner of an explanation (*apodeiktikôs*), with wit, with a syllogism (*syllogismos*), with an enthymeme, with an example (*paradeigma*), with a wish (*euchê*), in a symbolic manner (*symbolikôs*), in a figurative manner (*tropikôs*), with ambiguity, with a change of subject (*kata metalêpsin*), or by some combination of these. T. gives examples of all these types and details of how to practice them. He ends this chapter by remarking that the chreia should act as a thesis-statement; there should be an introduction, the chreia/thesis-statement, then the argumentation, with elaboration, digression, etc., as needed (206–16).

Commonplace (*topos*), the next exercise, is defined as an amplifying statement about an agreed-upon subject, one about either a wrong act or a brave act. Some commonplaces are simple (e.g. a traitor, tyrant, etc.), some not simple (e.g., a general/traitor, or a temple-robber/priest). It is called commonplace because we start from a familiar place, e.g. from the charge that someone is an insolent person. The commonplace differs from encomia and invectives in that the latter involve specific persons and have a proof (*apodeixis*), while the former is about general things and has no proof. In the latter introductions (*prooimia*) are required, in the former they are not (222–24). T. goes on to discuss the use of commonplace in a lawsuit (224–26).

Next come encomium and invective (*psogos*). Encomium is a speech setting forth the magnitude of the virtuous actions and other good aspects of some specific person. Encomium deals with the living, while the funeral speech (*epitaphios*) deals with the dead, and the hymn (*hymnos*) concerns the gods. But the procedure is the same. It is called *engkômion* because the ancients used to eulogize the gods in revelry (*kômos*) and at play (*paidia*). A review follows of various aspects of external and internal (psychic) qualities that may be praised. After the introduction, speak about good birth and then set forth external qualities and those of the body. Then mention deeds and successes. Encomia of inanimate things, e.g., honey, health, etc., should be handled similarly. Compose invective from the opposite arguments (226–31).

Comparison (*synkrisis*), the sixth exercise, shows what is better or worse. There are comparisons of persons (Ajax, Odysseus) and of subjects (wisdom, courage). Comparisons are made over matters that are similar but the object of disagreement. For persons we compare their good birth, education, children, public offices, reputation, health, etc. Compare actions by considering which are more noble, more enduring, done at the right time, etc. In comparing subjects we consider their discoverers, their nature, the region to which they belong, and the benefits that result from them. Use the opposites of these in seeking to uncover the worse of two things. Make comparisons of several things with several other things, e.g., males and females, by taking extreme examples of each side or choosing that class in which exceptional people are most numerous (231–35).

The seventh exercise, impersonation (*prosôpopoiia*), is defined as the introduction of a person who sets forth words suitable to himself and the circumstances. Panegyric (*panegyrikoi*), hortatory (*protreptikoi*), and epistolary (*epistolikoi*) speeches fall under this category. One should consider the character of the speaker and addressee, the speaker's age, the occasion, the place, the fortune, and the underlying material (*hylê*) about which the words are spoken (235–37). A detailed examination follows of impersonation in exhortation, dissuasion, and consolation (*parêgorêma*) and when asking for pardon (*sungnômê*, 237–39).

Eighth is vivid description (*ekphrasis*), defined as an account that creates a lively view what is being set forth. There are vivid descriptions of persons, deeds, places, times, ways (*tropoi*), and combinations of these. Both commonplace and vivid description involve generalities. They differ in that commonplace concerns motives as well as goodness or badness, whereas vivid description does not. They should be clear, lively, and concise, and the recitation of them should be appropriate to the subject (240–42).

Then to thesis, a reasoned inquiry (*episkepsis logikê*) into a dispute with no defined characters or circumstance, e.g,. whether one should marry. The thesis differs from the commonplace in that the latter is an amplification of a commonly accepted subject, whereas the thesis involves a disputed subject. The goal of the thesis is persuasion, that of the commonplace vengeance; the commonplace is usually delivered in a court of law, the thesis in the assembly and lecture room. Thesis differs from impersonation in that the former does not display a person, whereas the latter does. Theses are introduced by confirming them with an aphorism, chreia, story (*historia*), encomium, or invective. Theses do not have a narrative, since they involve no attendant circumstances. Some theses are theoretical (Are there gods?), some practical (Should one marry?). For one confirming, the main headings of the practical thesis are necessity, the noble, the beneficial, and the pleasurable. For one refuting, they are the opposite. A detailed list of possible topics follows. Advanced students should consider the testimony of the poets, philosophers, and statesmen. One should refute with the opposite topics (242–46). T. then gives an extended example of a practical thesis, whether a wise man participates in government, and one of a theoretical thesis, whether gods concern themselves with the world, using, as he says, many of the same arguments but not in the same order. Some theses are simple (Should one marry?), some combined (Should a king marry?). T. ends this section with remarks on devising words appropriate to the thesis (246–53).

Tenth and last is law (*nomos*), defined as a public decree (*dogma*) of an assembly or an esteemed man according to which all in the city should live, and not merely for a specific time. Laws are either being introduced and adopted, in which case examination (*dokimasia*) involves whether they should be approved, or they are already enacted, in which case disputants try to interpret them to their own advantage. We either refute or confirm laws. The work ends abruptly during a discussion of refutation from obscurity through ellipsis (254–57).

Texts and translations: James R. Butts, "The *Progymnasmata* of Theon: A New Text with Translation and Commentary" (Dissertation, Claremont Graduate School, 1987); Aelius Theon, *Progymnasmata*, ed. and trans. [into French] Michel Patillon with Giancarlo Bolognesi (Paris: Les Belles Lettres, Collection des Universités, 1997). Translation of the Introduction and "On the Education of Young Students" in *Readings from Classical Rhetoric*, ed. Patricia P. Matsen, Philip Rollinson, and Marion Sousa (Carbondal.: Southern Illinois Univ. Press, 1990), 253–62.

Select Bibliography

Bonner, S. F. *Declamation in the Late Republic and Early Empire.* Berkeley: Univ. of California Press, 1949.

Bowersock, Glen W. *Greek Sophists in the Roman Empire.* Oxford: Clarendon Press, 1969.

Brandes, Paul D. *A History of Aristotle's "Rhetoric."* Metuchen, N. J.: Scarecrow Press, 1989.

Calboli Montefusco, Lucia. *La dottrina degli Status nella retorica greca e romana.* Bologna: Dipartimento di Filologia Classica et Medioevale, 1984.

Clark, Donald Lemen. *Rhetoric in Greco-Roman Education.* New York: Columbia Univ. Press, 1957.

Cole, Thomas. *The Origins of Rhetoric in Ancient Greece.* Baltimore: Johns Hopkins Univ. Press, 1991.

Conley, Thomas M. *Rhetoric in the European Tradition.* 1990; rpt. Chicago: Univ. of Chicago Press, 1994.

Desbordes, Françoise. *La rhétorique antique.* Paris: Hachette, 1996.

Enos, Richard Leo. *The Literate Mode of Cicero's Legal Rhetoric.* Carbondale: Southern Illinois Univ. Press, 1988.

Enos, Teresa, ed. *Encyclopedia of Rhetoric and Composition.* New York: Garland, 1996.

Horner, Winifred Bryan. *Rhetoric in the Classical Tradition.* Boston: St. Martin's Press, 1988.

Kennedy, George A. *The Art of Persuasion in Greece.* Princeton: Princeton Univ. Press, 1963.

————. *The Art of Rhetoric in the Roman World.* Princeton: Princeton Univ. Press, 1972.

————. *Classical Rhetoric and Its Christian and Secular Tradition from Ancient to Modern Times.* Chapel Hill: Univ. of North Carolina Press, 1980.

————. *Greek Rhetoric under Christian Emperors.* Princeton: Princeton Univ. Press, 1983.

————. *A New History of Classical Rhetoric.* Princeton: Princeton Univ. Press, 1994.

Lausberg, Heinrich. *Handbook of Literary Rhetoric: A Foundation for Literary Study.* 2nd ed. Trans. Matthew T. Bliss, Annemiek Jansen, and David E. Orton. Ed. David E. Orton and R. Dean Anderson.Leiden: Brill, 1997.

Lentz, Tony M. *Orality and Literacy in Hellenic Greece.* Carbondale: Southern Illinois Univ. Press, 1989.

Martin, Josef. *Antike Rhetorik: Technik und Methode.* Munich: Beck 1974.

Murphy, James J., ed. *A Short History of Writing Instruction from Ancient Greece to Twentieth-Century America.* Davis, Cal.: Hermagoras Press, 1990.

———, and Richard A. Katula, eds. *A Synoptic History of Classical Rhetoric.* 2nd ed. Davis, Cal.: Hermagoras Press, 1995.

Ong, Walter J. *Orality and Literacy: The Technologizing of the Word.* London: Methuen, 1982.

Parks, E. Patrick. *The Roman Rhetorical Schools as a Preparation for the Courts under the Early Empire.* Baltimore: Johns Hopkins Univ. Press, 1945.

Porter, Stanley E. *A Handbook of Classical Rhetoric in the Hellenistic Period 330 B. C. -- A. D. 400.* Leiden: Brill, 1997.

Romilly, Jacqueline de. *Magic and Rhetoric in Ancient Greece.* Cambridge, Mass.: Harvard Univ. Press, 1975.

Russell, D. A. *Greek Declamation.* Cambridge: Cambridge University Press, 1983.

Scaglione, Aldo. *The Classical Theory of Composition from Its Origins to the Present.* Chapel Hill: Univ. of North Carolina Press, 1976.

Vickers, Brian. *In Defense of Rhetoric.* New York: Oxford Univ. Press, 1987.

Welch, Kathleen E. *The Contemporary Reception of Classical Rhetoric: Appropriations of Ancient Discourse.* Hillsdale, N.J.: Lawrence Erlbaum Associates, 1990.

Wisse, Jakob. *Ethos and Pathos from Aristotle to Cicero.* Amsterdam: Hakkert, 1989.

Index